What Readers Are Saying About *Using JRuby*

I was very happy to discover the JRuby project, my favorite program-ming language running on what's probably the best virtual machine in the world. This book really covers every in and out of this fantastic project.

► **Peter Lind**
Technical consultant, Valtech

I was floored by the amount of technical detail the authors managed to cram in here! And they did it with such an approachable and read-able tone that this book was both easy and fun to read. I can't remem-ber the last technical book that did that for me. The breadth of cover-age is astounding, too.

► **Kent R. Spillner**

My JRuby apps will go live in two weeks. Without your book and the Ruby community, I would never have gotten this far.

► **Pinit Asavanuchit**
Intersol Consulting Co., Ltd.

I really liked the clear structure of the book and all the covered libraries/dependencies (like Rake, Ant, Maven, testing frameworks). This clearly outlines the whole JRuby universe so that new users will immediately see what's available and how to start using it.

► **Vladimir Sizikov**
Senior engineer, Oracle

This book will open the eyes of any Java programmer who wants to take their art to the next level. Read it.

► **Geoff Drake**
Owner, Managed Design

This is one of those books that you don't want to put down and you can't wait to get back to. For a technical publication, that is extremely rare. Usually I find myself having a hard time trying to stay awake. After reading this book, I can say I have a very good understanding of what JRuby is, how it interacts with Java, and a working knowledge of many of the supporting tools to accomplish a wide range of tasks. The way this book is organized, it makes a great reference for future development.

► **Gale Straney**
Senior software design engineer, Tektronix

This book makes a compelling case for JRuby. A must-have to bring some Ruby goodness to your Java powerhouse.

► **Fred Daoud**
Author, *Stripes...and Java Web Development Is Fun Again*, and *Getting Started with Apache Click*

This book is an excellent resource for JRuby and will without a doubt facilitate JRuby adoption in Java-centric enterprises.

► **Bharat Ruparel**
Senior information architect, America's Test Kitchen

Using JRuby

Bringing Ruby to Java

Using JRuby
Bringing Ruby to Java

Charles O Nutter

Nick Sieger

Thomas Enebo

Ola Bini

Ian Dees

The Pragmatic Bookshelf
Raleigh, North Carolina   Dallas, Texas

Pragmatic Bookshelf

Many of the designations used by manufacturers and sellers to distinguish their products are claimed as trademarks. Where those designations appear in this book, and The Pragmatic Programmers, LLC was aware of a trademark claim, the designations have been printed in initial capital letters or in all capitals. The Pragmatic Starter Kit, The Pragmatic Programmer, Pragmatic Programming, Pragmatic Bookshelf and the linking *g* device are trademarks of The Pragmatic Programmers, LLC.

Every precaution was taken in the preparation of this book. However, the publisher assumes no responsibility for errors or omissions, or for damages that may result from the use of information (including program listings) contained herein.

Our Pragmatic courses, workshops, and other products can help you and your team create better software and have more fun. For more information, as well as the latest Pragmatic titles, please visit us at http://www.pragprog.com.

The team that produced this book includes:

Editor:	Jacquelyn Carter
Indexing:	Potomac Indexing, LLC
Copy edit:	Kim Wimpsett
Production:	Janet Furlow
Customer support:	Ellie Callahan
International:	Juliet Benda

ISBN-10: 1-934356-65-4
ISBN-13: 978-1-934356-65-4
Printed on acid-free paper.
P1.0 printing, January 2011
Version: 2011-1-10

Contents

Foreword by Matz

I love the term *diversity*. Di-ver-si-ty. Doesn't that sound great? JRuby surely embodies the value of diversity.

Some might think we can utilize our resources more efficiently without diversity. But in the open source world, the number of resources (that is, contributors) is not really limited. If a project is really attractive, we can get more people interested in it. If we had a less diverse ecosystem without projects like JRuby, I don't think we would get more resources. Instead, a lot of existing contributors would have dismissed Ruby for lack of diversity.

I created Ruby to make my programming happier. Since its creation, it has helped other programmers as well. I am proud that my masterpiece has made the world of programming a little bit better. JRuby made the Ruby language reach the Java world. JRuby made it possible to run Ruby on platforms like Google App Engine and Android. For this one thing, I will appreciate JRuby forever. Long live JRuby. Long live diversity in the Ruby world.

I hope you will enjoy Ruby on the JVM. Ruby will be with you. Enjoy programming, on whatever platform you love.

Yukihiro "Matz" Matsumoto
August 2010

Foreword by Bruce Tate

In late 2004, I was a Java author riding on an airport bus with Dave Thomas. At the time, I was frustrated with the increasing complexity of the Java language but thinking it was the only game in town. Dave convinced me to give Ruby a try. When I finally did, I found a language that was more expressive and productive than anything I'd ever used before. In a short year, I completed my first and second commercial Ruby applications and knew, beyond a shadow of a doubt, that Ruby was a better language for the types of applications I was writing. I wanted to share that idea with managers like the ones I encountered in my consulting practice, so I wrote *From Java to Ruby* [Tat06] to emphasize that Ruby wasn't just a smart move for programmers. Ruby made business sense.

Thankfully, I didn't have to lean solely on my own thin experience. To make the most critical points, I interviewed some important experts in complex areas such as design, adoption, and deployment. Among these people were Thomas Enebo and Charles Nutter, two of the earliest committers of the JRuby project. In those interviews, they elegantly made the case that a mature Ruby implementation on the JVM would lead to a powerful set of advantages.

You see, Ruby, the beautiful language, is only part of the story. Even this powerful, productive language needs a story that goes beyond the ideas embedded in the syntax and semantics. Real applications will have requirements encompassing performance, politics, and deployment. Truth be told, in 2006, Ruby was sometimes difficult to sell into the back office for some of these reasons.

What a difference four years makes. Thomas, Charles, and I have leaned hard on Ruby for these four years, supported by a growing community of many thousands of Ruby developers and customers. We've regularly run into each other in places like Austin, Texas, and Matsue, Japan. Each time, I've delightfully followed the progress of JRuby. This platform has delivered on every promise. Consider the following:

- JRuby is no longer a hobby. Though it holds fast to its open source foundations, it now has aggressive corporate sponsorship. Engine Yard has proven to be a wonderful steward, and several employees are dedicated to its success.
- Big customers have deployed major applications on JRuby, opening up the enterprise to Ruby. By allowing the back office to rely on the robust, reliable JVM, deploying Ruby is no longer the risk it once was. Each Ruby application becomes just bytecode, virtually indistinguishable from other Java applications.
- JRuby supports the Java frameworks that you need to support. Sure, the lower-level APIs are there, such as JDBC. But you can also build your nimble Ruby user interface directly on your Hibernate back end the way you want.
- ThoughtWorks, the dynamic consultancy that aggressively pushes the boundaries of developer productivity in the context of difficult problems, has used JRuby to deliver both products and customer applications on far more aggressive schedules than they could have with conventional languages.

So, JRuby is delivering on the promise of a marriage between the beautiful language on the robust and reliable JVM, and we've come full circle. Now, I'm writing a foreword for Thomas and Charles, and I could not be more thrilled. You see, the last missing piece of the JRuby puzzle is effective documentation. That's where *Using JRuby* steps in. This book tells the perfect story at the right time. This team of authors is uniquely positioned to give you the tips and tricks from the inside. They've nurtured this project from its infancy to where it is today. They've used JRuby to deliver real value to paying customers. And they're gifted communicators who can effectively tell this story.

I've been waiting for this day for a long time, and I could not recommend this book more highly. Congratulations, Charles, Thomas, Nick, Ola, and Ian. You've created something amazing and described it in a beautiful book.

Bruce Tate (Author, From Java to Ruby, 2006)
Austin, Texas, 2010

Preface

You know all the stereotypes of the Java and Ruby programming languages. The enterprise vs. the upstart. The staid, corporate safe choice against the free-wheeling new kid in town.

Look a little deeper, though, at what the languages have in common. They're about the same age (both had their 1.0 releases in 1996). Both their respective inventors were inspired by their favorite object-oriented language features. And both Java and Ruby have touched off an avalanche of Internet love-ins and flame-fests.

So, maybe it was inevitable that someone would try to combine the two. JRuby is an implementation of the Ruby programming language written in 100 percent Java.

Why JRuby?

JRuby is just another Ruby interpreter. It runs the same Ruby code you've been writing all along. But it's also a *better* Ruby interpreter. You get true multithreading that can use all your computer's cores from one process, plus a virtual machine that's been tuned for a decade and a half. All of this book's authors have seen our Ruby programs speed up just by moving them to JRuby.

JRuby is also just another .jar file. You don't need to install anything on your Java workstation to try it. And you don't need to do anything special to deploy your Ruby code to your production server. Just hand your sysadmin a .jar like you always do, and they might not even notice you used Ruby—except that you delivered your app in half the time and encountered fewer bugs down the road.

> **Ian Says...**
>
> **JRuby in Real Life**
>
> At work, we needed to sift through a mound of engineering data. Ruby was a natural fit for this task, and we had working code in minutes. But sharing this program with colleagues was a different story.
>
> With regular Ruby, we ran into trouble getting the code from one machine to another—even though they were both running Windows XP. We had to direct people to install a particular outdated version of MySQL, manually copy DLLs into Ruby's installation path, and then install another Ruby library. Even if they got all that right, they'd still encounter error messages like "msvcrt-ruby18.dll was not found."
>
> Enter JRuby. Its database drivers don't have to be compiled for each specific operating system and build environment, so things just worked out of the box. The installation procedure shrank to "copy the file, and then type java -jar ourprogram.jar."

What's in This Book

The first half of this book is about JRuby. In Chapter 1, *Getting to Know JRuby*, on page 3, we'll hit the ground running with a few quick examples that showcase JRuby's main features. In Chapter 2, *Driving Java from Ruby*, on page 15, we'll show you how to call into Java libraries from Ruby code. Then we'll go the other direction in Chapter 3, *Ruby from Java: Embedding JRuby*, on page 45 and extend a Java program using Ruby. Finally, Chapter 4, *The JRuby Compiler*, on page 63 will answer the question, "Isn't JRuby just a Ruby compiler for Java?" (Short answer: no.)

In the second half, we'll discuss how JRuby relates to the outside world of libraries, tools, and legacy code. We'll start with Chapter 5, *Introduction to Rails*, on page 85, in which you'll build a database-backed website in Ruby's most famous framework. Web development leads naturally to databases and deployment.Chapter 6, *JRuby and Relational*

Databases, on page 121 and Chapter 7, *Building Software for Deployment*, on page 153 will cover several Java and Ruby libraries in these areas.

In Chapter 8, *Testing Your Code with JRuby*, on page 187 and Chapter 9, *Beyond Unit Tests*, on page 207, you'll find out how to use Java tools to run Ruby tests and how to use Ruby frameworks to exercise Java code. You'll finish off the main part of the book in Chapter 10, *Building GUIs with Swing*, on page 229, where you'll find what many Rubyists have long sought: a cross-platform GUI toolkit.

Who This Book Is For

This book is for people looking to bring the Ruby and Java worlds together. Some of you are seasoned Java developers who are interested in seeing what the Ruby language can do for you. Others are familiar with Ruby and wondering what they need to know about running their code on the Java platform.

If your primary language has been Java up until now, you may want to start with the quick crash course on Ruby syntax in Appendix A, on page 263. If you're a Rubyist who's new to Java, a book like *Core Java* [HC07] can help fill in the gaps, without bogging you down in "how to program" lessons.

Online Resources

We encourage you to try the code samples you see in this book by typing them in by hand. If you get stuck or need a little more context, the source for the examples is available at http://pragprog.com/titles/jruby/source_code.

We designed these programs to run on JRuby version 1.5.5, with specific versions of various libraries we mention in the text. If you want to use a newer version of JRuby or one of the libraries, see http://github.com/jruby/using_jruby to track our updates to the example code.

If something isn't working or you have a question about JRuby that we haven't covered here, please let us know in the forums at http://forums.pragprog.com/forums/125. We'd love to hear from you.

Conventions

Let's skip the description of which fonts we're using for code and *emphasis*, shall we? You'll pick that up from context. But there are a couple of situations that your typical tech book doesn't have to face. It's probably worth adopting a few new conventions for those.

The first is function names. Books seem to have a tradition of spelling functions and methods with trailing parentheses, as in a Java class's main() method. In Ruby, though, parentheses tend to be optional—and there are some contexts where they're almost never used. So, we'll follow that dual convention in the print and PDF versions of this book. When we mention function names in the text, you'll see parentheses after someJavaMethod() but not after some_ruby_method.

The next convention we've adopted is a single notation for the command line, for the most part. Windows command prompts use something like C:\> as your cue to begin typing, while Mac and Linux machines typically use $ or %. Windows uses backslashes to separate directory names, while other platforms uses forward slashes. Other than that, there's little difference between invoking JRuby on one operating system or the other.

Accordingly, we're going to use the notation from bash, the default shell on the Mac and on many Linux distributions. When you see this:

```
$ jruby some_directory/program.rb
```

...you'll know not to type the dollar sign and to use whatever kind of slashes your system requires. (Actually, the latter is a bit of a moot point, because JRuby does fine with forward slashes on Windows.) For the few specific cases where the syntax is significantly different between Windows's cmd.exe and UNIX's bash, we'll spell out both cases.

Speaking of differences between systems, many UNIX-like systems require you to log in as the root user before installing software. Others have you preface any administration-level commands with sudo. Most of your authors run JRuby from regular (nonadministrator) directories in our own home directories, making sudo unnecessary. Accordingly, the commands to install software in this book will typically just say gem install some_library, rather than sudo gem install some_library.

Finally, a word on program output. We use three variations of the traditional Ruby "hash rocket" sign (which looks like this: # =>) to show the result of running a particular piece of code. These marks are just Ruby comments. JRuby ignores them, and you don't need to type them. But they come in handy for documenting how a function works.

```
# This line doesn't print
# anything, but the expression
# has a return value
result = 2 + 2                 # => 4

# This line prints a message
# when you run the program:
puts 'hello'.capitalize        # >> Hello

# This line causes an error
# message to appear:
Foo                            # ~> Uninitialized constant Foo
```

This way, we can show you what the values of different variables are in the middle of a code excerpt, without having to scatter a bunch of print functions all over.

Acknowledgments

To our initial tech reviewers—Fred Daoud, Steven Deobald, Geoff Drake, Yoko Harada, Peter Lind, David Rupp, Vladimir Sizikov, Kent Spillner, and Gale Straney—thank you for helping us sand down the rough edges. To folks who joined the beta release process and wrote to us in the forums—Matt Smith, David Mitchell, Arkadiy Kraportov, Sam Goebert, Robert Dober, Pinit Asavanuchit, Bharat Ruparel, Hans-Georg, and Paul Sideleau—the book is better because of your comments, and we thank you.

To our wonderful editor, Jackie Carter—thank you for being equal parts project champion, product manager, writing coach, and cheerleader. To Dave and Andy, the Pragmatic Programmers—thank you for giving this book a long runway and a chance to fly. To our ever-patient families—thank you for enduring our absence, obsession, and distraction. To Matz—thank you for creating Ruby, our favorite programming language. To Matz and Bruce—thank you for your support of this project and for the lovely forewords. To the entire community of JRuby fans, contributors, and users—thank you for your support of this, our favorite *implementation* of Ruby.

Ready to jump into JRuby? Let's go!

Part I

JRuby Core

Chapter 1

Getting to Know JRuby

You're now standing on the threshold of the JRuby universe, where you'll have your pick of the world's best Ruby and Java libraries. With the techniques in this book and the tools available to you, you'll be able to do amazing things with JRuby. Here are just a few possibilities:

- Deploy a Ruby on Rails web application to Google's App Engine service.[1]

- Target the latest Android smartphones with your Ruby code.[2]

- Create dazzling, cross-platform GUIs with clean, elegant code.[3]

- Build your project on solid libraries written in Java, Scala, Clojure, or other JVM languages.

Do these sound like intriguing projects? They'll all be within your grasp by the time you reach the end of this book. You'll see how to code, test, and package web applications for easy employment. You'll learn the nuances of compiling code and how to adjust to the limitations of mobile platforms. You'll design user interfaces using both graphical layout tools and straightforward code.

Before we get into those specific uses, we'd like to take you on a tour of the best of JRuby in this chapter. We'll start by showing you a couple of easy ways to get JRuby onto your system (including a hassle-free, no-installation option) and what to do with it once you have it.

---

1. http://rails-primer.appspot.com
2. http://ruboto.org
3. http://www.infoq.com/presentations/martin-jruby-limelight

When you have JRuby running, you'll see firsthand how JRuby is a top-notch Ruby environment. You'll try out code interactively in a live interpreter, which is a great way to learn the language and its libraries. You'll write a stand-alone script just like the ones you use for everyday system automation tasks.

We'll also show you how JRuby does a few things other Rubies can't do. You'll compile a Ruby program to a Java .class file. You'll call seamlessly into Java libraries just as easily as calling Ruby code.

Ready to begin your journey?

1.1 Installing JRuby

JRuby is built for easy deployment. After all, it needs to fit in environments ranging from your development laptop to a tightly controlled production server. Accordingly, there are a lot of ways to get it onto your system. We'll look at a couple of the more common ones here.

Using an Installer

The easiest way to install JRuby is to use one of the prebuilt installers available from the official download site.[4] These will take care of the "fit and finish" level of detail, such as setting up your PATH environment variable to make finding JRuby easier.

The JRuby team currently maintains installers for Windows and Mac machines. If you're on Linux, your distribution may package its own JRuby build. For example, on Ubuntu you can type this:

```
$ sudo apt-get install jruby
```

Most Linux distributions don't upgrade to the latest JRuby release the instant it comes out. If you want to stay with the latest and greatest, you might prefer installing from an archive instead; we'll describe how to do this later.

Using the Ruby Version Manager

The Ruby Version Manager (RVM) is a tool for Mac and Linux that can automatically install and switch among several different versions of

---

4. http://jruby.org/download

Ruby at once.[5] A large part of its audience consists of Ruby library developers, who need to test their software in many different Ruby environments.

Even if JRuby is the only Ruby you plan on using, you may want to take a look at RVM. As of this writing, here are the JRuby versions RVM knows about:

```
$ rvm list known | grep jruby
jruby-1.2.0
jruby-1.3.1
jruby-1.4.0
jruby(-1.5.5)
jruby-head
```

The last item, jruby-head, is a build from the latest bleeding-edge source code. The one before it, jruby-1.5.5 (or just jruby), is the latest stable release as of this writing. Here's how you'd install and start using 1.5.5:

```
$ rvm install jruby
$ rvm use jruby
```

If you're a long-time RVM user, you'll want to upgrade to the latest RVM version before using it to install JRuby.

From an Archive

If you have a heavily customized setup or just like doing things yourself, you can get a .zip or .tar.gz archive from the same download page. Extract the archive somewhere convenient on your system, such as C:\ or /opt. You can run JRuby straight from its own bin subdirectory, but you'll probably find it more convenient to add it to your PATH.

On UNIX (including Mac OS X), you can do the following:

```
$ export PATH=$PATH:/opt/jruby/bin
```

On Windows, you'll need to set both the PATH and JAVA_HOME variables:

```
C:\> SET PATH=%PATH%;C:\jruby\bin
C:\> SET JAVA_HOME="C:\Program Files\Java\jdk1.5.0_19"
```

You'll also need a recent version of the Java runtime, at least version 1.5.[6]

---

5. http://rvm.beginrescueend.com
6. http://java.com/en/download

From Source Code

If you're never satisfied with anything less than the latest features and bug fixes, you may want to try your hand at building JRuby from source. You'll need the following in addition to the Java runtime mentioned earlier:

- The Ant build system, version 1.7 or newer[7]
- The Git source control system[8]

First, grab the latest code with Git:

```
$ git clone git://github.com/jruby/jruby.git
```

Next, jump into the jruby directory that just got created:

```
$ cd jruby
```

If you want to compile the source of a specific release, such as JRuby 1.5.5, run the git checkout command:[9]

```
$ git checkout 1.5.5
```

Finally, build the software:

```
$ ant clean
$ ant
$ ant test
```

Assuming the tests pass, you're ready to run JRuby. It's perfectly valid to specify a full path to jruby or jruby.exe every time you run it—JRuby will automatically figure out where its support libraries are relative to the executable. But from here on out, the examples in this book will be written as if you've put the bin directory directly in your PATH, as described earlier.

1.2 Kicking the Tires

Ready to try it? First, make sure you have a good executable:

```
$ jruby --version
jruby 1.5.5 (ruby 1.8.7 patchlevel 249) (2010-11-10 4bd4200) (Java HotSpot(TM) ...)
```

If you have any problems getting to this point, check your PATH, and make sure you're running the latest release version of JRuby.

---

7. http://ant.apache.org
8. http://www.git-scm.com
9. To get out of building a specific release, type git checkout master.

It's time to run some code. The simplest way to try a simple Ruby excerpt, whether you're using plain Ruby or JRuby, is to pass the -e option to the interpreter:

```
$ jruby -e "puts 'This is a short program'"
This is a short program
```

Now that you're up and running, let's look at some more useful ways to execute JRuby.

1.3 The Interactive Shell

Just as Ruby ships with irb for trying code interactively, JRuby has jirb:

```
$ jirb
irb(main):001:0> ['Hello', 'world'].join ' '
=> "Hello world"
irb(main):002:0> "ybuRJ morf".reverse
=> "from JRuby"
irb(main):003:0>
```

As with the REPL[10] from any other dynamic language, jirb gives you instant feedback on the results of each command you type into it. Although this technique is a great way to explore the language, we're guessing that you're interested in running some actual programs, too.

1.4 The Command Line

To get a feel for running interpreted and compiled programs in JRuby, we're going to write a really trivial program and run it in a couple of different ways.

The Simple Case

Put the following code into a file called example.rb:

```
introduction/example.rb
```

```
puts "So, how are you liking the pace so far?"

pace = loop do
  puts "(1) Move it along"
  puts "(2) Just right"
  puts "(3) Not so fast!"
```

---

10. Read-eval-print loop, an interactive environment for programming

```
    res = gets.to_i
    break res if (1..3).include? res
end

puts (pace == 2) ?
  "Great; see you in the next section" :
  "Thanks; we'll see what we can do"
```

Now, run it from the command line like so:

```
$ jruby example.rb
```

Go ahead and give us an answer; we can take it.

```
⇒  So, how are you liking the pace so far?
   (1) Move it along
   (2) Just right
   (3) Not so fast!
⇐  1
⇒  Thanks; we'll see what we can do
```

jruby takes a wide range of command-line parameters to customize the way your programs run. A full discussion is outside the scope of this chapter, but it's worth talking about one of the more important ones.

Running Common Ruby Programs

If you've been coding Ruby for a while, you're used to having certain tools available as executables, such as gem and rake. A typical Ruby program will install itself into your Ruby distribution's bin directory. You may be tempted just to make sure JRuby's bin is at the front of your PATH and then run these commands directly just by typing in their names.

But it's best to invoke command-line tools through JRuby, rather than directly. In particular, Ruby's package manager, RubyGems, may not know whether to use plain Ruby or JRuby if you just type gem on the command line.

A much more reliable approach is to use Ruby's standard -S option for launching stand-alone scripts.[11] Instead of typing this:

```
$ gem install rspec
```

...you'd type the following:

```
$ jruby -S gem install rspec
```

---

11. For more information about this option, see Appendix C, on page 285.

Ian Says...

What Do We Use?

With all this talk of development environments, what do we the authors use to write code for our JRuby projects? By some strange cosmic coincidence, four out of the five of us are heavy users of the Emacs text editor.* The odd man out hops between Vim and TextMate.†,‡ All three of these editors have great support for Ruby, and all three of them stay out of our way while we're coding.

---

*. http://www.gnu.org/software/emacs/
†. http://vim.org
‡. http://macromates.com

This approach works for any Ruby command-line tool, including gem, rake, spec, and others.

There are a ton of other useful JRuby options; for more information, type jruby --help, or see Appendix C, on page 285.

1.5 IDEs

JRuby is easy to use from the command line—so much so that we'll be giving many examples of it in this book. But using an integrated development environment has its merits. In addition to the code completion features most people think of, IDEs can manage your JRuby installation and classpath for you.

Nearly every popular IDE has some support for Ruby, either directly or through a plug-in. If you're asking us for a recommendation, though, we have two.

RubyMine

RubyMine is a Ruby-specific IDE created by the JetBrains company.[12] It has the level of sophistication you'd expect from the folks who created IntelliJ IDEA, the beloved Java development environment.

---

12. http://www.jetbrains.com/ruby/index.html

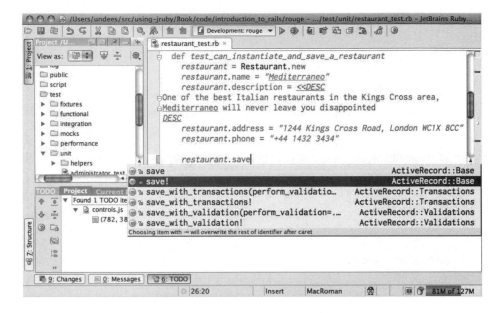

Figure 1.1: THE RUBYMINE IDE

As you can see in Figure 1.1, there's a lot to RubyMine. We'll just mention a couple of points that are hard to show in a screenshot. For one thing, the tool is aware of popular test and directory naming conventions for Ruby projects so you can jump automatically between a piece of code and its tests. It also supports several refactoring techniques on Ruby code.

NetBeans

NetBeans is an open source development environment with support for several different programming languages.[13] You can download a Ruby-specific build of the IDE and have everything you need to start coding.

With NetBeans, you can do some of the many things in Ruby that you're used to doing in less dynamic languages: automatically completing code, stepping through a program in a debugger, designing a GUI, and performing simple refactorings.

---

13. http://www.netbeans.org

Because NetBeans is cross-language, its level of Ruby-specific integration is not quite as deep or polished as RubyMine's. But it's a close second.

1.6 The Compiler

Throughout most of this book, we're going to run JRuby programs the same way people run programs in plain Ruby: hand the text of the program over to an interpreter. The interpreter walks through the program piece by piece, translating and running code as it encounters it.

If you spend time in the Java universe, you're probably wondering whether JRuby allows you to compile your Ruby code into .class files up front and treat them like compiled Java code.

The answer is yes. Here's how you'd compile the previous example:

```
$ jrubyc example.rb
Compiling example.rb to class example
```

The compiler supplies a main() method for you, so you can now run the program straight from the java command (adjust the path here to point to your JRuby installation):

```
$ java -cp .:/opt/jruby/lib/jruby.jar example
```

Note that your compiled program still depends on some JRuby-defined support routines, so jruby.jar needs to be on your CLASSPATH.[14] Also, the compiler compiles only the files you specifically pass to it. If you reference some_ruby_library.rb, you'll have to compile that extra .rb file yourself or ship it in source form alongside your .class file.

When you look at compilation in detail, there are a lot more shades of distinction between "no compilation at all" and "compile everything up front." JRuby may compile parts of your program to Java bytecode at runtime to improve performance. You'll find a detailed discussion of this and other aspects of compilation in Chapter 4, *The JRuby Compiler*, on page 63.

---

14. There's more on how JRuby uses the Java classpath in Chapter 2, *Driving Java from Ruby*, on page 15

1.7   Java Integration

JRuby can use Java objects much as if they were Ruby objects. Here's
a simple example that exercises Java's ArrayList class:

introduction/interop.rb

```
require 'java'

list = java.util.ArrayList.new

list << 'List of'
list << 3
list << :assorted_items

list.each do |item|
  puts "#{item.class}: #{item}"
end
```

As you can see, we can add a variety of objects, including native Ruby
types like Symbols, to the list. JRuby even provides appropriate Ruby
iteration idioms for Java collections, which is why we can call each()
on the list in this example.

Of course, Ruby has its own perfectly respectable collection classes.
Unless you're calling a Java library function expecting an ArrayList, it's
usually better just to use a Ruby Array instead. But bear with us and try
our slightly stilted example in jirb; you should see something like this:

```
⇒ String: List of
  Fixnum: 3
  Symbol: assorted_items
```

Now, let's try something we *couldn't* have done in plain Ruby. Let's hook
into some Java platform-specific functions and query a few properties
of the JVM:

introduction/jvm.rb

```
require 'java'

os   = java.lang.System.get_property 'os.name'
home = java.lang.System.get_property 'java.home'
mem  = java.lang.Runtime.get_runtime.free_memory

puts "Running on #{os}"
puts "Java home is #{home}"
puts "#{mem} bytes available in JVM"
```

```
⇒ Running on Mac OS X
  Java home is /System/Library/Frameworks/JavaVM.framework/Versions/1.5.0/Home
  1592320 bytes available in JVM
```

As you can see, we can access native Java classes, such as java.lang. Runtime and java.lang.System, using a dot notation similar to Java's import syntax. One thing to note is that JRuby gives you the option of calling Java functions like getProperty() by more Ruby-fitting names like get_property.

1.8 Wrapping Up

Now that you have JRuby installed and have taken it for a spin, it's time to get some real work done. In the upcoming chapters, we'll tackle some of the most common ways people bring the Java and Ruby worlds together.

Chapter 2

Driving Java from Ruby

It might be tempting to think of Java/Ruby integration as nothing more than calling from one language to another. But that's selling JRuby short. In a typical project, you're really *interacting* with both platforms. You might construct a Ruby object, pass it to a Java function, and watch the Java code call other Ruby methods you've defined.

In this chapter, we'll look at cases where the interaction starts in Ruby: calling Java methods from Ruby code, implementing Java interfaces in Ruby, and so on. In the next chapter, we'll start with a Java program and work our way back to Ruby.

2.1 Seeing Java Through Ruby Glasses

The first use case for JRuby, and still the most common one today, is calling a Java method from Ruby. Why would someone want to do this? There are thousands of reasons. Here are just a few of the things you can do with this interoperability:

- Visualize geographic data with NASA's World Wind project.[1] In Figure 2.1, on the following page, you can see a map of our hometowns that we put together with just a few lines of Ruby.

- Render beautiful SVG graphics with the Apache Batik project, like the folks at Atomic Object did for their cross-platform simulation app.[2] The elegant visuals they achieved are shown in Figure 2.2, on page 17. (Image used with permission of the Avraham Y. Goldratt Institute, LP.)

---

1. http://worldwind.arc.nasa.gov
2. http://spin.atomicobject.com/2009/01/30/ruby-for-desktop-applications-yes-we-can

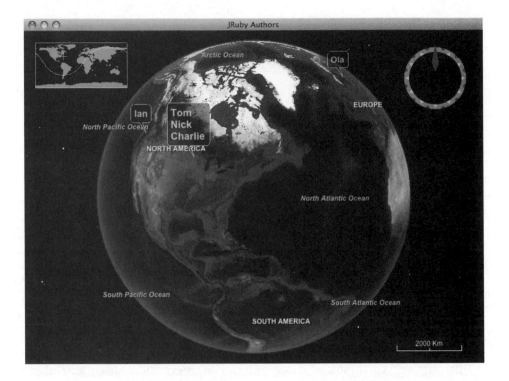

Figure 2.1: LOCATING JRUBY AUTHORS WITH WORLD WIND

- Handle a protocol or data format for which a Java library is the best fit. For example, you might choose the Java-based iText library to add PDF support to your Ruby program—especially if you need digital signatures or some other feature specific to iText.[3]

- Slay the "cross-platform Ruby GUI" dragon by writing a Swing or SWT program in Ruby.

- Boost the performance of a Ruby program. For example, the team behind the Redcar text editor knows they will always have the option of dropping down into Java for any performance-critical parts.[4]

---

3. http://www.itextpdf.com
4. http://redcareditor.com

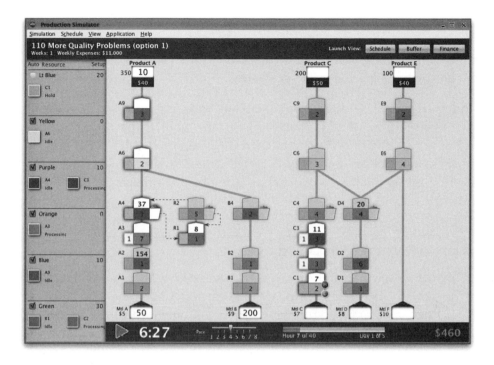

Figure 2.2: SIMULATING INDUSTRIAL PROCESSES WITH BATIK

- Tame a legacy Java project by walling off the old spaghetti code behind a clean Ruby interface.

- Sneak Ruby into a Java shop; after all, JRuby is "just another .jar file."

- Write great tests for your Java code, using one of Ruby's outstanding test frameworks.

- Index and search huge amounts of text with the Lucene search engine.[5]

- Write a database-backed web application in the Rails framework. Behind the scenes, Rails's database adapters call into Java's database libraries to do the heavy SQL lifting.

---

5. http://lucene.apache.org

All of these scenarios are the bread and butter of JRuby and are well supported. But as in any domain where two languages meet, there are some subtleties, gotchas, and impedance mismatches.[6] This chapter will address many of these edge cases.

First things first, though. We'll lead off with the basics of accessing Java classes from JRuby, starting with how your Ruby code can load and interact with Java libraries. Then we'll explore the details of parameter passing and automatic type conversions. Finally, we'll show a few tips and tricks to make Java classes and objects a natural part of your Ruby programs.

A Simple Example: Wrapping a Library

Let's start with a working program to drive a Java library. We'll expand on one of the examples we described earlier: using the iText library to generate a PDF file. This will be just enough to give a hint of the flavor of driving Java, without having to bang our heads against the more obscure edge cases (yet). Download the latest .jar (for example, iText-5.0.1.jar) from the official site, and copy it into the directory where you're following along in code.[7] Next, add this snippet to a file called pdf_demo.rb:

```
java_from_ruby/pdf_demo.rb
require 'java'

pdf  = com.itextpdf.text.Document.new
para = com.itextpdf.text.Paragraph.new 'Brought to you by JRuby'
file = java.io.FileOutputStream.new 'pdf_demo.pdf'

com.itextpdf.text.pdf.PdfWriter.get_instance pdf, file

pdf.open
pdf.add para
pdf.close
```

In the spirit of walking before we run, let's walk through the source before we run the program. In the opening lines, we create a few Java

---

6. The term *impedance mismatch* comes from electrical engineering. It refers to the power lost to reflection when two circuits are connected. It's also a poetic way to describe the conceptual losses between two different software domains.

7. http://sf.net/projects/itext/files

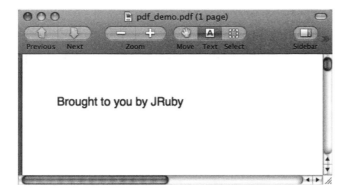

Figure 2.3: THE GENERATED PDF IN ALL ITS GLORY

objects the same way we'd create Ruby ones—by calling the class's new method. We use a typical full-package name for each class (for example, com.itextpdf.text.Document).

In JRuby, Java methods look and act like Ruby ones. All the method names you see in this snippet—open, add, and close—belong to Java classes. That includes get_instance, an alias JRuby has created for getInstance() to make it fit better in the Ruby universe.

Some Ruby types get converted into their Java counterparts automatically for you, such as the "Brought to you..." string. Others need a little hand holding; you'll see a few of those cases later.

Now that you've had a chance to look through the code, let's run it. You'll need to tell JRuby where the external iText library lives by setting the classpath. Java provides the -cp option for this purpose. JRuby will forward any option to the underlying Java runtime if you preface it with -J. Go ahead and try the following command, adjusting the version number of iText to match what you downloaded:

```
$ jruby -J-cp iText-5.0.1.jar pdf_demo.rb
```

That'll create a PDF file called pdf_demo.pdf in the same directory. If you open it, you should see something like Figure 2.3. It's not the most visually breathtaking use of the format, but you get the idea.

Another Simple Example: Extending a Ruby Program

Let's consider another big use case: taking an existing Ruby program
and rewriting part of it in Java for speed. Just for fun, we'll make this
one a GUI app, albeit a trivial one. We're going to build a calculator for
the famous stack-busting Ackermann function.[8] The Ruby code for this
reads like the official mathematical definition:

`java_from_ruby/ackerizer.rb`

```ruby
class Ackermann
  def self.ack(m, n)
    return n + 1                           if m == 0
    return ack(m - 1, 1)                   if n == 0
    return ack(m - 1, ack(m, n - 1))
  end
end
```

This implementation is far too slow for a production app, as will become
painfully clear after we wrap a Swing user interface around it. To build
our GUI, we're going to use a Ruby helper called Rubeus.[9] Go ahead
and install that now:

`$ jruby -S gem install rubeus`

We'll talk more about Rubeus in Chapter 10, *Building GUIs with Swing*,
on page 229. For this short example, the code is simple enough to show
without much explanation. It's just a couple of text inputs and a button:

`java_from_ruby/ackerizer.rb`

```ruby
require 'rubygems'
require 'java'
require 'rubeus'

include Rubeus::Swing

JFrame.new('Ackerizer') do |frame|
  frame.layout = java.awt.FlowLayout.new

  @m = JTextField.new '3'
  @n = JTextField.new '9'

  JButton.new('->') do
    @result.text = Ackermann.ack(@m.text.to_i,
                                 @n.text.to_i).to_s
  end
```

---

8. http://en.wikipedia.org/wiki/Ackermann_function
9. http://code.google.com/p/rubeus/

```
@result = JTextField.new 10

  frame.pack
  frame.show
end
```

Throw those two code snippets into a file called ackerizer.rb, and then launch the app. You'll most likely need to increase the JVM's stack size, using Java's standard -Xss setting together with JRuby's -J "pass-through" option:

```
$ jruby -J-Xss64m ackerizer.rb
```

You should see something like Figure 2.4, on the following page. Try clicking the button to calculate ack(3, 9). The results will probably take several seconds to appear in the window. Because our app is a one-trick pony, there's only one suspect worth investigating: the ack method.[10]

There's a lot we could try in Ruby before jumping into Java. At the very least, we should be storing our intermediate values so that we don't have to calculate them over and over. But let's say you've done all that, and you still need faster results. Here's how you'd move the calculation into a Java class:

`java_from_ruby/Ackermann.java`

```
public class Ackermann {
    public static int ack(int m, int n) {
        if (m == 0)
            return n + 1;

        if (n == 0)
            return ack(m - 1, 1);

        return ack(m - 1, ack(m, n - 1));
    }
}
```

...which you can then compile like so:

```
$ javac Ackermann.java
```

We need to make only one change to the Ruby code to use the new Java class. In the middle of the button's on_click handler, add the text Java:: to the beginning of the Ackermann.ack call.

---

10. On any nontrivial project, you'll want to profile your code, rather than relying on inspection and guesswork. See Appendix C, on page 285, for how to do that with JRuby.

Figure 2.4: THE ACKERMANN CALCULATOR

```
@result.text = Java::Ackermann.ack(@m.text.to_i,
                           @n.text.to_i).to_s
```

When you rerun the program and click the button, the result should appear immediately. Now that we've seen examples of the most common ways people use JRuby, let's look at each step of the process in more detail.

2.2 Dealing with the Classpath

Before you can use that piece of external library wizardry, you have to *find* it. When you bring Java code into your app, you're playing by Java's rules. Rubyists are used to saying require 'some_file_name' and counting on the file to show up inside one of Ruby's search paths. By contrast, Java looks for each class by its fully specified package name; the physical location of the file isn't as important.

For readers coming from the Ruby world, the *classpath* is the list of directories and .jar files where Java (and therefore JRuby) will look for external libraries. If you're doing a java_import (see Section 2.3, *By Importing*, on page 26) and JRuby can't find the class you're asking for, the classpath is usually the first place to make adjustments.

A lot of people code in an IDE that sets up their classpath for them and deploy to a server that has its own notions of where things should be; they'll never touch the classpath themselves. But if you're using the command line a lot on your own, you'll need to set the path up yourself. JRuby supports several ways of doing this to ensure that both Ruby developers and Java developers will find familiar ground.

From the Command Line

There's a strong parallel between the Ruby and Java ways of passing extra search paths on the command line. Ruby uses the -I switch:

```
$ ruby -I/path/to/library my_program.rb
```

Charlie Says...

The Default Package

Notice here we're using the Java:: prefix. In this case, it's because our Java-based Ackermann class is in the *default* package. Such classes can be accessed immediately under the Java namespace.

JRuby supports -I for Ruby code, naturally, but also understands Java's -cp/-classpath option for Java classes:

```
$ jruby -J-cp /path/to/library.jar
```

```
C:\> jruby -J-cp C:\path\to\library.jar
```

Remember that -J specifies that JRuby should pass the -cp option to the underlying Java runtime.

With an Environment Variable

As we did with the command-line arguments, we're going to draw a parallel between the ways Ruby and Java use environment variables. If you're a lazy typist like we are, you're probably used to storing your most commonly used Ruby search paths in the RUBYOPT environment variable:

```
$ export RUBYOPT=-I/path/to/common/libraries
```

```
C:\> set RUBYOPT=-IC:\path\to\common\libraries
```

JRuby supports RUBYOPT for finding Ruby code, and the Java equivalent (CLASSPATH) for finding Java classes:

```
$ export CLASSPATH=$CLASSPATH:/path/to/library.jar
```

```
C:\> set CLASSPATH=%CLASSPATH%;C:\path\to\library.jar
```

If you have both a CLASSPATH and a -J-cp option, the latter will take priority. Of course, you can always combine them by referencing the environment variable from inside the search path:

```
$ jruby -J-cp $CLASSPATH:/path/to/library.jar
```

```
C:\> jruby -J-cp %CLASSPATH%;C:\path\to\library.jar
```

Charlie Says...

A Gentle Reminder

Make sure you have called require 'java' *before* using the $CLASSPATH variable. JRuby doesn't prepare that variable unless it sees you're planning to use Java libraries.

Once JRuby has loaded your program, you can further manipulate the classpath from within Ruby.

In the Source Code

As an alternative or a supplement to the command-line classpath, you can add a .jar or directory to the $CLASSPATH variable inside Ruby itself (much as you're used to doing with $LOAD_PATH or $: for Ruby libraries):

`java_from_ruby/classpath.rb`

```
$CLASSPATH << '/usr/local/lib/jemmy/jemmy.jar'
```

To sum up what we've seen so far: in JRuby, you use Java techniques to find Java code, and you use Ruby techniques to find Ruby code. Now, we're going to do something a little different. We're going to cross the language barrier and use a *Ruby* technique to find *Java* code. The simplest way to do this is to use Ruby's require method to add a .jar to the search path:

`java_from_ruby/classpath.rb`

```
require '/usr/local/lib/jemmy/jemmy.jar'
```

You may be wondering whether other Ruby mechanisms can load Java code. Indeed, they can. Both the -I argument and the $LOAD_PATH variable work on both Ruby and Java libraries in JRuby:

```
$ jruby -I/path/to -e "require 'library.jar' ..."
```

```
C:\> jruby -IC:\path\to -e "require 'library.jar' ..."
```

`java_from_ruby/classpath.rb`

```
$LOAD_PATH << '/usr/local/lib/jemmy'
require 'jemmy.jar'
```

Now that JRuby knows where on disk to look for external libraries, how do we crack them open and get at the classes inside?

2.3 Loading Classes

Your Ruby code will see Java packages as Ruby modules. This is not surprising, because these are the fundamental namespace mechanisms of the two languages. Let's take a closer look at how this works.

By Namespace

The most reliable way to refer to a Java class in JRuby is by tacking Java:: onto the beginning of the full package name:

`java_from_ruby/loading_classes.rb`

```
Java::clojure.lang.Repl
# => Java::ClojureLang::Repl
```

Notice JRuby has translated the Java-like clojure.lang.Repl syntax into an internal name, Java::ClojureLang::Repl. It may be tempting to "cut out the middleman" and use the latter name directly in your code, but we don't recommend it. Internal formats are subject to change, but the package-name syntax will always work.

For the most commonly used namespaces, JRuby provides top-level functions like com, org, java, and javax. To use these, you have to require 'java' first:

`java_from_ruby/loading_classes.rb`

```
require 'java'

java.lang.StringBuffer
# => Java::JavaLang::StringBuffer
```

If the class you want to access lives in the default package (that is, no package specifier at all), just prepend Java:: directly to the class name:

`java_from_ruby/loading_classes.rb`

```
Java::MyTopLevelClass
# => Java::MyTopLevelClass
```

It's worth noting that the module/namespace for a given package is just another Ruby object.

You can stash it in a variable or pass it around at will:

> java_from_ruby/loading_classes.rb

```
swing = javax.swing
swing.JFrame
# => Java::JavaxSwing::JFrame
```

The techniques in the next section will build on this idea of treating module and class names like regular data.

By Importing

For classes nested deeply inside namespaces, you may get tired of typing out the full module or package name every time. A common convention is to define a new constant consisting of just the class name:

> java_from_ruby/loading_classes.rb

```
StringBuffer = java.lang.StringBuffer
```

JRuby provides a handy java_import shortcut that does exactly this kind of assignment. You can indicate the class you want using a Ruby constant, a Java package name, or a string:

> java_from_ruby/loading_classes.rb

```
java_import java.lang.StringBuffer
java_import 'java.lang.StringBuffer'
```

The latter is handy for importing a bunch of similarly named packages together:

> java_from_ruby/loading_classes.rb

```
['Frame', 'Dialog', 'Button'].each do |name|
  java_import "org.netbeans.jemmy.operators.J#{name}Operator"
end
```

You can also pass a block to java_import in case you need to do something else to the package name, such as renaming it to avoid a conflict with some existing Ruby class:

> java_from_ruby/loading_classes.rb

```
java_import 'java.lang.String' do |pkg, cls|
  puts "#{cls} lives in #{pkg}"
  'JString' # don't clobber Ruby's String class
end
```

You may encounter code in the wild that uses the shorter import alias. We recommend sticking with java_import to avoid conflicts with libraries such as Rake that define their own import method.

Finally, we can move on to actually calling external code.

2.4 Using Objects

It's taken a bit of housekeeping to get to this point. We've had to find libraries, load classes, and resolve names. Now comes the payoff: driving a Java object from Ruby.

Static Methods

Let's start with the easiest kind of Java method to invoke: static methods. Since these aren't attached to any particular class instance, we can punt on the whole issue of object creation for now. You can call a static Java method directly from JRuby:

`java_from_ruby/static.rb`
```
java_import java.lang.System
System.currentTimeMillis # => 1251075795138
```

But the Java convention of using camelCase looks out of place among Ruby's snake_case names. Your code will look more Ruby-like if you take advantage of JRuby's automatic mapping between Ruby names and Java names:

`java_from_ruby/static.rb`
```
java_import java.lang.System
System.current_time_millis # => 1251075795172
```

The mapping also knows how to deal with function names containing capitalized abbreviations, like "URL."

`java_from_ruby/static.rb`
```
java_import java.net.URL
# assume you've initialized some object "factory" here
URL.setURLStreamHandlerFactory(factory)
URL.set_urlstream_handler_factory(factory)
```

Static Fields

Static fields of Java classes are typically used to implement either singleton objects, such as Logger.global, or constants, such as Level.SEVERE. For the former case, you'll just treat the field like a Ruby class-level method, calling it with dot notation and a Ruby-style snake_case name. For the latter case, you'll treat the field like a Ruby constant, accessing it with double-colon notation and matching the Java capitalization.

Here's an example that shows both situations:

`java_from_ruby/static.rb`

```
java_import java.util.logging.Logger
java_import java.util.logging.Level

Logger.global.log Level::SEVERE, "It looks like you're writing a letter!"
```

Object Construction

JRuby adapts many Java idioms to "the Ruby way." Constructing Java objects falls right into this aesthetic; you just use the normal Ruby new class method. You might wonder how this is possible, since Java supports overloaded methods (including constructors) and Ruby doesn't. But JRuby sweeps this difference under the rug for you, looking at the parameters you pass to new and selecting the constructor that best matches those arguments. We'll see more detail on argument matching in a minute.

First, let's look at a concrete example. Java's URL class has several constructors, including these two:

```
new URL(String spec)
new URL(String protocol, String host, String file)
```

JRuby will choose the best match when you call new:

`java_from_ruby/instances.rb`

```
URL.new 'http://pragprog.com/titles'
URL.new 'http', 'pragprog.com', '/titles'
```

Instance Methods

Just as with static methods, JRuby maps instance methods to nice snake_case ones for you:

`java_from_ruby/instances.rb`

```
url.get_protocol # => "http"
```

As an added bonus, Java-style getters and setters are callable as Ruby-style attribute accessors. In other words, the following two lines are equivalent:

`java_from_ruby/attributes.rb`

```
car.setPrice(20_000)
car.price = 20_000
```

Instance Fields

On its own, JRuby doesn't seek out a class's fields and try to map them to Ruby attributes. After all, most fields are private—there's usually no need to get at them from outside the class, let alone outside the language. Still, there may be times when you really need this capability. If you have the following Java class:

`java_from_ruby/FieldDemo.java`

```java
public class FieldDemo
{
    private int somePrivateField = 0;

    public FieldDemo() {}
}
```

...you can reopen (that is, modify) the class in JRuby and specify a Java-to-Ruby mapping for the field:

`java_from_ruby/field_demo.rb`

```ruby
class FieldDemo
  field_accessor :somePrivateField => :some_field
end

obj = FieldDemo.new

obj.some_field = 1
obj.some_field
# => 1
```

This will always work for public fields of a particular Java type, and if your JVM's security settings are lenient enough (most default configurations are), it will work for protected, package-visible and private fields as well.

2.5 Passing Parameters

Even the simple method calls in the past few sections are the result of careful choreography on JRuby's part. As we saw with the URL constructors, JRuby seems to "know" which among several overloaded versions of a Java method is the best fit for the way you're calling it in Ruby.

What about method parameters? Unless it was written specifically for JRuby, a Java method will not expect to be passed a bunch of Ruby objects. So, JRuby will automatically convert certain parameters from the original Ruby types to the Java types needed by the method.

We're as mistrustful of magical thinking in programming as you are. Fortunately, there's no magic here, just some straightforward mappings between Java and Ruby types. Once you understand why and how JRuby selects methods and converts parameters, you'll always know how your code will behave.

Simple Type Conversion

For meat-and-potatoes types like numbers and strings, JRuby will copy each Ruby parameter into a reasonable Java equivalent. Consider this Java class:

`java_from_ruby/BigIntDemo.java`

```java
import java.math.BigInteger;

public class BigIntDemo {
    public static final BigInteger GOOGOL =
        new BigInteger("10").pow(100);

    public static boolean biggerThanGoogol(BigInteger i) {
        return (GOOGOL.compareTo(i) < 0);
    }
}
```

...and the Ruby code that calls it:

`java_from_ruby/big_int_demo.rb`

```ruby
a_big_number = 10 ** 100 + 1
BigIntDemo.bigger_than_googol(a_big_number)
# => true
```

Ruby's Bignum class and Java's java.math.BigInteger are distinct types, but JRuby seamlessly converts the Ruby data into its Java counterpart.

Arrays

Although JRuby adds a few conveniences to Java arrays to make them feel a little more at home in the Ruby world, Ruby arrays and Java arrays are actually distinct types:

`java_from_ruby/ArrayDemo.java`

```java
public class ArrayDemo {
    public static String whatTypeIsIt(Object o) {
        return o.getClass().getName();
    }
}
```

Charlie Says. . .

Ruby Arrays in Java

JRuby's implementation of the Ruby Array class provides a java.util.List interface for the Java world to use. So, there's really no expensive data conversion happening until some piece of Java code starts extracting individual elements from the Ruby array you passed in.

`java_from_ruby/array_demo.rb`
```ruby
ArrayDemo.what_type_is_it(['a', 'b', 'c'])
# => "org.jruby.RubyArray"

ArrayDemo.what_type_is_it(['a', 'b', 'c'].to_java)
# => "[Ljava.lang.Object;"
```

JRuby can convert Ruby arrays to Java ones for you, so this difference isn't much of an inconvenience in practice.

Plain Ol' Java Objects

When you've obtained a Java object from some API call, you can freely pass that object around in the Ruby world and hand it back to Java undisturbed. For example, let's say you wanted to construct a Java URL object, stash it in a Ruby variable, and then pass it into a Java method later:

`java_from_ruby/url_demo.rb`
```ruby
url = URL.new 'http://pragprog.com/titles'

add_url_to_some_ruby_list(url)

URLDemo.retrieve_url url
# => "big list of book titles"
```

There's no conversion going on in this case; the Java URL object is simply kept intact throughout its stay in Ruby-land.

Variable Arguments

JRuby can call Java methods with variable argument lists:

`java_from_ruby/variable_args_demo.rb`

```
VariableArgsDemo.longest_string "foo", "bazzles", "schnozzberry"
# => "schnozzberry"
```

The syntax is exactly like what you'd use for any other function.

Explicit Coercion

Though JRuby's mapping between Ruby and Java types will cover most of the cases you'll encounter, you may occasionally want to coerce Ruby types explicitly to specific Java ones. For instance, if JRuby's automatic conversion is likely to be time-consuming, you might want to pre-convert the object:

`java_from_ruby/string_demo.rb`

```
ruby_string = "This is a large string we don't want to convert frequently"
java_string = ruby_string.to_java

StringDemo.method_taking_a java_string
```

When you require 'java', every Ruby object gains a to_java method. Either you can call it with no parameters to get the nearest Java type or you can specify a particular Java class you want to convert to.

The Extra Mile

The Ruby/Java conversions we've seen so far have been like the simple translations in a tourist's phrasebook. They're fine for rudimentary communication. But as a seasoned traveler, you enjoy speaking in a more fluent, idiomatic way.

JRuby includes tons of extra conveniences for using Ruby idioms with Java classes, and vice versa. Here are a few of the most common ones.

Strings and Regular Expressions

Ruby's to_s and Java's toString() are a natural fit for each other. Define to_s on your Ruby object, pass it into Java, and any Java code expecting to find toString() in your class will be able to call it.

Java regular expressions can be used with Ruby's =~ operator:

`java_from_ruby/special_cases.rb`

```
java_import java.util.regex.Pattern
```

```
simple_us_phone = Pattern.compile "\\d{3}-\\d{3}-\\d{4}"
'Call 503-555-1212' =~ simple_us_phone # => 5
```

You can still match strings the Java way, through the various methods of Pattern and Matcher. But the Ruby syntax is much more convenient.

Collections

If you're accustomed to indexing Ruby Array and Hash objects with the [] operator, you'll find that the same technique works on Java Map and List objects as well:

java_from_ruby/special_cases.rb

```
# assume this came from some Java function
java_list.entries          # => ["lock", "stock", "barrel"]
first_item = java_list[0] # => "lock"
```

Moreover, all Java Collection objects gain the traditional Ruby array operators: +, -, <<, length, and join.

JRuby mixes the Ruby Enumerable interface into Java Collections and Iterables. So, you can use Ruby's functional programming idioms directly on Java classes:

java_from_ruby/special_cases.rb

```
# assume this came from some Java function
java_list_of_urls.entries
# => [#<Java::JavaNet::URL:0xacecf3>, #<Java::JavaNet::URL:0xf854bd>]

protocols = java_list_of_urls.map do |url|
  url.protocol
end
# => ["http", "ftp"]
```

Java and Ruby each have a notion of Comparable objects:

java_from_ruby/special_cases.rb

```
uris = [URI.new('/uploads'),
        URI.new('/images'),
        URI.new('/stylesheets')]
uris.sort.map {|u| u.to_string}
# => ["/images", "/stylesheets", "/uploads"]
```

JRuby maps the two concepts together so that you can sort Java objects inside Ruby collections.

Edge Cases

Before we move on, let's dip our toes into a few of the more obscure conversions. JRuby adds the to_proc Ruby method to Java Runnables so they can be passed around as blocks of code in Ruby. Here's a rather contrived example that hands off a Java thread to a Ruby one:[11]

java_from_ruby/special_cases.rb

```
runnable = java.lang.Thread.new
run_it = runnable.to_proc
Thread.new &run_it
```

Java InputStreams and OutputStreams can be converted to Ruby IO objects with the to_io method:

java_from_ruby/special_cases.rb

```
java_out = java.lang.System.out.to_io
java_out << 'Hello from JRuby!'
```

You can catch Java exceptions in a Ruby rescue clause:

java_from_ruby/special_cases.rb

```
begin
  java.text.SimpleDateFormat.new(nil)
rescue java.lang.NullPointerException
  puts 'Ouch!'
end
```

Believe it or not, there is an overall theme to this parade of examples: simplicity. JRuby supports so many different ways of passing data into Java, precisely so that your Ruby code can be as lucid as possible. Rather than trying to memorize every edge case, we recommend you take one more glance over the most common uses described earlier and then just let JRuby delight you. For those rare times when you really need to know exactly what's happening inside the machinery, you can turn to Appendix B, on page 281.

2.6 Calling Overloaded Methods

There are two reasons JRuby looks so closely at the parameters you pass into Java methods. The first, as we've just seen, is to expose your

---

11. Speaking of threads, we should mention that JRuby is not subject to the "Global Interpreter Lock" shared by some Ruby implementations. Your Ruby threads can run simultaneously on multiple cores.

Ruby data to Java in the most convenient way possible. The second is to select the best match for an overloaded method.

Automatic Resolution

The simplest case to consider is a set of overloads based on a single parameter, where the differences among types are obvious:

java_from_ruby/OverloadDemo.java

```java
import java.util.List;

public class OverloadDemo {
    public static String whatTypeIs(long value) {
        return "long";
    }

    public static String whatTypeIs(String value) {
        return "string";
    }

    public static String whatTypeIs(Object value) {
        return "object";
    }
}
```

Here, the Java types are radically different from one another, and JRuby is able to choose appropriate overloads with no assistance:

java_from_ruby/overload_demo.rb

```ruby
OverloadDemo.what_type_is 42        # => "long"
OverloadDemo.what_type_is "Fun!"    # => "string"
OverloadDemo.what_type_is Hash.new  # => "object"
```

Sometimes, though, things get a little hairier. In the following Java class, the overloaded methods both take integer types:

java_from_ruby/HowManyBits.java

```java
public class HowManyBits {
    public int neededFor(int i) {
        return 32;
    }

    public int neededFor(long l) {
        return 64;
    }
}
```

When we try to call the version that takes a 32-bit integer, JRuby ends up promoting our parameter to a long instead:

```
java_from_ruby/how_many_bits.rb
```

```
bits = HowManyBits.new

bits.needed_for 1_000_000
# => 64
```

How do we tell JRuby, "No, I really mean the int version?"

Forcing a Specific Overload

In Java, you can choose which overload you want by casting arguments to specific types. For instance, you might use System.out.println((char)70) to call the version of println that takes a character, rather than the one that takes an int. But Ruby has no casting syntax...are we stuck? Fortunately not. We can use JRuby's java_send method to specify the int version of the neededFor() method from earlier:

```
java_from_ruby/how_many_bits.rb
```

```
bits.java_send :neededFor, [Java::int], 1_000_000
# => 32
```

If you've used Ruby's built-in send method, the notation should look familiar. Notice that this is a bit more cumbersome than a plain method call. For this reason, JRuby provides a couple of shortcuts. The simplest is java_alias, which lets you choose a new name for the Java overload:

```
java_from_ruby/how_many_bits.rb
```

```
class HowManyBits
  java_alias :needed_for_int, :neededFor, [Java::int]
end

puts bits.needed_for_int(1_000_000)
```

The other alternative is to use java_method to get a reference to an overload. You can pass this reference around your program and call it at any time:

```
java_from_ruby/how_many_bits.rb
```

```
bits_needed_for = bits.java_method :neededFor, [Java::int]
bits_needed_for.call 1_000_000
# => 32
```

Not only will java_alias and java_method clean up your code, they'll also make it a little faster, since JRuby won't have to keep looking up the same Java overload.

Annotated Classes

Some Java methods expect the objects handed to them to have specific annotations. Assume we've defined a custom PerformedBy annotation containing the name of someone who performs a feat of skill:

java_from_ruby/Sorcery.java

```java
@PerformedBy(name="Charlie")
public class Sorcery {
    // Nothing up my sleeve...
}
```

If we wanted to describe the feat of skill at runtime, we could do so by reading the annotation:

java_from_ruby/Chronicler.java

```java
import java.lang.annotation.Annotation;

public class Chronicler {
    public static void describe(Class<?> c) {
        PerformedBy p = (PerformedBy)c.getAnnotation(PerformedBy.class);
        System.out.println(p.name() + " performs " + c.getName());
    }
}
```

How do we call this method from JRuby? There's no primitive Java type we can convert the parameter to. It's expecting a full-on Java class name with a runtime annotation attached. Fortunately, JRuby can create a Java class for us on the fly, based on our Ruby class:

java_from_ruby/mischief.rb

```ruby
require 'java'
require 'jruby/core_ext'

java_import 'PerformedBy'
java_import 'Chronicler'
java_import 'Sorcery'

class Mischief
  # ... more mischief here ...
end

Mischief.add_class_annotation PerformedBy => {'name' => 'Ian'}
Mischief.become_java!
```

```
Chronicler.describe Sorcery
# >>> Charlie performs Sorcery

Chronicler.describe Mischief
# >>> Ian performs ruby.Mischief
```

The add_class_annotation method, imported from JRuby's core_ext extensions, decorates the Ruby class with the necessary annotation. By itself, this doesn't mean much, since the Ruby universe won't know to look for this information. But when we use the become_java! method to "promote" Mischief to a real Java class, the Chronicler is able to see the PerformedBy annotation.

2.7 Implementing a Java Interface

What do you do when the function you're calling expects you to pass in a Java object implementing some specific interface? Consider Executors.callable, which wraps a Runnable up inside an object:

```
static Callable<Object> callable(Runnable task);
```

There are two main ways to pass an interface into a Java function.

Implementing the Methods

You can implement the Java interface completely in Ruby code. Just include it in your class definition, and any calls to the interface's methods become calls to your Ruby class. Runnable has just one required method, run:

```
java_from_ruby/runnable_demo.rb
```

```
Line 1   require 'java'
     -   java_import java.lang.Runnable
     -
     -   class Foo
     5     include Runnable
     -
     -     def run
     -       puts "foo"
     -     end
    10   end
     -
     -   callable = java.util.concurrent.Executors.callable(Foo.new)
     -   callable.call
```

Technically, you don't *have* to include the interface name at line 5. JRuby can detect that this instance of Foo implements Runnable's methods. But we like being explicit here.

Passing a Block

For single-method interfaces, there's an even more direct path from Ruby to Java. Instead of going through the mental overhead of creating and naming a Ruby class, you can just pass a block of Ruby code straight to the Java method:

java_from_ruby/runnable_demo.rb
```
callable = java.util.concurrent.Executors.callable do
  puts "foo"
end

callable.call
```

This also works with Proc objects, which are like blocks of code that can be stored in variables:

java_from_ruby/runnable_demo.rb
```
myproc = Proc.new { puts "foo" }
callable = java.util.concurrent.Executors.callable(myproc)

callable.call
```

This approach is suitable only for simple interfaces. If an interface has ten different methods in it, that poor little Ruby block is going to have to understand ten different ways in which Java might call it. In those cases, you're best off using the class approach described earlier.

One other thing to note about the block approach is that the interface passed into the Java world isn't quite a first-class citizen. For instance, the code on the other side of the wall won't be able to use features like introspection to interrogate your Ruby code.

2.8 Troubleshooting

It happens to the best of us. You're ready to tie together your masterpiece, and instead of passing tests, you get a 20-line stack trace. Here are some of the errors you might see on your path to JRuby bliss.

NameError

If your import fails with a NameError, like this:

`java_from_ruby/name_error.rb`

```
require 'java'

java_import 'com.example.Foo'
# ~> (eval):1:in `include_class': cannot load Java class com.example.Foo (NameError
```

...there are a couple of things you can check. First, try the obvious: make sure your classpath contains the directories where your Java classes live. Next, make sure the directory structure matches the Java package structure. If your Java class is part of the com.example package, the .class file needs to be nested in a com/example subdirectory.

Wrong Version of a Class

Maybe it's happened to you. You make a change to a Java class to fix a bug, and it doesn't work. You throw in some println() statements to find out what's going on, and nothing shows up on the console. Is JRuby even *calling* your code? Perhaps not. If some other implementation of that class, inside some other directory or .jar, is ahead in the classpath, JRuby might be loading that and not even seeing your work.

Errors at Construction Time

Sometimes JRuby will import a class just fine but will raise a NoClassDefFoundError or LinkageError when you try to instantiate it. This can happen when the class you need is in your classpath but one of its dependencies isn't. For example, imagine you have a file named consumer.jar containing a Consumer class. Even after JRuby finds the .jar, things can still go wrong:

`java_from_ruby/producer_consumer.rb`

```
consumer = Consumer.new
# ~> Consumer.java:2:in `<init>': java.lang.NoClassDefFoundError:
# ~>     Producer (NativeException)
# ~>     ...
# ~>     from -:7
```

Here, the backtrace provides a clue: Java couldn't find a Producer class, which Consumer apparently requires. Adding producer.jar (or wherever the class lives) to your classpath should fix the problem. If the backtrace doesn't give enough clues to figure out which .jar is missing, it's time to hit the documentation for the Java libraries you're using.

This kind of problem can also happen if a class you're directly or indirectly depending on was compiled for an incompatible JVM version.

Can't Find the Method

A lot of things can go wrong at method invocation time. The most obvious thing to check is the method name; if you can call a method by its original Java camelCase() name but not by its Ruby-style snake_case name, you may be looking at an edge case in the mapping between the two (like setURLForPage() → set_urlfor_page).

After spelling quirks, the most common cause of "vanishing methods" is type coercion. If JRuby can't automatically map your Ruby parameters to Java ones, it won't call the method. You'll need to convert some of the parameters yourself.

Wrong Method

A less frequent case, but no less baffling when it happens, is when JRuby invokes a different method than the one you want. As we saw earlier, JRuby tries to pick the closest match among overloaded functions. But some distinctions simply do not exist on the Ruby side.

Similar situations can come up when multiple overloads are all equally valid—such as when a Ruby object implements two interfaces and there are overloads for each. In cases like these, you'll need to use java_send or one of its cousins from Section 2.6, *Forcing a Specific Overload*, on page 36.

JRuby can also end up making the wrong call if your Java method names clash with common Ruby ones. Say you have the following class that just happens to have a method called initialize(), which is the name Ruby uses for constructors:

java_from_ruby/MethodClash.java

```java
public class MethodClash {
    public void initialize(String data) {
        System.out.println("Now we're set up with " + data);
    }
}
```

If you try to call this method the usual way, JRuby will think you want the no-argument Ruby initialize constructor:

`java_from_ruby/method_clash.rb`

```
the_clash = MethodClash.new

the_clash.initialize 'everything'
# ~> -:8: wrong # of arguments(1 for 0) (ArgumentError)
```

Actually, we got lucky this time. If the Java method had taken zero arguments instead of one, Ruby would have silently called the wrong method instead of reporting an error. Again, java_send comes to the rescue:

`java_from_ruby/method_clash.rb`

```
the_clash = MethodClash.new

the_clash.java_send :initialize, [java.lang.String], 'everything'
# >> Now we're set up with everything
```

Fortunately, there are very few cases like this one. object_id, __id__, and __send__ come to mind, but they are not likely to appear in a typical Java class.

Lost Monkeypatches

JRuby lets you monkeypatch Java classes, with a catch.[12] The Java side will be unaware of any new attributes or methods you define in Ruby. In fact, your additions will evaporate completely if Ruby lets go of all its references to the object. (The original Java part of the object will of course live on as long as the Java side holds a reference.)

If you've tried the techniques we've described here and are still stuck, you may want to peek at the relevant section of the JRuby wiki.[13]

2.9 Wrapping Up

We've been all over the map this chapter, from the basics of loading libraries to the minutiae of parameter passing. We've seen how JRuby

---

12. Monkeypatching (from a malapropism of "guerrilla patching") means modifying a class at runtime.
13. http://wiki.jruby.org/CallingJavaFromJRuby

sands off some of the rough spots where the two languages meet and how to steer around the remaining ones. And we've discussed what to do when things go wrong.

This broad set of topics might seem scattershot at first glance. But we've striven to show a common theme among them. The examples we've presented have all focused on the case where you're starting with a Ruby script that's calling into a Java library. Of course, there's been some back-and-forth, with Java occasionally calling back into a Ruby object we gave it.

We're about to shift the emphasis in the Java direction. In the next chapter, we'll start with a Java project and add Ruby to it. As with this chapter, there will still be plenty of places where the two worlds are calling back and forth to each other.

## Chapter 3

Ruby from Java:
Embedding JRuby

We've just seen several ways for Ruby to call into Java libraries. Now let's consider the other side of the coin: embedding Ruby code in a Java project.

There are several situations where this capability comes in handy. Here are a few examples:

- A Java program might need to perform some task for which there is no Java library (or for which the Ruby libraries are easier to use than their Java counterparts). For example, Ruby's image_voodoo library exposes a simpler API than the native Java2D framework.[1]
- Users might want to extend your Java game or animation program with their own scripts. With JRuby, you can use Ruby as your project's extension language.
- You might be deploying a Ruby program into an otherwise Java-heavy environment, where your team wants to test your Ruby code using their JUnit or TestNG harness.
- If you're wrestling with an existing Java code base, you might want to get the benefits of Ruby's flexibility by rewriting parts of your program in Ruby.

All these uses look the same from the Java side, so we're going to concentrate on the first case: using a Ruby library from a Java program.

---

1. http://rubyforge.org/projects/jruby-extras

3.1 A Real-Life Example: Source Control

Over the next several pages, we're going to build a Java app that calls into Ruby with increasing sophistication. We'll start with a simple "Hello world"–like program and end up performing a useful task.

What useful task? Glad you asked. We're going to build a source code history viewer in Java. The program—let's call it Historian—will use a Ruby library to peer into a Git repository and print patches.[2] In a delicious bit of recursion, we'll view the history of Historian's own source code.

Setting Up Your Workspace

Before we get started, let's quickly examine the layout of the Historian project. You can create this structure from scratch, but we strongly recommend following along with the book's source code.

- src/book/embed contains the Java source to our program, which is what we'll be spending most of our time looking at.
- lib contains the Ruby glue code we'll write to connect the Java world to the Ruby library we're wrapping.
- lib/git.rb and lib/git comprise a local copy of a popular Ruby Git library.[3] This library requires you to have Git installed on your system, so grab that if you don't already have it.[4]
- bin/get-jruby-libs downloads jruby-complete.jar, a bundle containing the parts of JRuby needed by our Java program, into the lib directory.[5] You'll need to run this script once at the beginning of the project or build your own .jar from source.[6]
- bin/make-history sets up a new Git repository in the current directory and adds a couple of revisions for Historian to play with. As with the previous script, you should run this once before you dive into the code.
- .git contains the history of the project's own source code. If you're creating this project from scratch, you'll need to create this history yourself by doing a git init, plus a few commits.

---

2. Java already has a library for accessing Git repositories, JGit. But let's say you were itching to use one of the many Ruby bindings to Git instead.
3. http://repo.or.cz/w/rubygit.git
4. http://git-scm.com
5. http://jruby.org.s3.amazonaws.com/downloads/1.5.5/jruby-complete-1.5.5.jar
6. http://wiki.jruby.org/DownloadAndBuildJRuby

As we proceed, you'll notice that we're building up this project in stages, from Historian1.java up to Historian8.java. You might find it slightly ironic that we're using such an old-school naming convention with such an advanced revision control system. We want the filenames on the printed pages of this book to be explicit about what stage of the process we're in.

We'll give instructions for building the project on the command line with Ant (see Chapter 7, *Building Software for Deployment*, on page 153). If you prefer the IDE experience, we've also included project files for NetBeans.

Getting the Two Worlds Talking

Let's start with the basics. Within the project structure we've described, create a file called Historian1.java in the src/book/embed folder. Put the following imports at the top (we won't need some of these classes until later, but let's go ahead and import them now):

ruby_from_java/historian/src/book/embed/Historian1.java

```java
package book.embed;

import java.util.Arrays;
import java.util.List;
import org.jruby.embed.InvokeFailedException;
import org.jruby.embed.ScriptingContainer;
```

Now, add the bare minimum connection to Ruby:

ruby_from_java/historian/src/book/embed/Historian1.java

```java
public class Historian1 {
    public static void main(String[] args) {
        ScriptingContainer container = new ScriptingContainer();

        container.runScriptlet("puts 'TODO: Make history here.'");
    }
}
```

This is the simplest way to drive Ruby from Java: pass in a chunk of Ruby code as a String, and let JRuby handle the rest (including output). The ScriptingContainer class is part of JRuby's core embedding API.[7]

You can compile the script using Ant:

```
$ ant
```

---

7. Embed Core is part of a collection of JRuby embedding APIs, known together as JRuby Embed or Red Bridge.

...and run it using the launcher we've provided:

```
$ ./bin/historian1
TODO: Make history here.
```

There's nothing mysterious going on inside this launcher. We're just setting up the classpath to contain both Historian and jruby-complete.jar. If you prefer, you can do this manually:

```
$ java -cp lib/jruby-complete.jar:build/classes book.embed.Historian1
```

Now that Java is at least able to run a trivial JRuby program, let's put some actual behavior in there. Here's the new body of the main() function. If you're using the same filenames as we are, make sure you name your new class Historian2 to match the file.

```
ruby_from_java/historian/src/book/embed/Historian2.java
ScriptingContainer container = new ScriptingContainer();

container.setLoadPaths(Arrays.asList("lib"));

String expr = "require 'git'\n" +
              "puts Git.open('.').diff('HEAD^', 'HEAD')";

container.runScriptlet(expr);
```

The call to setLoadPaths() adds the project's lib directory to the scripting container's Ruby search path so that the require line in Ruby can find the git.rb library. Next, we do a Git diff on our project home (which happens to be a Git repository) to see what has changed since the last commit.

Go ahead and run the new version of the app. The results should look something like this:

```
$ ./bin/historian2
diff --git a/lib/archive8.rb b/lib/archive8.rb
new file mode 100644
index 0000000..1d5967f
--- /dev/null
+++ b/lib/archive8.rb
@@ -0,0 +1,12 @@
+require 'git'
+
...
```

Our first real result! Let's ride this momentum as we charge into some of the details of the embedding API.

Passing Strings In and Out

Ruby is still in charge of the output, via its puts function. Let's get rid of that call and just have our script return the result to Java as a string:

ruby_from_java/historian/src/book/embed/Historian3.java

```
ScriptingContainer container = new ScriptingContainer();

container.setLoadPaths(Arrays.asList("lib"));

String expr = "require 'git'\n" +
              "Git.open('.').diff('HEAD^', 'HEAD')";

System.out.println(container.runScriptlet(expr));
```

You may be wondering how this works. Let's examine the signature of JRuby's runScriptlet() first:

```
java.lang.Object runScriptlet(String expression);
```

The return value is the result of the last expression in the Ruby code we passed in, converted to a Java Object. But what is the value of the following line?

```
Git.open('.').diff('HEAD', 'HEAD^')
```

It's a Ruby Array with one Git::Diff::DiffFile element per file in the Git changeset. How is Java supposed to work with this Ruby object?

Luckily, all we're doing is passing the result to println(), which doesn't care about the underlying type—as long as it implements toString(). As we discussed in Chapter 2, *Driving Java from Ruby*, on page 15, JRuby defines this method for us as a wrapper around the Ruby equivalent, to_s.

This example should produce the same output as the previous one; all we're doing is shifting the printing burden from Ruby to Java. Eventually, we'll be handing that data back in a format that Java can pick apart. But first, let's add a little flexibility.

It would be nice to be able to see the difference between any two revisions, not just the two most recent ones. So, we'll have the user supply two Git revision identifiers on the command line, and we'll pass them into Ruby together as a single Java object. As we've seen in the previous chapter, Ruby will have no problem calling methods on this Java object to extract the arguments.

First, create a very simple Revisions Java class, representing a pair of version identifiers:

```
ruby_from_java/historian/src/book/embed/Revisions.java
```
```java
package book.embed;

public class Revisions {
    private String start, finish;

    public Revisions(String start, String finish) {
        this.start = start;
        this.finish = finish;
    }

    public String getStart() {
        return start;
    }

    public String getFinish() {
        return finish;
    }
}
```

Now, add Ruby code to extract these fields and perform the diff. We could build this code up in Java as one big string like we've been doing. In the name of brevity, though, let's put this glue code in a separate file, lib/archive4.rb, which we'll later require:

```
ruby_from_java/historian/lib/archive4.rb
```
```ruby
require 'git'

def history
  git = Git.open('.')
  git.diff($revisions.start, $revisions.finish)
end
```

The history function refers to a global variable, $revisions, which holds a Revisions object from the Java side. We'll soon see how that value gets passed in.

First, though, note that we're calling the Revisions object's getStart() and getFinish() methods using the shorter start and finish names. We encountered this shortcut in Section 2.4, *Instance Methods*, on page 28; it's nice to be able to use it to keep our code clean here.

How does the assignment to the $revisions variable happen? Via the scripting container's put() method:

ruby_from_java/historian/src/book/embed/Historian4.java

```
ScriptingContainer container = new ScriptingContainer();
container.setLoadPaths(Arrays.asList("lib"));
container.runScriptlet("require 'archive4'");

container.put("$revisions", new Revisions(args[0], args[1]));
System.out.println(container.runScriptlet("history"));
```

Notice that the ScriptingContainer object remembers what's happened to it from one invocation of runScriplet() to another. The call to history works because it remembered the previous require of archive.

This continuity is incredibly useful. You can do expensive setup operations once at the beginning of a program and then later just consume those loaded Ruby features without having to reload them for every call to runScriptlet().

Go ahead and try the new Historian by passing in a couple of revision identifiers on the command line:

```
$ ./bin/historian4 HEAD~2 HEAD
diff --git a/lib/archive7.rb b/lib/archive7.rb
new file mode 100644
index 0000000..1d5967f
--- /dev/null
+++ b/lib/archive7.rb
@@ -0,0 +1,12 @@
+require 'git'
+
...
```

Our use of the embedding API is starting to look less like a "throw it over the wall and cross your fingers" approach and more like a real interaction between Java and Ruby. We're still using the blunt instrument of raw strings to pass data back and forth, though. Let's change that.

Real Java Data

Odds are that in any nontrivial application, you'll want something more substantial to chew on than just an Object you call toString() on. Let's change our example to return something useful to Java.

First, we'll make a Java interface to represent a diff for each file in a Git changeset:

ruby_from_java/historian/src/book/embed/GitDiff.java

```java
package book.embed;

public interface GitDiff {
    public String getPath();
    public String getPatch();
}
```

Of course, the Ruby Git library's DiffFile class was written long before the GitDiff Java interface. But we can reopen the Ruby class and *make it implement the interface*, using the techniques in Section 2.7, *Implementing the Methods*, on page 38:

ruby_from_java/historian/lib/archive5.rb

```ruby
require 'git'

class Git::Diff::DiffFile
  include Java::book.embed.GitDiff
end

def history
  git = Git.open('.')
  git.diff($revisions.start, $revisions.finish).to_a
end
```

The DiffFile class in Ruby already has path and patch methods defined. When we implement GitDiff by include-ing it in DiffFile, Java will automatically have access to the existing path and patch methods via getPath() and getPatch(). No need to write any wrappers or define any mappings!

As we saw earlier, the diff method will return a Ruby Array of DiffFiles—which are now also Java GitDiffs. Recall from Section 2.5, *Arrays*, on page 30 that Ruby Arrays are also java.util.List instances. Together, these two facts mean that our return value is now castable to List<GitDiff>.

Here's how the Java code will process the results now:

ruby_from_java/historian/src/book/embed/Historian5.java

```java
ScriptingContainer container = new ScriptingContainer();
container.setLoadPaths(Arrays.asList("lib"));
container.runScriptlet("require 'archive5'");

container.put("$revisions", new Revisions(args[0], args[1]));

List<GitDiff> files = (List<GitDiff>) container.runScriptlet("history");
```

```
for (GitDiff file: files) {
    System.out.println("FILE: " + file.getPath());
    System.out.println(file.getPatch());
}
```

Cool. One cast, and we are using the result like any other POJO.

Notice the sequence we're using now: stash the input arguments in a global and then call a top-level function that takes no parameters. That may do for BASIC programs written in the 1980s, but Ruby provides better abstractions. Let's pass the revision information into history as a parameter, instead of using a global. While we're at it, we'll move the function into a class:

ruby_from_java/historian/lib/archive6.rb

```
require 'git'

class Git::Diff::DiffFile
  include Java::book.embed.GitDiff
end

class Archive
  def history(revisions)
    git = Git.open '.'
    git.diff(revisions.start, revisions.finish).to_a
  end
end
```

So far, we've been calling the history method by building up a string in Java with the word *history* in it. But JRuby can actually call the method directly, using the callMethod() operation.

callMethod() takes the Ruby object whose method we're calling (the receiver), the method name, and whatever parameters you're passing in.

ruby_from_java/historian/src/book/embed/Historian6.java

```
ScriptingContainer container = new ScriptingContainer();
container.setLoadPaths(Arrays.asList("lib"));
container.runScriptlet("require 'archive6'");

Object archive = container.runScriptlet("Archive.new");

List<GitDiff> files = (List<GitDiff>)
    container.callMethod(archive,
                         "history",
                         new Revisions(args[0], args[1]));
```

```java
for (GitDiff file: files) {
    System.out.println("FILE: " + file.getPath());
    System.out.println(file.getPatch());
}
```

This is more like it! We're passing a parameterized list straight into a Ruby method. There's just one more thing we need to do before we call it a day.

So far, we have been running our program with valid Git revision identifiers like HEAD~2. What happens when we give it an invalid revision?

```
$ ./bin/historian6 PASTA NOODLES
ruby_from_java/historian/lib/git/lib.rb:700:in `command':
git diff "-p" "PASTA" "NOODLES"  2>&1:fatal: ambiguous argument 'PASTA':
... 28 lines of errors, including things like:
        at org.jruby.embed.internal.EmbedRubyObjectAdapterImpl.call(...)
        at org.jruby.embed.internal.EmbedRubyObjectAdapterImpl.callMethod(...)
        at org.jruby.embed.ScriptingContainer.callMethod(...)
        at book.embed.Historian6.main(Historian6.java:16)
```

OK, it got the job done, but...yuck! Fortunately, we can catch Ruby exceptions in Java, using JRuby's InvokeFailedException:

ruby_from_java/historian/src/book/embed/Historian7.java

```java
ScriptingContainer container = new ScriptingContainer();
container.setLoadPaths(Arrays.asList("lib"));
container.runScriptlet("require 'archive7'");

Object archive = container.runScriptlet("Archive.new");

try {
    List<GitDiff> files = (List<GitDiff>)
        container.callMethod(archive,
                             "history",
                             new Revisions(args[0], args[1]));

    for (GitDiff file : files) {
        System.out.println("FILE: " + file.getPath());
        System.out.println(file.getPatch());
    }
} catch (InvokeFailedException e) {
    // doSomethingSensibleWith(e);
    System.out.println("Couldn't generate diff; please see the log file.");
}
```

Here are the results:

```
$ ./bin/historian7 PASTA NOODLES
ruby_from_java/historian/lib/git/lib.rb:700:in `command':
git diff "-p" "PASTA" "NOODLES" 2>&1:fatal: ambiguous argument 'PASTA':
unknown revision or path not in the working tree. (Git::GitExecuteError)
Use '--' to separate paths from revisions
        from ruby_from_java/historian/lib/git/lib.rb:249:in `diff_full'
        from ruby_from_java/historian/lib/git/diff.rb:100:in `cache_full'
        from ruby_from_java/historian/lib/git/diff.rb:106:in `process_full'
        from ruby_from_java/historian/lib/git/diff.rb:64:in `each'
        from ruby_from_java/historian/lib/archive7.rb:10:in `history'
        from <script>:1
Couldn't generate diff; please see the log file.
```

So, there you have it: a program written in Java that calls a Ruby method to inspect the source code of...the program itself. We will be covering some more details for the rest of this chapter, but you largely have all the skills you need now. Go forth and make some simple embedded Ruby applications, or read on for the nitty-gritty details.

3.2 The Nitty-Gritty

There are always special circumstances and strange little details that a project runs into. If you find yourself wanting more control knobs for the embedding API than we've shown you so far, then read on.

Other Embedding Frameworks

All the examples we've seen so far have used Embed Core, the main embedding API that ships with JRuby. This API offers a great deal of interoperability. You can call a Ruby method, crunch the results in Java, and hand data back into Ruby. What makes this deep integration possible is that Embed Core was created just for JRuby.

There are times, however, when a general scripting API is a better fit than a Ruby-specific one. For instance, if your Java project already includes other scripting languages, you probably don't want to use a separate API for each language.

JRuby supports the two most popular Java embedding APIs. Bean Scripting Framework, the older of the two, began at IBM and is now hosted by the Apache Jakarta project. javax.scripting, also known as JSR 223, is part of the official JDK. Both have a similar flavor: you connect a general-purpose script manager to a language-specific scripting engine.

In case you're curious, here's how the final Historian example from earlier would look in JSR 223, minus the exception code. First, the imports at the top need to change a little:

`ruby_from_java/historian/src/book/embed/Historian8.java`

```java
package book.embed;

import java.lang.NoSuchMethodException;

import java.util.List;

import javax.script.Invocable;
import javax.script.ScriptEngine;
import javax.script.ScriptEngineManager;
import javax.script.ScriptException;
```

Now for the Ruby embedding code:

`ruby_from_java/historian/src/book/embed/Historian8.java`

```java
public static void main(String[] args)
    throws ScriptException, NoSuchMethodException {

    ScriptEngineManager manager = new ScriptEngineManager();
    ScriptEngine engine = manager.getEngineByName("jruby");
    Invocable invocable = (Invocable)engine;

    engine.eval("$LOAD_PATH << 'lib'");
    engine.eval("require 'archive8'");

    Object archive = engine.eval("Archive.new");

    List<GitDiff> diffs = (List<GitDiff>)
        invocable.invokeMethod(archive,
                               "history",
                               new Revisions(args[0], args[1]));

    for (GitDiff diff : diffs) {
        System.out.println("FILE: " + diff.getPath());
        System.out.println(diff.getPatch());
    }
}
```

JSR 223 is able to perform the same tasks for Historian that Embed Core does, in a slightly less expressive notation. BSF has a similar feel to what you saw previously, so we won't show a detailed example for it. Instead, we recommend you use JSR 223 for non-Ruby-specific embedding projects, because of its official position as part of the JDK.

Containers and Contexts

Each ScriptingContainer object that you create for embedding Ruby code has an associated *context* object, which JRuby uses for internal book-keeping. By "bookkeeping," we mean things like the Ruby interpreter instance, I/O streams, a special variable store, and configuration options.

The simplest ScriptingContainer constructor creates a context implicitly for you. In case you want a little more control, you can specify the kind of context you want:

```
new ScriptingContainer(); // defaults to SINGLETON

new ScriptingContainer(LocalContextScope.SINGLETON);
new ScriptingContainer(LocalContextScope.THREADSAFE);
new ScriptingContainer(LocalContextScope.SINGLETHREAD);
```

Singleton

SINGLETON, the default choice, creates one Ruby runtime shared by the entire JVM. No matter how many ScriptingContainers you create, they'll all share the same context if you use this option. You can either specify this type explicitly or use the no-argument form of the constructor.

Singleton contexts are simple to use, because you don't have to pass ScriptingContainer references all around your program. But they also have a big drawback: they're not thread-safe. Try to run two chunks of Ruby code in different Java threads, and...kaboom!

Thread-Safe

If you know multiple threads will be accessing the same ScriptingContainer (or if you're just feeling paranoid), then you should use a THREAD-SAFE context. This type synchronizes all access to the Ruby runtime so that multiple threads can safely call into it without crashing.

This mode is certainly safer than SINGLETON, but it doesn't automatically make your concurrency problems go away. Under a heavy load, you may end up with a lot of waiting threads. It's even possible to run into a deadlock situation. For instance, if an embedded script returns a Ruby object that, in turn, calls back into the embedding API, you

Tom Says...

What Type of Context Should You Use?

Even though it's a bit of extra work up front, I recommend starting your project off with THREADSAFE containers. This keeps you
in the habit of passing around the ScriptingContainer reference,
in case you later decide to switch to using to one of the other
two modes. It also makes it harder to accidentally kill your Ruby
runtime.

can end up with a call that never returns. Fortunately, this is a bit
of an extreme case. Just keep in mind the hazards of multithreaded
programs as you're writing your code.[8]

Single-Threaded

So, the first mode guaranteed a single Ruby runtime, and the second introduced some thread safety. The third mode does...none of the
above. Each time you create a ScriptingContainer with the SINGLETHREAD
option, you actually create a new context. This new context is completely unconcerned with concurrent access. Everything rides on you,
the programmer, to access the container from one thread at a time.

In truth, this kind of context is not such a dangerous beast if used in a
controlled environment. For example, if you are running a servlet that
spins up multiple threads, you can safely spawn one SINGLETHREAD-ed
ScriptingContainer per servlet thread in Servlet.init(). Some configurations
of the jruby-rack project use this strategy.

Ruby Version

JRuby supports both Ruby 1.8 and Ruby 1.9 syntax and semantics. By
default, a new ScriptingContainer uses Ruby 1.8 mode, but it's quite easy
to use 1.9 instead:

```
container.setCompatVersion(org.jruby.CompatVersion.RUBY1_9);
```

---

8. For more information on what some of these hazards are, see Ousterhout's "Why
Threads Are a Bad Idea (for most purposes)" at http://home.pacbell.net/ouster/threads.pdf.

Compile Mode

We hesitate even to bring up this option but have decided to give it a passing mention in case you encounter it in the wild or in documentation. In practice, we strongly recommend leaving it at the default setting.

The compile mode determines when, if ever, your ScriptingContainer object compiles individual Ruby methods down to JVM bytecode. It is tempting to set this option to force, meaning "always compile." After all, compiling just *sounds* faster, doesn't it?

Of course, real life is never so simple. The act of compilation takes time, so it only makes sense to compile a Ruby method if it's going to be called often enough for the time savings (if any!) to outweigh the initial delay. That's exactly what the default option, jit, tries to do.[9] There are times when compiling Ruby code makes sense but not when you're embedding a JRuby runtime in a Java project.

There are a few more options beyond these basic ones. You can control how an embedded JRuby runtime finds Ruby code, how it finds Java classes, how local variables are remembered from one invocation to the next, and more. Our goal, however, isn't to present a laundry list of every possible setting but to show you the ones you're most likely to encounter in the real world. For the rest, you may want to peek at the reference documentation.[10]

3.3 Embedding Strategies

In our Historian example, we saw several different ways to stitch the Java and Ruby sides together. You can pass a Java class into your Ruby script, make a Ruby class that implements/extends a Java type, or just use simple, coercible types such as strings.

There is no single best approach that applies in all situations. This section will break down some of the reasons why you may consider picking one strategy over another.

---

9. http://www.realjenius.com/2009/10/06/distilling-jruby-the-jit-compiler/
10. http://wiki.jruby.org/RedBridge#Configurations

Passing Java Data Into Ruby

How do you get data into your embedded Ruby script? Passing in a Java object is the easiest approach. The embedded script can call the object's methods just as if they were written in Ruby. You can even decorate the object with additional, easier-to-use methods that actually *are* written in Ruby.

When is passing data into Ruby as plain Java objects *not* a good fit? It depends on how often the Ruby script ends up calling back into Java. Calling from Ruby to Java is a little slower than staying inside the Ruby universe. In many cases the difference is unnoticeable, but in others, the type coercion cost (for example, copying a java.lang.String to a Ruby String) makes this approach too slow.

So if your Ruby code needs to call a string-returning Java method in a tight loop, consider reshaping your solution a bit. Perhaps the Java side could assemble a Ruby object with the data preconverted and pass that in instead. Or you could move that time-sensitive loop into your Java code.

We don't mean to scare you away from the direct approach. Start out by passing a Java object into Ruby. If this doesn't meet your performance goals, *then* measure and rework.

Returning Data to Java

Getting data back into Java-land is a little more involved; Java knows less about JRuby than JRuby knows about Java. In general, there are three options:[11]

- Return a Ruby object that implements a Java interface

- Return a Ruby object that extends a Java class (concrete or abstract)

- Construct a Java object in Ruby and return it

---

11. Technically, there's a fourth option: calling become_java! on a Ruby class. But we don't recommend it.

The first two options are similar, in that you are returning a Ruby object that is tied to the JRuby runtime it came from. If your Java code calls methods on the object, these invocations will land back in the same JRuby runtime.

As we saw in Section 3.2, *Containers and Contexts*, on page 57, this reuse of runtimes can have interesting consequences for multithreaded Java programs. If you are passing objects between threads without using THREADSAFE mode, you can crash the Ruby runtime.

The third option is much less prone to threading issues than the other two choices. It can also be slightly faster, since you're not dispatching function calls from one language to another.

The obvious downside is inelegance. If you have a small, clean Ruby script, then the extra step of constructing a Java class for the sole purpose of returning results will feel like makework.[12] If, on the other hand, you can build a simple Java class that doesn't look too out of place alongside your Ruby code, then go for it.

Type Coercion Pitfalls

JRuby strives to do the right thing with type coercions. As you call into Ruby code and as that Ruby code returns data back to Java, many types will get implicitly converted to similar types in the other language.

This approach is not, however, immune to mishaps. Once an object is coerced to another type, no matter how similar, it really is a different object. Code that relies on object identity will not work right. For example, Maps may not work as you expect.

We've discussed a lot of "doom and gloom" scenarios in this section. While these are important to keep in mind, remember that, for the most part, things will just work. If you go about your project armed with the knowledge of which subtleties can bite you and what to do about them, you'll be fine.

---

12. Anyone remember the original EJB specification?

3.4 Wrapping Up

In this chapter, we looked at the various ways to call from Java into Ruby, all in the context of a real-life example. We then highlighted a couple of specific features of JRuby embedding that may help you in your own projects. Finally, we zoomed out to discuss the general trade-offs among embedding approaches.

We hope this discussion has whet your appetite to introduce Ruby into your Java project. In the next chapter, we're going to take the next logical step and compile Ruby programs down to JVM bytecode.

Chapter 4

The JRuby Compiler

By now, you've had the chance to run a few Ruby applications on the JVM. You've tried a few of the many Ruby libraries available in the wild. You're probably becoming a whiz at calling from Ruby into Java, and vice versa.

We hope you're getting the feel for how a JRuby application fits into the Java ecosystem and how you can start using it for your applications today.

Ready to take the next step toward JRuby mastery?

4.1 Compiler 101

A common theme in this book is that JRuby offers both sensible defaults and advanced control. For quick scripts where you don't care what's going on under the hood, you can just jump in and treat JRuby like a faster Ruby. But when you have to plug into a legacy system or squeeze a little more performance into a complex system, JRuby rewards further exploration.

The compiler is no exception. JRuby ships with a compiler that's always looking for chances to optimize your code, without any explicit instructions from you. When the need arises, you can override the defaults and tap into this power directly.

We'll talk about how this happens in a moment. But first, we need to get into a bit of compiler-nerd theory.

Running Without a Compiler

Most implementations of the Ruby programming language run programs directly from the source code, by following a series of steps:

1. Read the text of the program from an .rb file on disk.

2. Parse the source code into an in-memory form called an *abstract syntax tree* (AST).[1]

3. Execute (interpret) the AST directly by walking through its structure and performing the instructions at each node.

The first two steps happen when the application first starts. The third happens continually while the program is running.

This is how nearly all Ruby development happens. Most Ruby gems ship as a collection of .rb files, which remain in their unaltered source form straight through deployment. Most Ruby developers never need to write or run anything but .rb files.

JRuby supports this method of running programs, of course. Interpreting code works just fine for most applications, and it's the most direct route from source code sitting on disk to a running program.

However, interpreters are generally not the fastest way to execute code. At each node of the AST, JRuby's runtime must make a decision about how to react, make several calls to the Java runtime, and eventually perform the requested action. Is there a better way?

Introducing the Compiler

Most interpreted languages that need to perform well eventually incorporate a compiler. A compiler generally takes some intermediate interpreted form (like JRuby's AST) and converts it to a faster, more direct representation.

The textbook definition of a compiler is somewhat more specific than we have time or space for here. For now, it's fine to think of a compiler as a tool for converting code from one form into another form.

Compiling a Ruby program is conceptually similar to compiling a Java program.

---

1. http://en.wikipedia.org/wiki/Abstract_syntax_tree

The process involves several stages of compilation:

1. From .rb source to JVM bytecode—the resulting bytecode may live in memory or in a .class file

2. From JVM bytecode to a VM-specific internal representation

3. From the internal representation to native machine code

4. ...and conceptually several smaller phases at each level

The compilers used at each stage can be roughly classified into two kinds: just-in-time (JIT) and ahead-of-time (AOT).

Just-in-Time Compilation

You've probably had more exposure to JIT-compiled languages than you realize. Just-in-time compilation is the act of taking executable code (often code that's already running in an interpreter) and compiling it quietly behind the scenes, without any user intervention.

Some platforms, such as Microsoft's .NET runtime, have no interpreter. Their JIT compilers run immediately before the program is executed. Other platforms, including many JVM implementations, perform JIT compilation only as code becomes "hot," in other words, gets called frequently. This approach can speed up application startup. It can also boost performance down the road, because the compiler can use live runtime information to make optimization decisions.

JRuby includes a JIT compiler that optimizes your application as it executes. Later, we'll see how to make the most of its power.

Ahead-of-Time Compilation

If you've ever manually run a compiler against a piece of source code to create an executable file, you've performed ahead-of-time (AOT) compilation. AOT compilers often represent the first phases of a program's life cycle—especially if the program's source code form is not generally executable on its own (as is the case for languages like C or Java).

Most Ruby implementations (including the standard implementation) do not incorporate AOT compilers into their life cycle. Instead, they either walk through an AST at runtime (as Ruby 1.8 does) or run a lower-level intermediate form of the code (as Ruby 1.9 does).

AOT compilers often do less to optimize code than their JIT cousins, since they can only usc information available at compile time. They are useful for languages that don't have interpreters or that need to expose a standard compiled form to other libraries and languages. They are also sometimes used for code obfuscation, since the compiled form is usually not human-readable.

JRuby also includes an AOT compiler usable for obfuscation, for generating "real" Java classes from Ruby code, or for deployment to environments that don't support the JIT compiler. (The Android mobile platform is an example of such an environment.) We'll explore JRuby's AOT compiler later in the chapter.

JRuby's Compiler

In JRuby, almost all code starts out interpreted. But as the program runs, JRuby looks for functions that would benefit from being compiled —and compiles them. (Readers used to the HotSpot JVM will find this approach familiar.)

Let's look at an example. Here's a simple benchmark that iterates through all the permutations of a string:

`compiler/jit/permute.rb`
```ruby
require 'benchmark'

def do_something_with(data)
  # Your favorite operation here
end

5.times do
  timing = Benchmark.measure do
    letters = ['f', 'a', 'c', 'e', 't', 's']
    letters.each_permutation do |p|
      do_something_with(p)
    end
  end

  puts timing
end
```

The implementation uses Ruby's blocks to perform the iteration.[2]

---

2. For more on how blocks work, see Appendix A, on page 263.

compiler/jit/permute.rb

```ruby
class Array
  # Calls the attached block of code once for each permutation.
  def each_permutation(&block)
    # We'll need to permute the array L! times.
    factorial = (1..length).inject(1) { |p, n| p * n }

    # Make a copy, so we don't modify the original array.
    copy = clone
    block.call copy

    (factorial - 1).times do
      copy.permute!
      block.call copy
    end
  end
end
```

For each iteration, we permute the array once using an algorithm from Dijkstra's *The Problem of the Next Permutation* [Dij76]:

compiler/jit/permute.rb

```ruby
class Array
  # Generate one permutation by Dijkstra's algorithm.
  def permute!
    i = length - 1

    i -= 1 while at(i - 1) >= at(i)
    j = length
    j -= 1 while at(j - 1) <= at(i - 1)

    swap(i - 1, j - 1)

    i += 1
    j = length

    while i < j
      swap(i - 1, j - 1)
      i += 1
      j -= 1
    end
  end

  def swap(a, b)
    self[a], self[b] = [self[b], self[a]]
  end
end
```

Here are the results of running the benchmark:

```
compiler/sessions/jit.txt
```

```
$ jruby permute.rb
  0.381000   0.000000   0.381000 (  0.255000)
  0.117000   0.000000   0.117000 (  0.117000)
  0.017000   0.000000   0.017000 (  0.017000)
  0.017000   0.000000   0.017000 (  0.017000)
  0.010000   0.000000   0.010000 (  0.011000)
```

You can immediately see one very noticeable result: the numbers get faster over time. Where the initial run takes around 0.255s of real time, the subsequent runs take anywhere from 0.011s to 0.117s. What you are seeing is the effect of JRuby's JIT (and the JVM's JIT, too) compiling code as it runs to improve performance.

Getting the Best Out of JIT

Most JRuby users will never need to think about the JIT. It will run quietly behind the scenes, optimizing hot code and leaving cold code alone. Over time, JRuby will incorporate more runtime information into those optimizations, and long-running programs well seem to "magically" get faster.

With a little insider information on JRuby, though, you can write code that will get the best performance out of the JIT.

Avoid Generating Code at Runtime

For JRuby's JIT to run, code needs to get "hot." If you're repeatedly calling the same method, for example, JRuby will notice that and switch from interpreting the AST to running real JVM bytecode. This will generally improve the performance of that piece of code, many times over.

On the other hand, if you are constantly generating new Ruby code (for example, by passing a string to eval or one of its cousins), there will be no hot spots for JRuby to optimize.

If you need the flexibility of runtime Ruby code generation, try to limit it to the early phases of your application's life cycle. Keep evaluated code out of the critical path.

Prefer Smaller Methods

JRuby's JIT operates on method boundaries. It makes decisions about whether to JIT-compile a piece of code only when it is about to be called.

This works well for code with many moderately sized methods. However when you have a few very large methods instead, optimization gets trickier. A large method might get called infrequently but do performance-critical work in a loop. A complicated method might get called frequently but have many cold paths through the code. An extremely long method can exceed limits set by JRuby or the JVM itself.

In all these situations, a method will remain interpreted forever. Both JRuby's JIT compiler and the principles of good software design favor breaking large algorithms into smaller methods.

Moving On to AOT

As we've seen, JRuby usually runs in "full auto" mode. You don't have to decide when to interpret or compile a particular section of your code.

There are, however, times when you want to invoke JRuby's ahead-of-time compiler yourself and generate bytecode. Just as Java programmers are used to typing javac SomeJavaProgram.java to generate SomeJavaProgram.class, you can type jrubyc some_ruby_program.rb to generate some_ruby_program.class.

Why would you want to do this? There are a few different situations where this technique comes in handy:

- You're deploying to a system that requires your code to be in .class files.

- You don't want your original Ruby source code to appear in your finished program.

- You're writing a plug-in for a tool that isn't sophisticated enough to call the Ruby Embed API.

- You're looking at one of those rare cases when AOT compilation really is faster, such as the Android platform.

It's not difficult to take an existing Ruby library, compile it, and call it from Java. In fact, it's only a short step beyond the techniques you used in Chapter 3, *Ruby from Java: Embedding JRuby*, on page 45. In the next section, we'll get to know the AOT compiler by trying it on a simple project.

4.2   A Simple Compiled Example

Over the course of this section, we'll start with a simple Ruby example and explore different ways to compile it for the JVM.

Compiling a Single JRuby Class

Let's say you're a home audio enthusiast and want to make some basic measurements of your setup. In particular, you may be interested in the root-mean-square (RMS) voltage of a signal you've captured:

```
compiler/waveform/waveform.rb
class Waveform
  def initialize(points)
    @points = points
  end

  def rms
    raise 'No points' unless @points.length > 0
    squares = @points.map {|p| p * p}
    sum     = squares.inject {|s, p| s + p}
    mean    = sum / squares.length
    Math.sqrt(mean)
  end
end
```

What does it mean, exactly, to ask JRuby to compile this code?

```
$ jrubyc waveform.rb
Compiling waveform.rb to class waveform
```

This will place a waveform.class file in your project directory. This file can be used in place of the original .rb file. Go ahead and try it. Rename your Ruby file to backup.rb or something, and then run the following:

```
compiler/waveform/waveform_test.rb
require 'waveform'

sine_wave = (0..360).map do |degrees|
  radians = degrees * Math::PI / 180.0
  Math.sin radians
end

waveform = Waveform.new sine_wave

puts waveform.rms
# >> 0.706126729736776
```

What else can we do with the compiled .class file? Not much. It might be tempting to try to drive this code from Java, like this:

```
public class WaveformNaiveTest {
    public static void main(String[] args) {
        double[] triangleWave = {0.0, 1.0, 0.0, -1.0, 0.0};
        waveform w = new waveform(triangleWave);
        System.out.println(w.rms());
    }
}
```

Unfortunately, that doesn't work:

```
$ javac -cp jruby.jar:. WaveformNaiveTest.java
WaveformNaiveTest.java:4: cannot find symbol
symbol  : constructor waveform(double[])
location: class waveform
        waveform w = new waveform(triangleWave);
                     ^
WaveformNaiveTest.java:5: cannot find symbol
symbol  : method rms()
location: class waveform
        System.out.println(w.rms());
                             ^
2 errors
```

Java was able to find the waveform class (note that the capitalization follows the Ruby filename), but none of its methods. Consider the constructor. Java will be looking for a constructor taking an array of doubles. Ruby parameters can be anything, and we haven't yet discussed how to tell JRuby what parameter types to write into the .class file.

The mismatch doesn't stop at the constructor. This Java code is expecting the waveform class to have an rms() method taking no parameters and returning a double. But the .class file has no such method. If you use javap to look at the waveform class, you get a long list of methods—including this one:

```
$ javap waveform
...
    public static org.jruby.runtime.builtin.IRubyObject
    method__2$RUBY$rms(waveform, org.jruby.runtime.ThreadContext,
    org.jruby.runtime.builtin.IRubyObject, org.jruby.runtime.Block);
```

As you can see, these methods are meant for JRuby's consumption only. It would be possible to whip up all those private data structures and pass them in. But as we'll soon see, there are much more pleasant ways to accomplish this task.

Charlie Says...
Word to the Wise
_____

When you compile several Ruby classes with the --java option, the generated Java classes all share one instance of the Ruby runtime. This is similar to the SINGLETON context we discussed in Chapter 3, *Ruby from Java: Embedding JRuby*, on page 45, so the same warnings about thread safety apply.

Calling Compiled Ruby from Java

Let's back up for a second. The purpose of the regular jrubyc command is to compile Ruby code so that Ruby can use it. Trying to call that Ruby-specific compiled class from Java is cutting against the grain.

In Chapter 3, *Ruby from Java: Embedding JRuby*, on page 45, we saw a much more straightforward way of calling Ruby from Java: JRuby Embed. If we insisted on doing everything by hand (there's no need, as we'll soon see), here's how we might use the embedding API to drive our Ruby class:

`compiler/waveform/WaveformWrapper.java`

```java
import org.jruby.embed.ScriptingContainer;

public class WaveformWrapper {
    static ScriptingContainer rubyContainer;
    Object waveform;

    static {
        rubyContainer = new ScriptingContainer();
        rubyContainer.runScriptlet("require 'waveform'");
    }

    public WaveformWrapper(double[] points) {
        Object waveformClass = rubyContainer.runScriptlet("Waveform");
        waveform = rubyContainer.callMethod(waveformClass, "new", points);
    }

    public double rms() {
        return (Double)rubyContainer.callMethod(waveform, "rms");
    }
}
```

This code requires you to have a definition of the Waveform Ruby class sitting around, either in waveform.rb or in waveform.class. What if you want all the waveform-related code in a single .class file? The simplest way to do that is just embed the Ruby code straight in the .java file, by replacing the static section with something like this:

`compiler/waveform/WaveformComplete.java`

```
static {
    String source = new StringBuilder(
        "class Waveform\n" +
        "  def initialize(points)\n" +
        "    @points = points\n" +
        "  end\n" +
        "\n" +
        "  def rms\n" +
        "    raise 'No points' unless @points.length > 0\n" +
        "    squares = @points.map {|p| p * p}\n" +
        "    sum     = squares.inject {|s, p| s + p}\n" +
        "    mean    = sum / squares.length\n" +
        "    Math.sqrt(mean)\n" +
        "  end\n" +
        "end\n").toString();

    rubyContainer = new ScriptingContainer();
    rubyContainer.runScriptlet(source);
}
```

The advantage of this approach is that it's simple and reliable. The disadvantage is that it takes a lot of manual work. You have to paste your tested Ruby code into the .java file, write a bunch of methods with names matching the Ruby ones, and possibly add a bunch of conversion code to get your Java data into Ruby-compatible structures.

Fortunately, JRuby's compiler makes all those manual steps unnecessary. If you pass the --java option to jrubyc, it will generate a .java file instead of a .class file. You can then fall back on familiar Java tools to finish the job.

```
$ jrubyc --java waveform.rb
Generating Java class Waveform to Waveform.java
$ javac -cp jruby.jar:. Waveform.java
```

As you can see, we generated a file called Waveform.java and then compiled this file like any normal Java source code. But it's not obvious how to call it.

Look at the signatures of the generated methods:

```java
public  Waveform(Object points) {
    // ...
}

public Object rms() {
    // ...
}
```

Recall that Ruby function definitions don't specify argument types. Without this information, jrubyc has to fall back on Object for the parameters and return values. The Ruby code to initialize a Waveform instance is expecting an array of numbers. How do we inform the compiler of that expectation?

All we have to do is tag the Ruby functions with java_signature, followed by a string containing a Java function declaration. Here's how that would look for the Waveform class:

compiler/waveform/waveform_with_sigs.rb

```ruby
require 'java'

class Waveform
  java_signature 'Waveform(double[] points)'
  def initialize(points)
    @points = points
  end

  java_signature 'double rms()'
  def rms
    raise 'No points' unless @points.length > 0
    squares = @points.map {|p| p * p}
    sum     = squares.inject {|s, p| s + p}
    mean    = sum / squares.length
    Math.sqrt(mean)
  end
end
```

At this point, you could retry the compilation step from earlier, by running jrubyc --java to generate a .java file and then running javac to compile that to a .class. Or you could combine the two steps into one. The --javac option will compile the generated Java code for you.

```
$ jrubyc --javac waveform.rb
Generating Java class Waveform to Waveform.java
javac -d . -cp jruby.jar:. Waveform.java
```

Charlie Says...

Filenames and Case Sensitivity

The java_require directive has an interesting quirk on non-case-sensitive file systems (the default on Mac and Windows). These systems can't tell the difference between Waveform.class (which is a generated Java wrapper around Ruby code) and waveform.class (which is just compiled Ruby code). When some piece of Ruby code tries to require 'waveform', JRuby will try to load Waveform.class instead—which will throw an error.

The solution to this is easy: make sure your generated Java class has a different name than your Ruby source file. For example, we placed the Ruby source for the Waveform class into a file called waveform_with_sigs.rb (instead of just waveform.rb).

If you look inside Waveform.java, you'll see something similar to the JRuby Embed example we cooked up earlier. A simple Java wrapper class contains the full Ruby source embedded as a string, plus a few methods that hand off their implementation to the Ruby class.

This approach has the advantage of being self-contained: a single .java file is all you need to throw at your build system. But there may be times when you don't *want* your Ruby source pasted into your Java class. For these situations, add the text java_require plus the Ruby filename (minus extension) anywhere in your .rb file. For this example, you might put something like this right before the start of the Waveform class definition:

`compiler/waveform/waveform_with_sigs.rb`

```ruby
require 'java'
java_require 'waveform_with_sigs'
```

Now, when you recompile, the generated Java code will have method signatures easier to call from Java:

```java
public Waveform(double[] points) {
    // ...
}

public double rms() {
    // ...
}
```

Charlie Says...

Why Does the Class Name Need to Be a String?

Remember that the jrubyc --java command first generates a Java source file and then compiles that to bytecode. JRuby just copies the class name as a string from your Ruby file into the generated text. In other words, this requirement is just a side effect of the way JRuby generates source code.

And there you have it: one Ruby class compiled to JVM bytecode, in a form that's easy to use from Java. We're sure you have lots of questions about where to go from here: how to use other Java classes, implement interfaces, and so on. In the next section, we'll get into several of these details.

4.3 The Details

Now that you have some simple Ruby code compiled into a Java project, let's explore a few things you might do to help this code fit into the broader Java universe.

Importing Classes

If your compiled Ruby code is going to be part of a larger system, you'll probably want to import other Java classes into your Ruby code. To do this, you'll use the same java_import syntax from Chapter 2, *Driving Java from Ruby*, on page 15, with a twist. You'll need to use a string, rather than a Java-style package name, to refer to the class:

```
# Original style:
java_import com.example.MyClass

# Compiler style:
java_import 'com.example.MyClass'
```

Here's an example of how to apply this technique to the Waveform class:

compiler/waveform/waveform_with_import.rb
```
require 'java'

java_import 'java.io.PrintStream'
```

```
class Waveform
  # ... other methods here ...

  java_signature 'void print(PrintStream)'
  def print(stream)
    stream.write("The RMS is #{rms}")
  end
end
```

This new print method can write out the RMS voltage to a standard Java PrintStream.

Specifying a Package

It's standard Java practice to avoid name clashes by putting compiled code into packages. JRuby has you covered here. Since most of the other compiler hints have names that start with java_..., perhaps you've guessed that the way to specify a Java package name is to use the java_package directive:

compiler/waveform/waveform_with_package.rb

```
java_package 'com.example'
```

If you add the previous line to your Ruby file, the resulting Java class will be generated into the com.example package.

Implementing an Interface

Most Java-based systems will eventually need to implement an interface. For jrubyc, you can do this by specifying java_implements inside the body of the class.

compiler/waveform/waveform_with_interface.rb

```
require 'java'

java_package 'com.example'

class Waveform
  java_implements 'Runnable'

  # ... other methods here ...

  java_signature 'void run()'
  def run
    puts 'inside runnable implementation'
    puts rms
  end
end
```

Remember, since jrubyc generates Java source, you must implement all of the interface's required methods. Otherwise, you'll get a compiler error from javac.

Adding Annotations to a Class or Method

Many Java frameworks require you to add annotations to your classes or methods. These annotations may be used to tag tests, indicate dependency injection points, or configure a database mapping.

In jrubyc, you can specify annotations using the java_annotation line. Here's a simple example of a JUnit 4 test, which uses annotations to indicate which methods are tests:

```ruby
compiler/waveform/test_waveform.rb
require 'java'
require 'waveform_with_sigs'

java_import 'org.junit.Test'

class TestWaveform
  java_annotation 'Test'
  java_signature  'void testRms()'
  def test_rms
    dc = [1.0]
    rms = Waveform.new(dc).rms
    org.junit.Assert.assert_equals rms, 1.0, 0.001
  end
end
```

Like most of the other java_... directives, the annotation line must be specified as a string so it can be inserted into the generated Java output.

This technique isn't just for spelling out test cases. It's fully compatible with more complex uses, like the Jersey framework.[3] With Jersey, you can serve requests with a simple Java object, thanks to a few annotations that tell the server the URL that goes with each method.

Deploying Compiled Code

We've talked about compiling Ruby code to make it more pleasant to run—faster execution, integration with frameworks, and so on. Now, let's talk about compiling Ruby to make it easier to *deploy*.

---

3.   http://blog.headius.com/2010/06/restful-services-in-ruby-using-jruby.html

Compiling Several Files at Once

For larger projects, you will likely have a carefully arranged directory of Ruby source code, with each component in its own folder. What's the easiest way to compile an application with this kind of setup? It would certainly be possible to write a build script (see Chapter 7, *Building Software for Deployment*, on page 153) to search recursively through your project directory for source files and compile each one individually. But there's an easier way.

As an alternative to passing a single .rb filename to jrubyc, you can pass a directory name. If you couple this technique with the -t option and a target directory, JRuby will make the compiled Java package names mirror the directory structure of the Ruby source.

In other words, if you have com/example/gui.rb and com/example/database.rb and you type the following:

```
$ jrubyc . -t build
```

...then the resulting gui and database classes will be part of the com.example package.

Hiding the Source

Many JRuby users simply want to compile their .rb files to hide the source code. In simple cases, the simple jrubyc command works fine for this purpose. It takes .rb source files and outputs .class files (either in their own dedicated location or alongside the .rb files).

In JRuby, the require 'foo' method will load either foo.rb or foo.class. So, you can usually just leave the .rb files out of your deployment and run entirely from .classes.

Avoiding Name Clashes

On a bigger project, you may run into a few issues with running from .class files. The hairiest of these is the difference between the way Ruby loads code (by looking for .rb files) and the way Java loads code (by looking for classes—which may have nothing to do with their filenames).

For example, the following two lines of Ruby code refer to the same file:

```
require 'some_library'
require 'sub/directory/../../some_library'
```

Ian Says...

Does the SHA-1 Really Hide the Source?

The SHA-1 hash is generated from the Ruby source. Does this mean you're once again stuck with shipping a bunch of .rb files alongside your compiled code?

Well, for now, yes. But the compiler will soon support stripped-down .rb files that contain the SHA-1 value and nothing else. So, you'll be protected from name collisions without having to ship your source code.

...but the Java universe doesn't know that. The next two lines of Ruby code refer to different files:

```
require 'math/sin'
require 'mortal/sin'
```

...but to Java, these would both be in classes called sin. Clearly, we need some way other than just the filename to distinguish between two different compiled Ruby files. We need to know something about the file contents, not just the name.

JRuby offers a way to name compiled files based on their source contents. The --sha1 flag calculates a SHA-1 hash—a 40-digit hex number that is overwhelmingly likely to be unique for each Ruby file in your program—and uses that for the filename instead. So, JRuby could tell that two uses of some_ruby_class are referring to the same code, because the contents would be the same. The resulting .class file would be named something like 804618fe4c994ba2b7a39b949cae81c9301327.class.

Deploying to Mobile Platforms

When you compile a Ruby class to bytecode, JRuby normally saves one last stage of code generation for runtime. This stage builds "method handles"—one tiny Java class per Ruby method, basically. Some platforms place restrictions on this kind of last-minute generation. For example, the Android mobile operating system forbids any runtime code generation.

For these cases, you can pass the --handles option to jrubyc. You'll typically use this alongside the previously discussed --sha1 flag:

```
$ jrubyc --sha1 --handles
```

When you use this option, you'll see lots of extra little .class files. There's nothing to be alarmed about; these are just the method handles that JRuby would normally have generated at runtime.

4.4 Wrapping Up

We started this chapter with a heady discussion of compiler-nerd theory. But it was for a good cause. That background information was useful to keep in mind as we considered all the different ways that JRuby can compile your Ruby code. Most of the time, your Ruby code can coast through JRuby's just-in-time compiler. If you need more control for a particular project, jrubyc and its many options are there for you.

By this point, you've been through all the core pieces of JRuby: calling Java from Ruby, embedding Ruby into Java, and now using the compiler. Where do we go from here?

Out into the world! There's a rich set of Java and Ruby libraries out there, ready for you to tame and bring into your own applications. In the second part of the book, we'll visit some of the more interesting libraries in both languages.

Our goal isn't to cover all the popular libraries but to highlight the ones that people new to JRuby usually ask about first. We'll start off by getting Rails, the blockbuster web development framework, up and running on JRuby. We'll then look at popular libraries in both languages for building and testing software. Finally, we'll top things off with various approaches to designing Ruby GUIs on top of the Swing toolkit.

Part II

JRuby and the World

## Chapter 5

Introduction to Rails

Rails is the most-cited reason that people are turning to Ruby from other languages. It has—with good reason—been called Ruby's killer application. From the initial release in July 2004 up to now, the increase of Rails adoptions, products, books, blogs, and articles has been staggering.

In this chapter, we will first take a quick look at the different parts of Rails and where all the buzzwords and slogans fit into the picture. Next, we'll create a simple JRuby on Rails application from scratch—the focus will be on getting up and running quickly, rather than providing encyclopedic coverage of the API.

5.1 What Is Rails?

Rails is a web application framework. It has seen great success in the past few years, because of several revolutionary differences from earlier web frameworks. It has given countless developers the tools to create web applications in an easy and intuitive way. Rails removes the need for giant configuration files, gives you a set of reasonable defaults, uses Ruby's expressiveness to keep your code readable, and focuses on making the most common use cases dead simple.

When you combine the rapid development of Rails and the power of the JVM, you can do the following:

- Handle an entire site's worth of traffic in a single Rails instance, thanks to Java's multithreading

- Connect to a huge range of legacy databases without struggling with native database drivers

- Use one of Java's many libraries for persistence, messaging, or image processing from your Rails app

- Deploy clean, compact Ruby code to a Java-only server environment

- Wrap a web interface around a legacy application, such as the Tracker 7 software that's keeping the world safe from nuclear proliferation[1]

Principles

Although the success of Rails can be credited to the way it changed how we build web applications, Rails is also distinguished by brilliant marketing, including the propagation of several slogans and buzzwords. Here are a few of the more common slogans, together with their meanings in the context of Rails:

Don't Repeat Yourself (DRY)
> According to the DRY principle, each piece of information should live in exactly one place.[2] If you're writing a payroll app where each Employee needs a name and a salary, you shouldn't have to define those fields in the database *and* your Ruby class. And indeed, in Rails, you don't—property information resides only in the database.

Convention over Configuration
> Also known as "sensible defaults"—when you do things the way Rails expects you to, you won't need to configure much. For example, Rails will automatically find the table for your Recipe class, provided the table is named recipes in the database. It will also implicitly assign URLs like http://example.com/recipes to Ruby methods like RecipesController#index.

> This idea is closely related to the DRY principle. After all, the best way of not repeating yourself is to not say anything at all.

---

1. http://exportcontrol.org/library/conferences/2657/9._Tracker_7_System_Overview.pdf
2. See *The Pragmatic Programmer* [HT00].

Ola Says...

The ABCs of MVC

Rails embodies the Model-View-Controller (MVC) software pattern—understanding this pattern will help you learn Rails.

A frequent trap for application developers is letting business logic creep into user-interface code. MVC tries to avoid this problem by providing three different buckets for your code: the model, the view, and the controller.

The model contains the business logic and data—this may include connecting to a database.

The controller is responsible for providing the view with all the data needed for the current interaction with the user. It also responds to user actions by evaluating them and dispatching to a model. A controller should be small—think of it as the switch-board between the models and the views.

The view displays data in different formats. Rails apps often implement this layer using eRuby, a mix of Ruby and HTML.

These are the central parts of Rails—everything else is just the plumbing necessary to make everything work.

In Rails, your models are usually ActiveRecord classes (see Section 6.1, *ActiveRecord*, on page 122) kept in app/models. The views are usually .html.erb, .xml.erb, or .js.rjs files, and they live in app/views. Finally, the controllers are regular Ruby classes that are placed in app/controllers. This division makes it very easy to know where code should be placed and what the responsibility of each piece is.

Agile

Though Agile is of course a general computer-industry buzzword, it has specific connotations in Rails. With the Ruby language, you can get off the ground quickly with clear, understated code. With built-in test harnesses, you can safely change directions in the middle of a project. It's all about bringing more value to your application in less time.

Opinionated Software

All of these slogans and buzzwords tie into each other. They all have the common goal of establishing the easiest and best way to develop web applications, according to one opinionated person: David Heinemeier-Hanson. He started the Rails project with very specific ideas about what's good and what's bad in a web framework. Of course, thousands of volunteers have improved Rails over the years, but its overall shape is still guided by these opinions.

One example of opinions in Rails is the lack of support for composite primary keys in the database.[3] If you really need them, they're available as a plug-in, but the Rails team has resisted bloating the core libraries with them.

Most things are possible in Rails, but dubious practices result in uglier code than sound practices do. Suspect code will therefore really stand out when you're writing it.

Components

Under the hood, Rails is not really one framework. Rather, it's a composition of several loosely tied libraries that happen to work well together.

Here are the major Rails libraries:

ActiveRecord

The ActiveRecord library covers the model part of the MVC pattern, by pairing database tables with simple wrapper classes that embody your program's logic. The implementation makes particularly good use of Ruby language features and takes most of the pain out of defining model classes.

---

3. For a discussion, see http://lists.rubyonrails.org/pipermail/rails-core/2006-February/thread.html#794.

ActiveRecord supports most standard database features but notably omits foreign-key relationships and composite primary keys. (Most of these can be added with the use of plug-ins.) For more details on this component of Rails, see Chapter 6, *JRuby and Relational Databases*, on page 121.

ActionPack

ActionPack takes care of presenting your models to users and responding to the actions they perform. It consists of three parts: ActionView and ActionController correspond to the view and controller parts of MVC, while ActionDispatch is responsible for connecting a request to a controller.

A controller in Rails is just a regular class that inherits from ActionController; each public method is an action triggered by something the user does. ActionView is there in the background, but your Ruby classes don't interact directly with it. Views in Rails are templates with names ending in .html.erb by default (the exact suffix varies with the templating system).

ActionPack and ActiveRecord do most of the work in Rails.

ActiveSupport

Rails includes a large number of extensions to the Ruby core classes. It also includes libraries to handle internationalized text, helpers for working with times and dates, and lots of other things.

A lot of these smaller features aren't necessarily tied to web development. Date/time math crops up in a lot of applications, on the Web or elsewhere. With ActiveSupport, you can express a time difference as easily as (2.months + 1.day + 3.hours + 15.minutes).ago. Compare that to old-school time arithmetic: Time.now - (2*30*24*3600 + 24*3600 + 3*3600 + 15*60)—and that doesn't even take into account that different months have different lengths.

ActiveSupport is chock full of nice things like this. As you become familiar with it, you'll often find that some utility function you've been wishing for is already included.

ActiveResource

In the bad old days, we tended to think of web apps as little computer programs churning out HTML tag soup. You can write a program like this with Rails, of course. But you will find it far easier to "cut with the grain" and think in terms of *resources* instead of pages or scripts. This style is known as Representational State Transfer (REST).

Rails makes it easy for you fit your app into this structure. Action-Pack helps you create REST services, and ActiveResource helps you consume them—both under similar APIs.

ActionMailer

ActionMailer is a small package that helps you create uniform mail templates. You can send mail from your controllers and use .erb files as templates for your messages.

ActiveModel

ActiveModel is a new component created in Rails 3 that is basically an extraction of the best bits of ActiveRecord, such as data validations and callbacks. With ActiveModel, you can easily make any Ruby object (not just database classes) at home in Rails.

Bundler

Although not part of Rails, Bundler is a utility developed in parallel with the Rails 3 release to aid in gem dependency management in any Ruby project (even a non-Rails one). Bundler locks down your dependencies to make sure you can repeatably deploy the same configuration across different environments and machines. You'll get comfortable with Bundler in the tutorial shortly.

Most parts of Rails work fine on their own, even in non-Rails applications. For instance, ActiveRecord is widely used in other frameworks and applications. That said, some components are more reusable than others.

There's a lot functionality just in the Rails core. Thanks to the plug-in architecture, there's also a universe of extensions available to take Rails in more directions (or sometimes fewer directions—the Rails team will often spin off a seldom-used feature into a plug-in).

What About JRuby on Rails?

The previous sections described how Rails is put together, and we will soon take a look at how to actually create an application using JRuby on Rails. But first, why would you want to use JRuby together with Rails? The short answer: for exactly the same reasons you would want

 **Ian Says. . .**

A First Look at REST

A RESTful web service provides a set of discoverable, uniquely named documents (*resources*). Client code—which may or may not be a browser—can read and modify resources by using the HTTP protocol's four simple verbs: POST, GET, PUT, and DELETE.*

For example, suppose you're creating a photo-editing site. With a traditional approach, you might send a GET request to http://example.com/show.php to display an image or send POST requests to new.php, edit.php, or delete.php to upload, modify, or remove an image.

With REST, you'd present each photo as a resource with a unique ID, such as http://example.com/photos/12345. All operations—viewing, modifying, and so on—would take place through GET, POST, PUT, and DELETE requests to that same address.

Think of it as "convention over configuration" applied to your API design.

---

*. This is not the same thing as the four CRUD (create, read, update, destroy) operations performed by many web apps; see http://jcalcote.wordpress.com/2008/10/16/put-or-post-the-rest-of-the-story.

---

to use JRuby on *any* project—speed, stability, infrastructure, and so on.

The slightly longer answer is that Rails in its current incarnation is very good at many things but not absolutely everything. JRuby can smooth over some of the remaining rough spots. Deployment is probably the most interesting of these. Deploying a Rails application is fairly well documented, but getting everything right can still be difficult. With JRuby, you can package your Rails application as a standard .war file and deploy it to any compliant Java web container.[4]

---

4. Web application archives, or .war files, are a standard way of deploying web applications on Java servers.

Rails supports several different databases, but in practice, most shops use either MySQL or PostgreSQL. Since JRuby on Rails allows you to use any database that has a JDBC driver, you have access to a wider range of databases, plus features such as data sources and connection pooling. JRuby on Rails also works very well with JavaDB, the in-memory database that is distributed with Java.

The best way to think of JRuby on Rails is like regular Rails with a few intriguing new possibilities.

5.2 Going Rouge

It's time to get started with some code. Through the rest of this chapter, we'll build Rouge, a simple web-based restaurant guide. By the time we've finished, you should be able to build your own JRuby on Rails application. We can't cover all or even most of the functionality that Rails provides—there are other books that can teach you this.[5]

Getting Started

Before starting the tutorial, we need to install Bundler and Rails. The example code in this chapter was written using Rails 3.0.1, Bundler 1.0.2, and activerecord-jdbc-adapter 1.0.1.

To install Bundler and Rails, just type this command:

introduction_to_rails/output/gem-install.txt

```
$ jruby -S gem install bundler rails
Successfully installed bundler-1.0.2
Successfully installed activesupport-3.0.1
Successfully installed builder-2.1.2
Successfully installed i18n-0.4.1
Successfully installed activemodel-3.0.1
Successfully installed rack-1.2.1
Successfully installed rack-test-0.5.6
Successfully installed rack-mount-0.6.13
Successfully installed tzinfo-0.3.23
Successfully installed abstract-1.0.0
Successfully installed erubis-2.6.6
Successfully installed actionpack-3.0.1
Successfully installed arel-1.0.1
Successfully installed activerecord-3.0.1
Successfully installed activeresource-3.0.1
```

---

5. See *Agile Web Development with Rails* [RTH08].

```
Successfully installed mime-types-1.16
Successfully installed polyglot-0.3.1
Successfully installed treetop-1.4.8
Successfully installed mail-2.2.7
Successfully installed actionmailer-3.0.1
Successfully installed rake-0.8.7
Successfully installed thor-0.14.3
Successfully installed railties-3.0.1
Successfully installed rails-3.0.1
24 gems installed
```

Our restaurant guide will make it easy for someone who's considering a restaurant to find reviews for it. They'll want to search restaurants, read reviews, and comment on either a review or a restaurant. Visitors will be generating most of this content, but we'll also need an administrator account for creating restaurants. You'll see later how to offer these two different views of the same data.

Deciding on Our Models

From the previous short description, we can deduce some potential models:

- Restaurant
- Administrator
- Reviewer
- Review
- Comment (attached to a Restaurant)
- Comment (attached to a Review)

We will use a common Comment model for both restaurant comments and review comments—it seems unnecessary to have two different models for essentially the same idea.

Establishing Structure

Rails emphasizes a particular structure for your code. The first step in creating a new application is to generate this structure. The rails new command will build a minimal (but well-organized!) app from scratch, using the directory name you provide on the command line. We'll choose the name rouge for our project directory.

```
$ jruby -S rails new rouge --template http://jruby.org
      create
      create  README
      create  Rakefile
      create  config.ru
      create  .gitignore
      create  Gemfile
      create  app
      create  app/controllers/application_controller.rb
      create  app/helpers/application_helper.rb
      create  app/views/layouts/application.html.erb
      create  app/mailers
      create  app/models
      create  config
      create  config/routes.rb
```

Rails tells you exactly which directories and files get created. Reproducing the entire list here would take more than two pages; for the trees' sake, we've truncated the output. As you can see by the directory names, there is one specific place for each piece of functionality you would want to add to your application.

The directories you will spend most of your time in from now on are the following:

- app: Contains most of the application's functionality—models, controllers, and views.

- config: Holds configuration settings, such as the database server location.

- test: Go on, guess!

You'll notice we passed an extra --template http://jruby.org option when we generated the application. This flag tells Rails to apply some extra JRuby-specific configuration to the new application.

If you are following along and ran the command yourself, you might have noticed a couple of extra lines at the bottom of the rails new command output:

```
apply  http://jruby.org
apply     http://jruby.org/templates/default.rb
 gsub     Gemfile
```

Nick Says...
You Have Options

The rails new command supports a number of options. A couple of the more interesting ones are --database mysql for setting up an application for use with MySQL and --skip-active-record for avoiding using ActiveRecord or databases at all. See jruby -S rails help new for more information.

JRuby needs to use the activerecord-jdbc-adapter gem to connect to databases via Java's JDBC API, so JRuby has made some small modifications to the default Rails application's Gemfile. What goes in the Gemfile, you say? We're glad you asked!

Installing Dependencies with Bundler

Bundler's stated goal is to "manage an application's dependencies through its entire life across many machines systematically and repeatably."[6] In more pragmatic terms, it helps prevent conflicting or missing gems. Although you can use Bundler with any Ruby application, the integration story is particularly good with Rails 3.

As we hinted in the previous section, one of the files the rails new command creates is called Gemfile. Let's take a look inside:

introduction_to_rails/output/Gemfile

```
source 'http://rubygems.org'

gem 'rails', '3.0.1'

# Bundle edge Rails instead:
# gem 'rails', :git => 'git://github.com/rails/rails.git'

if defined?(JRUBY_VERSION)
  gem 'activerecord-jdbc-adapter'
  gem 'jdbc-sqlite3', :require => false
else
  gem 'sqlite3-ruby', :require => 'sqlite3'
end
```

---

6. http://gembundler.com/

The Gemfile is just a place to declare the gems and libraries your application needs. Bundler shines when it's time to configure those dependencies at install time and runtime. To make Bundler install the dependencies, run the bundle install command:

introduction_to_rails/output/bundle-install.txt

```
$ jruby -S bundle install
Fetching source index for http://rubygems.org/
Using rake (0.8.7)
Using abstract (1.0.0)
Using activesupport (3.0.1)
Using builder (2.1.2)
Using i18n (0.4.1)
Using activemodel (3.0.1)
Using erubis (2.6.6)
Using rack (1.2.1)
Using rack-mount (0.6.13)
Using rack-test (0.5.6)
Using tzinfo (0.3.23)
Using actionpack (3.0.1)
Using mime-types (1.16)
Using polyglot (0.3.1)
Using treetop (1.4.8)
Using mail (2.2.7)
Using actionmailer (3.0.1)
Using arel (1.0.1)
Using activerecord (3.0.1)
Installing activerecord-jdbc-adapter (1.0.1)
Using activeresource (3.0.1)
Using bundler (1.0.2)
Installing jdbc-sqlite3 (3.6.14.2.056)
Using thor (0.14.3)
Using railties (3.0.1)
Using rails (3.0.1)
Your bundle is complete! Use `bundle show [gemname]`
to see where a bundled gem is installed.
```

The beauty of having the dependencies stored in Gemfile is that you can ensure that anyone else working on your application has the same set of libraries. Everyone simply needs to remember to run bundle install (the first time) or bundle update (when someone changes the Gemfile).

Configuring the Database

The next step after creating a new Rails application is to configure your database. Open config/database.yml. It will consist of three sections named after the three standard environments Rails creates for you:

 **Ola Says...**

Whitespace in Config Files

Be very careful when editing YAML files (files that end in .yml or .yaml)—one single tab character in these files will render them unreadable to Ruby. If you see strange errors after editing database.yml, check your whitespace for tabs.

test, development, and production. Here's the setup for the development database, which is the one you'll use during most of this chapter:[7]

introduction_to_rails/rouge/config/database.yml

```
development:
  adapter: sqlite3
  database: db/development.sqlite3
  pool: 5
  timeout: 5000
```

If you were developing the application with a database server such as MySQL or PostgreSQL, you'd edit this file to change the connection information. Since we'll be using the embedded SQLite database, there's no need to change anything here for now.

Before you start the application, we should point out there is another step you'd need to perform had we started with MySQL: creating the databases. Rails provides a handy command that will create a separate database for each environment. As with many maintenance tasks, you run it using Rake, the Ruby build and maintenance tool.[8] This step is unnecessary with SQLite, which will create the files for us the first time our Rails app hits the database. If you're really curious, you can safely run the command anyway:

introduction_to_rails/output/rake-db-create.txt

```
$ jruby -S rake db:create:all
(in code/introduction_to_rails/rouge)
```

---

7. Your automated tests will use the test database instead. It's important to keep this one separate, since Rails destroys and re-creates it every time you run the tests.
8. We'll cover Rake in more detail in Chapter 7, *Building Software for Deployment*, on page 153.

The Rails application is now ready to start:

```
$ jruby script/rails server
=> Booting WEBrick
=> Rails 3.0.1 application starting in development on http://0.0.0.0:3000
=> Call with -d to detach
=> Ctrl-C to shutdown server
[2010-10-15 11:08:40] INFO  WEBrick 1.3.1
[2010-10-15 11:08:40] INFO  ruby 1.8.7 (2010-10-13) [java]
[2010-10-15 11:08:40] INFO  WEBrick::HTTPServer#start: pid=6137 port=3000
```

You should be able to visit http://localhost:3000 and see the standard Rails welcome page.

5.3 Building Our Models

Now that we know Rails works correctly and your application is configured as it should be, it's time to sketch out our models. You're probably not surprised to hear we'll be using Rails code generation again.

That First Step Is a Doozy

You will see several things get generated in the following interaction. These include a nearly empty Ruby file containing your model and another Ruby file called a *migration*. Rails won't actually put anything in the database for you, until you specifically ask it to do so. The migration defines exactly what gets added.

introduction_to_rails/output/script-generate-model.txt

```
$ jruby script/rails generate model Restaurant
      invoke  active_record
      create    db/migrate/20101014180911_create_restaurants.rb
      create    app/models/restaurant.rb
      invoke    test_unit
      create      test/unit/restaurant_test.rb
      create      test/fixtures/restaurants.yml
```

As usual with Rails, you get several things for free, including a basic test file and a skeleton in which to put the database definitions for the model. Since Rails defines models by their database structure, we need to create a table before using the model. This is done in the file db/migrate/..._create_restaurants.rb. For now, you should edit it to look like this code example:

introduction_to_rails/edits/001_create_restaurants.rb

```ruby
class CreateRestaurants < ActiveRecord::Migration
  def self.up
    create_table :restaurants do |t|
      t.string :name
      t.text :description
      t.string :address
      t.string :phone
      t.timestamps
    end
  end

  def self.down
    drop_table :restaurants
  end
end
```

Notice that the migration describes the data's structure in Ruby, without referring to any particular database product. Each migration should perform a single unit of database work and should include a way to undo that work (so that the migration can be rolled back). In the previous example, we create or remove a table called restaurants.

The next step is to run this migration and thus create the database table. We do so using rake with the db:migrate target:

introduction_to_rails/output/rake-db-migrate-1.txt

```
$ jruby -S rake db:migrate
(in code/introduction_to_rails/rouge)
==  CreateRestaurants: migrating ===============================================
-- create_table(:restaurants)
   -> 0.0290s
   -> 0 rows
==  CreateRestaurants: migrated (0.0290s) ======================================
```

As you can see, rake reports that it successfully created the restaurants table in the database. If you don't specify an environment, the migration will run in development mode. You should see the results in the rouge_development database, complete with columns for the ID, name, description, address, phone number, and time stamp fields.

Before we proceed, let's take a look at the other files Rails created for us. First, there's the actual model file, app/models/restaurant.rb. At this stage, it doesn't really look like much, since it gets all the information it needs from the database.

introduction_to_rails/output/restaurant.rb

```
class Restaurant < ActiveRecord::Base
end
```

This seemingly empty class already has some functionality. When the app starts up, Rails will reach out to the database, find out the column names (name, description, address, and phone), and add methods to the class with the same names—all at runtime. We will add even more functionality in a minute. First, a brief word on testing.

Testing the Model

Take a peek inside the test directory. By default, Rails generates a test file for every model and controller. Let's add a few tests to demonstrate some common ActiveRecord operations. Open test/unit/restaurant_test.rb. Right now, it just contains a single no-op test case:

introduction_to_rails/output/restaurant_test.rb

```
require 'test_helper'

class RestaurantTest < ActiveSupport::TestCase
  # Replace this with your real tests.
  test "the truth" do
    assert true
  end
end
```

There are two ways to run this test: directly or through Rake. The Rake approach is the simplest:

introduction_to_rails/output/rake-test.txt

```
$ jruby -S rake
(in code/introduction_to_rails/rouge)
Loaded suite .../gems/rake-0.8.7/lib/rake/rake_test_loader
Started
.
Finished in 0.044 seconds.

1 tests, 1 assertions, 0 failures, 0 errors
```

Without any parameters, this command will run all the tests. You can run just unit tests or functional tests by using the target test:units or test:functionals. On UNIX, you can narrow things down to one file or even one test case, by adding something like TEST=test/unit/restaurant_test.rb or TESTOPTS=--name=test_can_create_restaurant to the command line.

The second way to test the components of your Rails app is just to run a test file directly from the jruby command. This avoids the overhead of rake and is usually a bit quicker:

`introduction_to_rails/output/jruby-single-test.txt`

```
$ jruby -Itest test/unit/restaurant_test.rb
Loaded suite test/unit/restaurant_test
Started
.
Finished in 0.292 seconds.

1 tests, 1 assertions, 0 failures, 0 errors
```

Now that we have successfully run an empty test, let's actually exercise the Restaurant model. First, we'll check that we can create a restaurant (all of these tests should be added inside the RestaurantTest class in test/unit/restaurant_test.rb):

`introduction_to_rails/rouge/test/unit/restaurant_test.rb`

```ruby
def test_can_create_restaurant_with_only_name
  Restaurant.create! :name => "Mediterraneo"
end
```

There are several ways to create new instances with ActiveRecord. In this case, we'll use the create! method, which will save a new object to the database immediately. The exclamation mark signifies that the method will raise an exception if something goes wrong. By contrast, the nonpunctuated create method will ignore errors. In test cases, it's usually easier to let ActiveRecord raise an exception so that the test harness can record it as a failure.

In the next test, we'll make some changes to a restaurant and save! it to the database:

`introduction_to_rails/rouge/test/unit/restaurant_test.rb`

```ruby
  def test_can_instantiate_and_save_a_restaurant
    restaurant = Restaurant.new
    restaurant.name = "Mediterraneo"
    restaurant.description = <<DESC
One of the best Italian restaurants in the Kings Cross area,
Mediterraneo will never leave you disappointed
DESC
    restaurant.address = "1244 Kings Cross Road, London WC1X 8CC"
    restaurant.phone = "+44 1432 3434"

    restaurant.save!
  end
```

Now, let's make sure our app can recognize incomplete data. We'll use the valid? method to see what happens when we create a restaurant without a name:

`introduction_to_rails/rouge/test/unit/restaurant_test.rb`

```
def test_that_name_is_required
  restaurant = Restaurant.new
  assert !restaurant.valid?
end
```

If you run this test, it will fail. We haven't yet told Rails that every restaurant is required to have a name. To get the behavior we want and make sure that no one enters a blank name, we'll need to add a validation to the model. A validation is a condition that ActiveRecord will check before saving an object to the database. Objects that fail their validations don't get saved. Make the following change to app/models/restaurant.rb:

`introduction_to_rails/edits/restaurant1.rb`

```
class Restaurant < ActiveRecord::Base
  validates_presence_of :name
end
```

After you've added this validation, rerun the test and make sure it passes.

Filling Out the Roster

Now that we have the Restaurant model in place, it's time to add the remaining ones. We can get the job done quickly by way of a shortcut in the model generator, which lets us specify the columns and their types on the command line. This saves us from having to edit all those migration files directly. Here's what that looks like:

`introduction_to_rails/output/script-generate-more-models.txt`

```
$ jruby script/rails g model Administrator \
                          username:string password:string
$ jruby script/rails g model Reviewer \
                          name:string description:string \
                          username:string password:string
$ jruby script/rails g model Review \
                          restaurant_id:integer reviewer_id:integer \
                          title:string content:text
$ jruby script/rails g model Comment \
                          said_by:string content:text \
                          commentable_id:integer commentable_type:string
```

Note that the Comment model doesn't have a restaurant_id or a review_id column. Instead, it has a commentable_id and a commentable_type. Rails will use these fields to track whether a particular comment was made about a restaurant or about a review. We'll see how in a moment— first, though, we need to migrate the database:

introduction_to_rails/output/rake-db-migrate-2.txt

```
$ jruby -S rake db:migrate
(in code/introduction_to_rails/rouge)
==  CreateAdministrators: migrating =========================================
-- create_table(:administrators)
   -> 0.0060s
   -> 0 rows
==  CreateAdministrators: migrated (0.0080s) ================================

==  CreateReviewers: migrating ==============================================
-- create_table(:reviewers)
   -> 0.0050s
   -> 1 rows
==  CreateReviewers: migrated (0.0060s) =====================================

==  CreateReviews: migrating ================================================
-- create_table(:reviews)
   -> 0.0060s
   -> 1 rows
==  CreateReviews: migrated (0.0060s) =======================================

==  CreateComments: migrating ===============================================
-- create_table(:comments)
   -> 0.0060s
   -> 1 rows
==  CreateComments: migrated (0.0070s) ======================================
```

The models are looking pretty good on their own. So, let's make some associations between them. We do this by modifying the various files in app/models.

Adding Associations

Let's begin with the Restaurant model. Each restaurant will need both reviews and comments. Here's how to express that relationship:

introduction_to_rails/edits/restaurant2.rb

```
class Restaurant < ActiveRecord::Base
  validates_presence_of :name

  has_many :reviews
  has_many :comments, :as => :commentable
end
```

The first line we added reads almost like English: "A restaurant has many reviews." The next line needs a little extra wording, since a comment can be associated with either a review or a restaurant.

The Administrator model is so easy that we don't need to make any changes at all to what Rails generated for us. So, let's move on to the Reviewer model:

`introduction_to_rails/rouge/app/models/reviewer.rb`

```
class Reviewer < ActiveRecord::Base
  has_many :reviews
end
```

Now, on to the Review model. You've probably guessed that, since both restaurants and reviews can take comments, this class will need the same :as => :commentable declaration that we gave the Restaurant model:

`introduction_to_rails/rouge/app/models/review.rb`

```
class Review < ActiveRecord::Base
  belongs_to :restaurant
  belongs_to :reviewer

  has_many :comments, :as => :commentable
end
```

That just leaves the Comment model:

`introduction_to_rails/rouge/app/models/comment.rb`

```
class Comment < ActiveRecord::Base
  belongs_to :commentable, :polymorphic => true
end
```

As you can see, most of the code used to specify models in Rails is self-explanatory. The only complication is the Comment model's polymorphic association (in other words, its ability to belong to more than one kind of owner). Following Rails conventions, we've named the commentable relationship after the adjective form of the Comment model's name.

Interacting with the Console

Ideally, this example has given you an idea of how to put together a few simple models in Rails. Now, to get a taste of how easy it is to work with these models, let's fire up the Rails console and add some data to our database:

```
$ jruby script/rails console
Loading development environment (Rails 3.0.0.rc)
>> mac = Restaurant.create :name => "Chez MacDo"
>> mac.comments.create :said_by => "Ola",
     :content => "I think this place is great!"
>> chef = Reviewer.create :name => "Swedish Chef",
     :description => "The Swedish Chef has dazzled audiences for years."
>> chef.reviews.create :restaurant => mac, :title => "A fine blend",
     :content => "Sometimes you find one of these exquisite experiences ..."
```

As you can see, a few lines of ActiveRecord declarations have given us
a nice internal API for our app. Let's put that API to work now.

5.4 Restaurant Administration 101

We're going to add the web front end now, starting with the administrative interface. Once we have that in place, we can use it to add data
(restaurants and reviewers) for regular visitors to see.

Scaffolding

Much as construction workers will set up scaffolds to support their
work in progress, Rails developers can take advantage of scaffolding
code to support their newly created applications. A Rails scaffold consists of views and a controller for the standard CRUD operations (Create, Read, Update, and Delete). It gives you a basic web interface for
your data, which you can lean on as you gradually add your real business code. By the end of the project, the scaffolding will have served its
purpose and will be completely replaced.

We'll build scaffolds for three of our models: Administrator, Restaurant,
and Reviewer. These are easy to create, and they'll give us the chance
to show off all four CRUD operations. Let's start with the scaffold for
the Administrator model:

introduction_to_rails/output/script-generate-scaffold.txt

```
$ jruby script/rails g scaffold Administrator \
                    username:string password:string \
                    --migration false --skip

      invoke  active_record
   identical    app/models/administrator.rb
      invoke    test_unit
   identical      test/unit/administrator_test.rb
   identical      test/fixtures/administrators.yml
       route  resources :administrators
```

```
invoke   scaffold_controller
create     app/controllers/administrators_controller.rb
invoke     erb
create       app/views/administrators
create       app/views/administrators/index.html.erb
create       app/views/administrators/edit.html.erb
create       app/views/administrators/show.html.erb
create       app/views/administrators/new.html.erb
create       app/views/administrators/_form.html.erb
invoke     test_unit
create       test/functional/administrators_controller_test.rb
invoke     helper
create       app/helpers/administrators_helper.rb
invoke       test_unit
create         test/unit/helpers/administrators_helper_test.rb
invoke   stylesheets
create     public/stylesheets/scaffold.css
```

The --migration false and --skip options tell Rails that we've already written the migrations for this model. The username and password fields determine what goes into the generated HTML form.

Go ahead and start the web server using the script/server command we saw earlier, and visit http://localhost:3000/administrators in your browser. Poke around the scaffolding interface, and create at least one new administrator for later.

As you might notice, there are a few problems with this simple scaffold. The biggest one is that we're displaying the password in plain sight. Let's fix that. Open the view file at app/views/administrators/_form.html.erb, and change text_field to password_field in the following place:

```
introduction_to_rails/rouge/app/views/administrators/_form.html.erb
```
```
<div class="field">
  <%= f.label :password %><br />
  <%= f.password_field :password %>
</div>
```

Now, modify app/views/administrators/index.html.erb and app/views/administrators/show.html.erb to show asterisks instead of passwords. To do so, replace occurrences of this:

```
administrator.password
```

...with this:

```
administrator.password.gsub(/./, '*')
```

Note that these changes affect only the display of the password, not the storage. We're still keeping the password in the database in clear text, which is a good way to get our site compromised. Password hashing is a fascinating topic, but definitely one for another day. We encourage you to check out a Rails security package such as Devise for your own apps.[9]

With a simple but functional account creation page in place, we can move on to the rest of the administrative section. The Restaurant administrative user interface is much simpler:

```
$ jruby script/rails g scaffold Restaurant
                        name:string address:string \
                        phone:string description:text \
                        --migration false --skip
```

You don't really *need* to do anything to this scaffold, although in order to save screen space, you may want to remove the description column from app/views/restaurants/index.html.erb.

Since you're running in development mode, there's no need to restart the web server. Just visit http://localhost:3000/restaurants.

Finally, here is the scaffolding for reviewers:

```
$ jruby script/rails g scaffold Reviewer \
                        name:string description:text \
                        username:string password:string \
                        --migration false --skip
```

Since this scaffold has a password field, you'll need to change the generated views in app/views/reviewers to hide the password, just like you did for the Administrator views.

May We See Your ID, Please?

Right now, any visitor to the site can edit the page for any administrator, restaurant, or reviewer. Let's add HTTP Basic Authentication to control access.

---

9. http://github.com/plataformatec/devise

First, we'll create a new base class for admin-only controllers; let's call it AuthenticatedController:

`introduction_to_rails/rouge/app/controllers/authenticated_controller.rb`

```ruby
class AuthenticatedController < ApplicationController
  before_filter :authenticate

  private

  def authenticate
    authenticate_or_request_with_http_basic do |user_name, password|
      Administrator.find_by_username_and_password(user_name, password)
    end
  end
end
```

Notice the before_filter declaration. With this in place, Rails will call our authenticate method before any action on an AuthenticatedController or on one of its subclasses. Inside authenticate, we check for any HTTP Basic Authentication credentials and look for a matching administrator account. The final step is to make all three controllers inherit from AuthenticatedController instead of ActionController. For example, the first line of app/controllers/administrators_controller.rb should look like this:

```ruby
class AdministratorsController < AuthenticatedController
```

At this point, we have a utilitarian but working administrative user interface in place. One thing we can do to spruce things up a little bit is add a common link bar for the administration options. Open the three controller files back up, and on the second line of each, add this line of code:

```ruby
layout 'authenticated'
```

Then add a new file called app/views/layouts/authenticated.html.erb with the following:

`introduction_to_rails/rouge/app/views/layouts/authenticated.html.erb`

```erb
<!DOCTYPE html>
<html>
<head>
  <title>Administration</title>
  <%= stylesheet_link_tag :all %>
  <%= javascript_include_tag :defaults %>
  <%= csrf_meta_tag %>
</head>
<body>
```

```
<table width="50%">
  <tr>
    <td><%= link_to "Administrators", administrators_path %></td>
    <td><%= link_to "Restaurants", restaurants_path %></td>
    <td><%= link_to "Reviewers", reviewers_path %></td>
  </tr>
</table>

<p style="color: green"><%= flash[:notice] %></p>

<%= yield %>

</body>
</html>
```

All three of the 'authenticated' controllers will share this common HTML structure. If you reload any of the administration pages in your browser, you should now be able to switch among them with the link bar.

5.5 Open to the Public

Now that we have an interface for the administrator, it's time to turn our attention to the general visitor. As a first step, we need to remove public/index.html so we can have dynamic content on the front page. Once that's done, we need to change the routing.

Routes to Success

The routing system is what Rails uses to decide which controller to call when a request arrives. It maps URLs, such as http://localhost/show/index, to controller actions, such as ShowController's index method. It's quite a flexible system, but for now, we only need a tiny piece of its power. Open config/routes.rb, and add these two lines anywhere inside the main block:

```
introduction_to_rails/rouge/config/routes.rb
```

```
root :to => "guide#index"
match 'guide/:action/:id' => 'guide'
```

This new code tells Rails to route requests for http://localhost:3000/ and http://localhost:3000/guide/... to the GuideController class. This controller doesn't exist yet, so let's generate it now:

```
$ jruby script/rails generate controller guide
```

If you start up the server again and visit http://localhost:3000, you will notice that the regular Rails welcome page is no longer there. Instead, you'll get an error page, because we haven't defined any GuideController actions yet. We want the main page to display a list of restaurants that the user can choose from. Edit app/controllers/guide_controller.rb to look like this:

```
introduction_to_rails/edits/guide_controller1.rb
class GuideController < ApplicationController
  def index
    @restaurants = Restaurant.all
  end
end
```

We also need to create the view for this action, by editing app/views/ guide/index.html.erb:

```
introduction_to_rails/rouge/app/views/guide/index.html.erb
<h1>Welcome to Rouge</h1>
<table>
  <tr>
    <th align="left">Name</th>
  </tr>

  <% @restaurants.each do |restaurant| %>
    <tr>
      <td><%=link_to restaurant.name, :action => :show, :id => restaurant %></td>
    </tr>
  <% end %>
</table>
```

If you reload the page, you should see a simple list of all the restaurants you've added so far. Clicking a link won't take you to a restaurant's page, though. For that, we'll need a new view and controller action.

A Restaurant with a View

Add the following method to GuideController:

```
introduction_to_rails/rouge/app/controllers/guide_controller.rb
def show
  @restaurant = Restaurant.find(params[:id])
  @comment = Comment.new
end
```

Why are we creating a new comment here? It will help us fill in some default form values in a moment. Before we get to that, though, add a new view by creating app/views/guide/show.html.erb and putting the following code in it:

```
introduction_to_rails/rouge/app/views/guide/show.html.erb
<h1><%= @restaurant.name %></h1>

<p><b>Address:</b> <%= @restaurant.address %></p>
<p><b>Phone:</b> <%= @restaurant.phone %></p>

<p><%= @restaurant.description %></p>

<h2>Reviews</h2>
<table>
<tr>
  <th>Title</th>
  <th>Author</th>
</tr>
<% @restaurant.reviews.each do |review| %>
  <tr>
    <td><%= link_to review.title, :action => 'review', :id => review %></td>
    <td><%= review.reviewer.name %></td>
  </tr>
<% end %>
</table>

<h2>Comments</h2>
<% @restaurant.comments.each do |comment| %>
  <p><b>By:</b> <%= comment.said_by %><br/>
  <%= comment.content %></p>
<% end %>

<h2>Add comment</h2>

<%= render :partial => 'shared/comment', :locals => {:target => 'restaurant'} %>
```

There are several things going on in this view. First, we display information about the restaurant itself. Below that, we link to reviews and comments people have posted. At the bottom of the page is a form for adding new comments. That form will be shared between restaurants and reviews, so we're keeping it in a separate file and using Rails's render method to reference it. We've followed Rails conventions and named the file shared/_comment.html.erb.

```
introduction_to_rails/rouge/app/views/shared/_comment.html.erb
```

```erb
<%= form_for(@comment, :url => { :action => "comment_on_#{target}",
                                 :id => params[:id] } ) do |f| %>
  <% if @comment.errors.any? %>
    <div id="error_explanation">
      <h2><%= pluralize(@comment.errors.count, "error") %>
          prohibited this comment from being saved:</h2>

      <ul>
        <% @comment.errors.full_messages.each do |msg| %>
        <li><%= msg %></li>
        <% end %>
      </ul>
    </div>
  <% end %>
  <p>
    <b>By</b><br />
    <%= f.text_field :said_by %>
  </p>

  <p>
    <b>Content</b><br />
    <%= f.text_area :content %>
  </p>
  <p>
    <%= f.submit "Comment" %>
  </p>
<% end %>
```

See the @comment instance variable at the top? That's the value we
created with the Comment.new line in the controller so that we could fill
in the fields with their correct defaults.

This user interface is not particularly fancy. But with some small
touches of CSS, it could be perfectly servicable. Of course, not everything is hooked up yet. If we want to be able to save a new comment,
we'll need to add an action to the GuideController:

```
introduction_to_rails/rouge/app/controllers/guide_controller.rb
```

```ruby
def comment_on_restaurant
  @restaurant = Restaurant.find(params[:id])
  @restaurant.comments.create params[:comment]
  @comment = Comment.new

  flash[:notice] = 'Comment created'
  render :action => 'show'
end
```

We're almost finished with the app now. The only major feature missing is reviews.

Reviewers and Reviews

We'll start with a scaffold, as before:

```
$ jruby script/rails g scaffold Review \
                           title:string content:text \
                           --migrate false --skip
```

The first change we need to make is to confine each reviewer to editing only their own reviews. We'll use HTTP Basic Authentication as we did for the admin interface but with a twist: we need to remember *which* reviewer is logged in. Open app/controllers/reviews_controller.rb, and add this at the top (after the class declaration):

introduction_to_rails/rouge/app/controllers/reviews_controller.rb

```
before_filter :authenticate
```

Now, add this near the bottom, just before the end of the class declaration:

introduction_to_rails/rouge/app/controllers/reviews_controller.rb

```
private

def authenticate
  authenticate_or_request_with_http_basic("Reviews") do |user_name, password|
    @reviewer = Reviewer.find_by_username_and_password(user_name, password)
  end
end
```

This code will make sure that reviewers are authenticated separately from administrators and will also store the logged-in reviewer in the @reviewer instance variable. Our other controller actions can use that instance variable to decide whether to allow access. For instance, here's the new index method in ReviewsController:

introduction_to_rails/rouge/app/controllers/reviews_controller.rb

```
def index
  @reviews = Review.find(:all, :conditions => ['reviewer_id = ?', @reviewer.id])

  respond_to do |format|
    format.html # index.html.erb
    format.xml  { render :xml => @reviews }
  end
end
```

As you can see, we're limiting our listing to show only the reviews associated with the current reviewer. We'll also want to restrict the show action, which displays a single review's details:

```
introduction_to_rails/rouge/app/controllers/reviews_controller.rb
  def show
    @review = Review.find_by_id_and_reviewer_id(params[:id], @reviewer)

    raise "Couldn't find Review with ID=#{params[:id]} \
and reviewer=#{@reviewer.name}" unless @review

    respond_to do |format|
      format.html # show.html.erb
      format.xml  { render :xml => @review }
    end
  end
```

Now, consider the three other controller actions: edit, update, and destroy. All three of these act on an existing review, and all three need modifications identical to the previous one.

The create action requires a slightly different change, because it builds a new review instead of searching for and updating an existing one:

```
introduction_to_rails/rouge/app/controllers/reviews_controller.rb
def create
  @review = @reviewer.reviews.build(params[:review])

  respond_to do |format|
    if @review.save
      format.html { redirect_to(@review,
                                  :notice => 'Review was successfully created.') }
      format.xml  { render :xml => @review,
                           :status => :created,
                           :location => @review }
    else
      format.html { render :action => "new" }
      format.xml  { render :xml => @review.errors,
                           :status => :unprocessable_entity }
    end
  end
end
```

In the previous excerpt, it wouldn't have been enough just to call Review.new to create a new review. We have to reach into the reviewer's reviews collection to make sure the new review gets associated with the right reviewer.

Matching Reviews to Restaurants

As it stands, there's no way for the user to specify which restaurant his review goes with. Let's fix that. First, we need to tell our controller to grab a list of all the restaurants, so the view can show them in a selection box. Open reviews_controller.rb, and add a single line to the beginning of both the new and edit actions. We'll just show the new action here:

introduction_to_rails/rouge/app/controllers/reviews_controller.rb
```
def new
  @restaurants = Restaurant.alphabetized
  @review = Review.new

  respond_to do |format|
    format.html # new.html.erb
    format.xml  { render :xml => @review }
  end
end
```

Restaurant.alphabetized will be a sorted list of restaurants. We say "will be," because this is new functionality we need to add to the Restaurant model. What should this method look like? Well, we could use bread-and-butter techniques like Ruby's sort method:

```
def Restaurant.alphabetized
  Restaurant.all.sort {|r| r.name}
end
```

This code would return the correct results, but it ignores the fact that we already have a screamingly fast data sorter sitting underneath our app: the database. So, should we construct an entire SQL query ourselves and send it to the database? ActiveRecord offers us something much better: *relations*. To add an alphabetized relation to the Restaurant model, modify restaurant.rb to look like this (the new code is in the second-to-last line):

introduction_to_rails/rouge/app/models/restaurant.rb
```
class Restaurant < ActiveRecord::Base
  validates_presence_of :name

  has_many :reviews
  has_many :comments, :as => :commentable

  scope :alphabetized, order("restaurants.name ASC")
end
```

Ian Says...

Relations in Rails

Relations are Rails 3's way of expressing database operations like sorting or filtering. They let the database do what it's good at (slicing and dicing data), and they let Ruby do what it's good at (readable notation).

One nice feature of relations is that they're *composable*. If you defined two relations called in_zip_code and alphabetized, you could write Restaurant.in_zip_code('97201').alphabetized.

For more on what relations can do, take a look at AREL ("A Relational Algebra"), the muscle behind ActiveRecord.*

∗.   http://github.com/rails/arel

Now we need to put this list of restaurants in the view so that the reviewer can choose among them. Rails's collection_select method will construct the right HTML <select> tag for us. Add the following lines just above the restaurant title in app/views/reviews/_form.html.erb:

```
introduction_to_rails/rouge/app/views/reviews/_form.html.erb
<div class="field">
  <%= f.label :restaurant %><br />
  <%= collection_select :review, :restaurant_id, @restaurants, :id, :name %>
</div>
```

As you can see, we've had to pass in five somewhat opaque parameters. These become less mysterious once you have the decoder ring.[10] Together, they specify what gets saved (the :review object's :restaurant_id field) and where the list contents come from (the @restaurants collection's :id and :name fields).

That takes care of the details of the form. Let's zoom out to the overall structure for a moment. Each review should feature the restaurant name prominently. We can accomplish this by snazzing up the header at the top of the page.

---

10. http://api.rubyonrails.org/classes/ActionView/Helpers/FormOptionsHelper.html

Here's what the resulting show.html.erb looks like:

`introduction_to_rails/rouge/app/views/reviews/show.html.erb`

```erb
<h1>Review for <%= @review.restaurant.name %></h1>

<p>
  <b>Title:</b>
  <%= @review.title %>
</p>

<p>
  <b>Content:</b>
  <%= @review.content %>
</p>


<%= link_to 'Edit', edit_review_path(@review) %> |
<%= link_to 'Back', reviews path %>
```

While we're at it, the overall list of reviews should also include restaurant names:

`introduction_to_rails/rouge/app/views/reviews/index.html.erb`

```erb
<h1>Listing reviews</h1>

<table>
  <tr>
    <th>Restaurant</th>
    <th>Title</th>
  </tr>

<% @reviews.each do |review| %>
  <tr>
    <td><%= review.restaurant.name %></td>
    <td><%= review.title %></td>
    <td><%= link_to 'Show', review %></td>
    <td><%= link_to 'Edit', edit_review_path(review) %></td>
    <td><%= link_to 'Destroy', review, :confirm => 'Are you sure?',
                                :method => :delete %></td>
  </tr>
<% end %>
</table>

<br />

<%= link_to 'New Review', new_review_path %>
```

After reviewers have gone to all the trouble of writing their reviews, it would be nice for the general public to be able to read and comment on them. Add the following two actions to the GuideController:

introduction_to_rails/rouge/app/controllers/guide_controller.rb
```ruby
def review
  @review = Review.find(params[:id])
  @comment = Comment.new
end

def comment_on_review
  @review = Review.find(params[:id])
  @review.comments.create params[:comment]
  @comment = Comment.new

  flash[:notice] = 'Comment created'
  render :action => 'review'
end
```

The code should look pretty unsurprising, since it's similar to what we did for viewing restaurants. The final view (which is in app/views/guide/review.html.erb) is similarly straightforward:

introduction_to_rails/rouge/app/views/guide/review.html.erb
```erb
<h1><%= @review.title %></h1>

<p><b>About:</b> <%= @review.restaurant.name %></p>
<p><b>By:</b> <%= @review.reviewer.name %></p>

<p><%= @review.content %></p>

<h2>Comments</h2>
<% @review.comments.each do |comment| %>
  <p><b>By:</b> <%= comment.said_by %><br/>
  <%= comment.content %></p>
<% end %>

<h2>Add comment</h2>

<%= render :partial => 'shared/comment', :locals => {:target => 'review'} %>
```

And there you have it—a working application! Of course, you're probably tempted to add some visual styling, nice navigational features, and so on. We highly encourage you to do so. Have fun, and drop us a line in the forums to show us what you've come up with.

5.6 Wrapping Up

In this chapter, we introduced the Rails framework and built a simple Rails application on JRuby. We also discussed a few differences from regular Ruby on Rails. For the most part, there hasn't been much of a distinction, other than a couple of configuration settings. Over the next couple of chapters, we'll see where JRuby on Rails really shines: database access and deployment options.

Chapter 6

JRuby and Relational Databases

These days, any upstart programming language has to have some kind of persistent storage support to be taken seriously. Ruby is no exception; in fact, developers tout its fluid database connectivity.

Many of the techniques for connecting Ruby to databases work basically the same in JRuby. Over the coming pages, we'll turn our attention to relational databases (as opposed to key-value or other data stores). You'll see how to use Ruby's more popular data frameworks and what kinds of adjustments to make when you're running them in JRuby.

In regular Ruby, SQL libraries typically depend on a database-specific C module. The APIs differ widely depending on the database, and framework authors are left with the task of papering over these differences. With JRuby, you'll still install a binary driver for your choice of database, but at least all these drivers are written to one common API: Java's JDBC standard.

You can call JDBC routines directly from Ruby, and later, we'll see a situation where you might want to do just that. But it's usually more convenient to work with a higher-level library. It's worth keeping in mind, though, that all these library calls percolate down to JDBC under the hood.

6.1 Ruby Database Frameworks

Let's take a look at the most commonly used Ruby frameworks for database connectivity. From a bird's-eye view, there's little difference between using these in plain Ruby or JRuby.

Ola Says...

Throwback to JDBC

In many ways, both DBI and Sequel remind me of JDBC, in that they try to abstract away some of the differences between different databases engines, while still acknowledging that you're working with a database.

The main database libraries for Ruby are quite different from one other. ActiveRecord is a high-level framework that allows you to work with the database abstracted away (at least to a degree). Its name comes from a pattern in Martin Fowler's *Patterns of Enterprise Application Architecture* [Fow03].[1]

DBI and Sequel both allow you to work much closer to the database. Although you won't have to deal with a specific database product's wire protocol or file format, you'll have much more control over the exact SQL queries your Ruby program will be running.

The differences listed earlier should make it clear that these libraries are suited for very different circumstances, and it's good to keep a couple of them in your toolbox. But wait with that decision until you have seen the tools available only on JRuby!

ActiveRecord

In Chapter 5, *Introduction to Rails*, on page 85, we saw just enough ActiveRecord to get a Rails app running. Let's dive in a little deeper now. We've said that this library is an implementation of the Active Record software pattern; what does that mean?

For the purposes of this chapter, we're going think of object-oriented programs in terms of *model classes* and *utility classes*. Model classes represent the ideas behind your program, in language similar to what you'd use with an end user: blog posts, employees, appointments, and

---

1. Another great Ruby data library, DataMapper, also gets its name from Fowler's book. Its JRuby support is a work in progress; still, you might want to take a peek at http://datamapper.org if you like living on the bleeding edge.

so on. Utility classes perform auxiliary tasks, such as drawing graphics or parsing wire protocols. Clearly, model classes are what you'd typically want to keep around in a database.

In the simplest incarnation of the Active Record pattern, each model class is represented by one database table. Each instance of that class corresponds to one row in the table and typically has one property for each column.

For instance, a program for cataloging different species of trees might have a Tree class with name, max_height, and maybe a few other fields. If the program follows the Active Record pattern, it will keep all its trees in a trees table—which might look something like this after a user enters the first couple of species:

```
+----+-----------------+------------+--------------+
| id | name            | max_height | is_evergreen |
+----+-----------------+------------+--------------+
| 1  | Canyon Live Oak | 30         | 1            |
| 2  | Post Oak        | 15         | 0            |
+----+-----------------+------------+--------------+
```

In a less flexible programming language, you might end up writing a lot of repetitive code to support this pattern. For instance, you'd need a getMaxHeight() method to fetch the value of the max_height column for a particular database record and convert it to an integer. Fortunately, the ActiveRecord library automates much of this mapping for you. In the simplest cases, if you follow the naming conventions, you won't have to write anything except the class name.

There's a lot more to ActiveRecord than what's in Fowler's original design pattern. These extra features allow ActiveRecord to handle the most common database-related tasks you're likely to encounter. Broadly speaking, the library can be divided into four parts:

- Migrations

- Model descriptions

- Validations

- Model usage

We'll describe and give examples each of these parts soon, but first we need to talk about how JRuby and ActiveRecord work together.

JRuby has supported ActiveRecord for quite a long time. A collection of gems gives you a choice among various JDBC drivers to use with ActiveRecord. You can choose to use either a driver specific to your database or a general driver; it doesn't make much difference either way. To install the general gem, run this command (the exact version number may vary):

```
$ jruby -S gem install activerecord-jdbc-adapter
Successfully installed activerecord-jdbc-adapter-1.0.2-java
1 gem installed
```

To use a database-specific gem instead, first do a search for available gems:

```
$ jruby -S gem search -r activerecord-jdbc

*** REMOTE GEMS ***

ActiveRecord-JDBC (0.5)
activerecord-jdbc-adapter (1.0.2 java, 0.9.2)
activerecord-jdbcdbf-adapter (0.9.7.2 java)
activerecord-jdbcderby-adapter (1.0.2 java, 0.9.2)
activerecord-jdbch2-adapter (1.0.2 java, 0.9.2)
activerecord-jdbchsqldb-adapter (1.0.2 java, 0.9.2)
activerecord-jdbcmssql-adapter (1.0.2 java)
activerecord-jdbcmysql-adapter (1.0.2 java, 0.9.2)
activerecord-jdbcpostgresql-adapter (1.0.2 java, 0.9.2)
activerecord-jdbcsqlite3-adapter (1.0.2 java, 0.9.2)
...
```

...and then install the driver for your database. For example, if you were using MySQL, you'd type this:

```
$ jruby -S gem install activerecord-jdbcmysql-adapter
```

If you're using a commercial database like Oracle or Microsoft SQL Server, you'll also need to download your vendor's JDBC driver and copy it into JRuby's lib directory. For example, with Oracle 10g, you'd look for ojdbc14.jar on the official download site.[2]

For the most part, your Ruby code will look the same whether you use the generic driver or a specific one. We'll note the few places where you need to do something different between the two.

---

2. http://www.oracle.com/technetwork/database/enterprise-edition/jdbc-10201-088211.html

Once you have chosen and installed your database adapter, you can finally install ActiveRecord itself:

```
$ jruby -S gem install activerecord
```

At this point, it's a good idea to check that everything is working by connecting to a database and executing some raw SQL. Here's how you'd do that using the general adapter:

databases/simple_connect.rb

```
require 'rubygems'
require 'active_record'

ActiveRecord::Base.establish_connection(
  :adapter => 'jdbc',
  :driver => 'com.mysql.jdbc.Driver',
  :url => 'jdbc:mysql://localhost/using_jruby',
  :username => 'root',
  :password => ''
)

ActiveRecord::Base.connection.execute("CREATE TABLE FOO1(id INTEGER)")
p ActiveRecord::Base.connection.execute("SHOW TABLES")
```

You may need to change some of the parameters to suit your circumstances. The code assumes that you've done the following:

1. Install and start the MySQL server.[3]

2. Download and extract the MySQL JDBC drivers, and copy the .jar to JRuby's lib directory.[4]

3. Use the MySQL server's admin tools to create a database called using_jruby:

```
$ mysql --user=root
Welcome to the MySQL monitor.  Commands end with ; or \g.
Your MySQL connection id is 4
Server version: 5.1.44 Source distribution

Type 'help;' or '\h' for help. Type '\c' to clear the current input statement.

mysql> CREATE DATABASE using_jruby;
Query OK, 1 row affected (0.00 sec)

mysql> \q
Bye
```

---

3. http://dev.mysql.com/downloads/mysql
4. http://dev.mysql.com/downloads/connector/j

Once those steps are complete, you're ready to run the code:

```
$ jruby simple_connect.rb
[{"Tables_in_using_jruby"=>"F001"}]
```

If you choose to use the specific MySQL adapter, the establish_connection part should look like this instead:

`databases/specific_connect.rb`

```
ActiveRecord::Base.establish_connection(
  :adapter => 'jdbcmysql',
  :database => 'using_jruby',
  :host => 'localhost',
  :username => 'root',
  :password => ''
)
```

This configuration looks more like the regular Ruby version of the same code, because it omits the ugly JDBC URL and driver specification.

It's also possible to fetch your database connection from JNDI.[5] You do this by providing a parameter named jndi, which has the name of the JNDI object to get the database connection from.[6] If you do that, you can leave out most of the other parameters:

`databases/jndi_connect.rb`

```
ActiveRecord::Base.establish_connection(
  :adapter => 'jdbc',
  :jndi => 'jdbc/using_jruby',
  :driver => 'com.mysql.jdbc.Driver'
)
```

We won't describe in detail all the features of ActiveRecord here—there are better places to find that documentation.[7] It's worth highlighting some of the main features, though, so you know what's possible.

Migrations

The original Active Record pattern suggests a structure for your database. How do you create that structure in the first place, and how do you modify it as your data model changes? This is where the ActiveRecord library's notion of *migrations* comes in. A migration is a piece of

---

5. Java Naming and Directory Interface, a way for Java services to discover one another. See http://java.sun.com/products/jndi.
6. See your JNDI implementation's instructions for how to create and name this object.
7. http://api.rubyonrails.org/classes/ActiveRecord/Base.html

Ola Says...

Migrations

Migrations are so useful that I often use them outside the context of Rails applications, whenever I want to be able to make controlled changes to my database structure.

code that runs when you're creating your database for the first time or when you're rearranging it later as your app evolves.

A typical migration will create a new table (to represent a new class you're adding to your program) or add a column to an existing table. Migrations can also run in reverse, dropping tables when you need to roll back to a previous version of your code.

Migrations are named with a timestamp so that they run in the order in which you created them. This sequencing allows you to grow your database organically. If you need a table, you add a new migration for it. If you need a new column, add a new migration to add that column.

It just so happens that most of the complexity in activerecord-jdbc-adapter lies in the code related to migrations. The reason is that Data Definition Language (DDL) is the least-specified part of SQL, and all vendors have different ways of manipulating the database structure. That said, most standard databases work fine when combining migrations and JDBC.

Let's take a look at an example migration. Rails uses a structure of one file per migration, and that works really well. But if you want to do something ad hoc or maybe just see how migrations work in a code example, it's fine to put several migrations in one file, as in the upcoming example.

Assuming you have an establish_connection call at the beginning of your file, as we've discussed on the previous pages, you can define a series of migrations like this:

`databases/ar_migrations.rb`

```ruby
class AddFooTable < ActiveRecord::Migration
  def self.up
    create_table :foo do |t|
      t.string  :foo
      t.text    :bar
      t.integer   :qux
    end
  end

  def self.down
    drop_table :foo
  end
end

class AddBlechColumnTable < ActiveRecord::Migration
  def self.up
    add_column :foo, :flax, :string
  end

  def self.down
    remove_column :foo, :flax
  end
end
```

Once you've defined your migrations, you can run them normally (:up) or in reverse (:down):

`databases/ar_migrations.rb`

```ruby
AddFooTable.migrate(:up)
AddBlechColumnTable.migrate(:up)
AddBlechColumnTable.migrate(:down)
AddFooTable.migrate(:down)
```

The code will generate simple output like this, provided everything was configured correctly. Behind the scenes, your SQL database will contain the new tables and columns:

```
$ jruby ar_migrations.rb
==  AddFooTable: migrating =============================================
-- create_table(:foo)
   -> 2.1932s
   -> 0 rows
==  AddFooTable: migrated (2.1963s) ====================================
```

```
==  AddBlechColumnTable: migrating =============================================
-- add_column(:foo, :flax, :string)
   -> 0.1170s
   -> 0 rows
==  AddBlechColumnTable: migrated (0.1190s) ====================================

==  AddBlechColumnTable: reverting =============================================
-- remove_column(:foo, :flax)
   -> 0.0081s
==  AddBlechColumnTable: reverted (0.0092s) ====================================

==  AddFooTable: reverting =====================================================
-- drop_table(:foo)
   -> 0.0026s
   -> 0 rows
==  AddFooTable: reverted (0.0048s) ============================================
```

Migrations are definitely handy to have in your tool chest, and making use of JDBC and JNDI to attach to different databases makes it much easier to do any of the DDL tasks you might want to do repeatedly.

Model Descriptions

ActiveRecord includes a very rich DSL-like syntax for describing your model classes and their associations with one other. Creating a new model class is as simple as inheriting from ActiveRecord::Base and then using certain class methods to tell ActiveRecord some facts about your model.

Instead of taking each piece in isolation, we will show you a model class that uses most of the common definitions and then describe them afterward.

databases/ar_description.rb

```ruby
require 'rubygems'
require 'active_record'

class Blog < ActiveRecord::Base
  set_table_name 'WP_BLOG'
  set_primary_key 'blog_id'

  belongs_to :owner,     :class_name  => 'Person'
  has_one    :audit_log, :foreign_key => 'watched_id'

  has_many :posts
  has_many :authors, :through => :posts
end
```

This code defines a Ruby model class named Blog, sets the table name to WP_BLOG (the default would have been blogs), and sets the primary key to be blog_id (instead of the default primary key of id). We don't have to say anything at all about the blog's basic properties. If, for example, the WP_BLOG table has a name, a creator, and a visit_count column, each of these will automatically be accessible in Ruby with the same name it has in the database.

We see four different examples of associations in this code. First, let's look at belongs_to and has_one. Each of these indicates a foreign-key relationship. In the case of belongs_to, the foreign key will be a column called owner_id in this model's own WP_BLOG table.

The has_one declaration, on the other hand, shows that the watched_id foreign key lives in a separate audit_logs table and points back at this model. As you can see, ActiveRecord uses sensible naming conventions for column, table, and class names but allows you to override them.

The final two definitions—the ones beginning with has_many—describe collections. The first one is simple and says that every blog has zero or more posts. The assumption here is that there also exists a Post model class and that the blog posts will be a collection of these.

The second has_many declaration creates a many-to-many association. It doesn't use a typical join table (you can do that too, using has_and_belongs_to_many). Instead, it uses another Ruby class, the Post model, as the intermediate object. Here, a blog's authors are the set of people who have ever written a post on that blog.

There are definitely more nuances and fine-tunings of data models, but these pieces represent the most common uses of ActiveRecord.

Validations

Nearly all database-driven programs require data validation at some point. Sometimes, you want to apply constraints that are more stringent than a typical RDBMS's primitive type checking. Or you might want to catch errors before the database ever sees them. ActiveRecord provides a declarative way to get this behavior, by describing validations on your model class.

Although you can put almost anything in a validation, there are several common checks you end up doing quite often. This code gives a few examples of what you can specify in your model:

Ola Says...
Validate Anything

ActiveRecord allows you to validate just about any property you can think of. I made an example in Rails once that was a database of Ruby scripts. As one of the validations, I added a check to make sure that the Ruby script saved was actually valid Ruby code.

`databases/ar_validations.rb`

```ruby
require 'rubygems'
require 'active_record'

class Blog < ActiveRecord::Base
  validates_presence_of :title, :message => "should be provided"

  validates_numericality_of :age, :only_integer => true

  validates_length_of :title, :in => 5..35
  validates_length_of :posts, :maximum => 30

  validates_uniqueness_of :title

  validates_inclusion_of :blog_type, :in => %w(work personal)

  validates_format_of :contact, :with => /^.+?@.+?$/

  validates_each :title, :text do |record, attr, value|
    unless value.buddha_nature?
      record.errors.add attr, "doesn't have the Buddha nature"
    end
  end
end
```

This example checks quite a lot of things on the Blog model. Let's take them in order:

- validates_presence_of: This method will make sure that the named attributes are not nil or blank. All validations allow you to provide a custom message if you don't like the one provided, and in this case an error message would say "title should be provided".

- validates_numericality_of: As the name says, it checks that an attribute is a number. You can decide if any kind of number is fine or if you only want to allow integers. The default is to allow any kind of number.

- validates_length_of: Checking the length of something can be done either by comparing to a maximum or by comparing to a range. Anything that responds to the message length can be used, so a String value works fine, and so does an association.

- validates_uniqueness_of: This validation is a bit different in that it doesn't check any property of the value itself but instead makes sure that there is nothing else with the same value for that property.

- validates_inclusion_of: If you want to make sure that a value is in a range of values, you can use this validation. You can give it any kind of object that has the include? method, so arrays and ranges both work fine.

- validates_format_of: You may sometimes find it necessary to check that a string field matches a specific format. In this example, we've used an extremely simple regular expression to make sure that a string looks a little bit like an email address.

- validates_each: There are several ways to do custom validation. The low-level way is to override validate, validate_on_create, or validate_on_update. The better way is to just define a custom validation with validates_each.

With this approach, you simply provide the names of the properties to be checked, plus a block that actually does the testing. The block gets three arguments: the model instance under validation, the name of the property that is being checked, and the new value that is about to be inserted into the database.

You signal a failed validation by adding one or more errors to the errors attribute of the model instance. If you add no errors, ActiveRecord will consider the validation a success. We strongly recommend validates_each over the low-level mechanisms. If you make a mistake with the latter, your other validations might not run.

As you can see, the possibilities for validation are considerable. You can go totally crazy and validate each and every aspect of the data before it ever gets into the database. But one detail is missing. When should the validations actually run? There are some alternatives here. The basic rule is that during regular model usage (you will see more about this in the next section), ActiveRecord will run your validations just before an object gets saved to the database. If you need more control, you can call the valid? on a model instance at any time.

Model Usage

You have now seen most of the important parts of the ActiveRecord puzzle—except for how to actually use it, that is.

In keeping with the blogging theme we've started, let's take a look at some examples of how to create blogs and add posts:

`databases/ar_usage.rb`

```ruby
require 'rubygems'
require 'active_record'

b1 = Blog.new :author => 'Ola Bini'
b1.title = 'My first blog'
b1.save

Blog.create :title => 'My second blog'

b2 = Blog.find(2)
b2.title = 'My second blog, revisited'
b2.posts.create(:title => 'First post',
                :body  => 'This is a post about something')
b2.save

my_blogs = Blog.where(:author => 'Ola Bini')
my_blogs.first.destroy
```

This example shows only a small extent of what's possible to do with an ActiveRecord model, but it shows enough to get you started. Let's run through the interesting parts of this code snippet.

First, a model object can be created using new, exactly as any other Ruby object. You can also give this call a hash of initial values for attributes. Any attribute can be set by just using a setter. ActiveRecord provides these for columns in the table (such as title), *and* for associated objects (like posts).

To push a newly created object to the database, just call save or save!. The difference between them is that the first one returns false if it couldn't validate the object or save it to the database for some reason. The "bang" version will throw an exception instead.

If you want to initialize an object and save it to the database in one step, you can use create or create!.

To retrieve an object from the database, you use the find method with the blog's unique ID. You'll notice we didn't supply any IDs when we created the blogs; this is a detail that ActiveRecord prefers to take care of.

The next lines update some attributes and also put a new Post into the blog's collection of posts. There are lots of ways of sticking together two associated objects. For this case, it makes sense just to call create on the associated posts collection and let ActiveRecord take care of the potentially tricky process of wiring them together.

A database mapping wouldn't be very useful if the only way to look up objects were through their IDs. ActiveRecord models support a mind-boggling number of ways to slice and dice data. Here, we're filtering blogs by author and then taking the first one that matches. The documentation for ActiveRecord is full of examples of other techniques for searching through databases.

In the final line, we delete the first Blog in the filtered list by calling destroy. This will also make the instance immutable, so if you try to modify any of the attributes of the instance after destroying it, it will raise an exception.

This is really the minimum you need to know to be able to use ActiveRecord models. Armed with this information, you should be able to add, search for, update, or remove objects from your own databases. In the next few sections, we'll take a quick look at the other database libraries for Ruby and see how they compare. While ActiveRecord is the premier Ruby database library, there are times when one of the alternatives is a better fit.

DBI

DBI is a very lightweight framework, in that it tries to get really close to the database. It is not a mapping framework like ActiveRecord; instead, it allows you to work with a thin wrapper over the direct database driver.

It was originally heavily inspired by the Perl DBI library but has now diverged a bit, with the addition of more idiomatic Ruby features. DBI works well with JDBC, and once you are connected to the database using JDBC, you can use the standard DBI interface to work with your data.

The JDBC interface for working with DBI is still quite young, so make sure to play around with it before committing to it.

To use DBI, you first need to install the dbi and dbd-jdbc gems:

```
$ jruby -S gem install dbi dbd-jdbc
```

Once you have these in place, you can connect to a database and grab some data. The multirow select_all method is the workhorse of DBI:

databases/dbi_test.rb
```
require 'rubygems'
require 'dbi'

DBI.connect('DBI:Jdbc:mysql://localhost/using_jruby',
            'root',
            '',
            'driver'=>'com.mysql.jdbc.Driver') do |dbh|
  p dbh.select_all('SELECT * FROM foo')
end
```

For single-row queries, you use the select_one method instead. Here's how to get the current version of a MySQL server:

databases/dbi_version.rb
```
require 'rubygems'
require 'dbi'

DBI.connect('DBI:Jdbc:mysql://localhost/using_jruby',
            'root',
            '',
            'driver'=>'com.mysql.jdbc.Driver') do |dbh|
  row = dbh.select_one('SELECT VERSION()')
  puts "Server version: #{row[0]}"
end
```

If you want to run a script that updates the database, say, to drop or create a table, you can call the do method on the database handle.

```
databases/dbi_table.rb
```

```ruby
require 'rubygems'
require 'dbi'

DBI.connect('DBI:Jdbc:mysql://localhost/using_jruby',
            'root',
            '',
            'driver'=>'com.mysql.jdbc.Driver') do |dbh|
  dbh.do("DROP TABLE IF EXISTS blogs")

  dbh.do(<<SQL)
CREATE TABLE blogs(
  id INT UNSIGNED NOT NULL AUTO_INCREMENT,
  name VARCHAR(255),
  author VARCHAR(255),
  PRIMARY KEY (id))
SQL

  dbh.do(<<SQL)
INSERT INTO blogs (name, author)
 VALUES
  ('Languages', 'Ola Bini'),
  ('Politics', 'Roy Singham'),
  ('Environment', 'Al Gore')
SQL
end
```

This code will drop the table if it exists and then create the table from scratch and add some data to it. The do method will return the number of updated rows after the command has finished. This can be useful when checking whether an UPDATE statement actually did something, for example. Note that we're using the Ruby "heredoc" syntax to make the SQL statements more readable.[8]

We're going to show a few more examples on how to use DBI. As you will see, DBI is actually much closer to JDBC than any of the other database tools described in this chapter. When you extract values from the database, DBI doesn't automatically give you back everything in one collection—instead, you get a handle to a result set, so you can traverse the results in any way you want. There are performance advantages to this approach, but it does tend to make for more low-level code to handle everything.

---

8. http://en.wikipedia.org/wiki/Here_document

When performance and memory usage are not an issue, you can gloss over results sets and just use the select_all and select_one methods shown earlier.

So, let's see how this works:

```
databases/dbi_result.rb
require 'rubygems'
require 'dbi'

DBI.connect('DBI:Jdbc:mysql://localhost/using_jruby',
            'root',
            '',
            'driver'=>'com.mysql.jdbc.Driver') do |dbh|
  sth = dbh.prepare("SELECT * FROM blogs")
  sth.execute

  while row = sth.fetch
    puts "Values from DB: #{row.inspect}"
  end

  sth.finish
end
```

Not much difference, really. You call fetch on the statement object, and it will return a new row every time, until there are no more rows to return. It's important to call finish after you're finished with the statements—otherwise, the database will stop responding at some point. Not fun.

The statement object actually has a Ruby-style each method, so you can iterate over it like a traditional Ruby collection instead, if that strikes your fancy.

DBI also supports preparing statements with placeholders for data. This works like in JDBC: the data will be quoted correctly, based on what kind of column it's going into. This is very convenient and also makes it much easier to avoid security holes. ActiveRecord has taken a lot of flak because it used to encourage quoting in Ruby, instead of letting the database take care of it.

To prepare and use such a statement, we use the prepare method, like we did earlier.

```
databases/dbi_prepare.rb
require 'rubygems'
require 'dbi'

DBI.connect('DBI:Jdbc:mysql://localhost/using_jruby',
            'root',
            '',
            'driver'=>'com.mysql.jdbc.Driver') do |dbh|
  sth = dbh.prepare("INSERT INTO blogs (name, author) VALUES(?, ?)")

  sth.execute("Architecture", "Richard Gabriel")
  sth.execute("Physics", "Lee Smolin")
  sth.execute("Memes", "Richard Dawkins")

  sth.finish
end
```

Here, we prepare an INSERT statement and then run it with three different pieces of data. This technique is not limited to INSERTs, of course.
You can use it with any kind of SQL statement.

DBI also allows you to get lots of metadata associated with a current
connection, result set, or table. This information is readily available
from DBI's online documentation.[9]

With these pieces in place, you have everything you need to get started
with DBI for low-level database tasks.

Sequel

Sequel is a relatively new database framework for Ruby. It's quite different from both ActiveRecord and DBI, sitting somewhere in between
them on the ladder of abstraction. It's closer to the database than
ActiveRecord but more abstract than DBI. You generally don't work
with raw SQL commands as much in Sequel as you do in DBI.

The goal for Sequel was to layer a Ruby-like interface over some of the
cases that ActiveRecord didn't handle so well in the past (such as large
data sets). Sequel also includes model and migration features similar to
those of ActiveRecord, albeit more integrated with the rest of the library
than their ActiveRecord counterparts.

Before we start looking at some examples of Sequel, it's important to
know that not everything that looks like familiar Ruby will actually be

---

9. http://ruby-dbi.rubyforge.org

executed as it reads. There are some circumstances where Sequel does exceedingly clever things with Ruby code—such as transforming it into SQL for later execution in the database. This can cause some of the examples to look a bit unusual.

To be able to use Sequel, you just need to install the sequel gem:

```
$ jruby -S gem install sequel
```

Now, you can use something like this to take a look at the database:

databases/sequel_simple.rb

```
require 'rubygems'
require 'sequel'

url = 'jdbc:mysql://localhost:3306/using_jruby?user=root&password='
DB = Sequel.connect(url)

DB[:blogs].each do |row|
  p row
end
```

Each row comes back as a Ruby Hash:

```
$ jruby sequel_simple.rb
{:id=>1, :name=>"Languages", :author=>"Ola Bini"}
{:id=>2, :name=>"Politics", :author=>"Roy Singham"}
{:id=>3, :name=>"Environment", :author=>"Al Gore"}
{:id=>4, :name=>"Architecture", :author=>"Richard Gabriel"}
{:id=>5, :name=>"Physics", :author=>"Lee Smolin"}
{:id=>6, :name=>"Memes", :author=>"Richard Dawkins"}
```

Note that we specify the connection information just like we would when connecting to JDBC. That's because JDBC is actually used under the covers—so this is really a JDBC URL.

Once we have a connection, there are lots of ways of getting data out of it. The shortcut used in this code allows us to get a dataset that points to a specific table. DB[:blogs] is more or less a shorter way of saying DB['select * from blogs']. Sequel includes quite a lot of clever shortcuts like this. The goal is to allow you to write Ruby code for most things where you would have needed SQL in other frameworks.

Once you have a dataset, you can do some clever things with it. Say you want to get aggregate information, such as a count, or maybe you're just interested in a specific entry.

databases/sequel_functions.rb

```
require 'rubygems'
require 'sequel'

url = 'jdbc:mysql://localhost:3306/using_jruby?user=root&password='
DB = Sequel.connect(url)

p DB[:blogs].count
p DB[:blogs].map(:name)
```
```
$ jruby sequel_functions.rb>
6
["Languages", "Politics", "Environment", "Architecture", "Physics", "Memes"]
```

There are a huge amount of these simplifying methods all over Sequel. Once you master them, Sequel ends up being a really powerful tool for working with databases.

What about executing arbitrary SQL? Well, it depends on whether you want a dataset back. As we saw earlier, you can use the square brackets format to do SELECTs. If you want to do a raw INSERT, you can do it like this:

databases/sequel_insert.rb

```
require 'rubygems'
require 'sequel'

url = 'jdbc:mysql://localhost:3306/using_jruby?user=root&password='
DB = Sequel.connect(url)

DB << "INSERT INTO blogs (name, author) VALUES('Music', '_why')"
```

The left-shift operator is overloaded to execute any SQL statement sent to it. You can also use the execute method if that feels more natural.

You might be worried about the lively use of datasets in these examples. As it turns out, the datasets in Sequel are extremely lazy, meaning that they don't do anything at all until you want to get some real data out of them—at which point Sequel tries really hard to do things in the database if possible. So, count and map will actually send out two very different SQL statements to do these operations, rather than fetching an entire table into Ruby and doing the operations in memory.

If you want to get all the records as an array of hashes, you call all on the dataset. Searching in a table for a specific data item can be as simple as DB[:blogs][:id => 1].

Sequel has very powerful filtering capabilities. You won't even have to resort to SQL to do subselects. This capability can be very powerful, but it also makes the library really easy to use.

You can run DELETE and INSERT statements in pure Ruby as well:

```
databases/sequel_delinsert.rb
require 'rubygems'
require 'sequel'

url = 'jdbc:mysql://localhost:3306/using_jruby?user=root&password='
DB = Sequel.connect(url)

blogs = DB[:blogs]

blogs.insert(:name => 'Databases',
             :author => 'Pramod Sadalage')

blogs.filter(:name => 'Databases').delete
```

This code does an INSERT using the parameters specified, filters the table, and then deletes the blogs selected by the filter. This just scratches the surface on what is possible with filters in Sequel.

Sequel also offers models, like ActiveRecord does:

```
databases/sequel_simple_model.rb
require 'rubygems'
require 'sequel'

url = 'jdbc:mysql://localhost:3306/using_jruby?user=root&password='
DB = Sequel.connect(url)

class Blog < Sequel::Model
end

blog = Blog[1]
p blog
```

Here, we first define a class that will become a Sequel model. By default, it will use the same naming conventions as ActiveRecord, so this code will connect to the table called blogs, using the existing database connection. The square brackets allow us to get a specific blog instance based on the primary key. Sequel is fine with composite primary keys but also "scales down" in simplicity: it will default to an id column as the primary key.

 Ian Says...

The Lazy Arms Race

Since Sequel came out, ActiveRecord has gained similar "lazy loading" features. Starting with version 3, ActiveRecord will put off as much work as it possibly can, until you absolutely need to hit the database.* This allows both Sequel and ActiveRecord to optimize their queries and avoid creating an excessive number of Ruby objects.

*. http://m.onkey.org/2010/1/22/active-record-query-interface

You can use square brackets to find a model based on conditions. For example, you could call Blog[:name => 'Music'] to find any blog with the name Music. Most of the familiar Sequel filtering operations work fine inside square brackets. Sequel Model is quite a thin wrapper over regular Sequel, so most of the concepts should be recognizable.

Sequel models allow you to specify associations between them, much in the same way as ActiveRecord does. This is very well documented on the Sequel website, and it works exactly the same in JRuby as it does in regular Ruby.[10]

All in all, Sequel is a really nice database library. It takes a very different approach than both DBI and ActiveRecord, but this approach makes it a really advanced tool.

6.2 Ribs

Database libraries for Ruby generally share the same goal of making the most common cases achievable with very little code, which is why we have the table naming conventions, automatic primary keys, and so on.

Sometimes, however, you have legacy databases, unconventional column names, inconvenient mappings, or high-performance caching needs. In these situations, wedging exotic behavior into ActiveRecord

---

10. http://sequel.rubyforge.org

would be more difficult than using a database framework that was designed for this kind of use—like the Java Hibernate library.[11]

The overhead of using Hibernate can be inconvenient, especially for small projects. That's what the Ribs project aims to change.[12] Simply put, Ribs allow you to persist your Ruby objects using Hibernate. It's a wrapper around the real Hibernate database framework, not a port. This means that Ribs is for JRuby only.

Using Hibernate means that you get a large amount of power out of the box. But Ribs tries really hard to make its interface more Ruby-like, intuitive, and easy to use. The goal is to be able to scale Ribs from the absolutely simplest applications, all the way up to extremely complex systems interacting with legacy databases.

Ready to get started? You can install a prebuilt Ribs gem, but we recommend building with the latest source instead. Either way, the installation will bring in Hibernate and its dependencies for you (the version number in the last line may vary):

```
$ git clone git://github.com/olabini/ribs.git
$ cd ribs
$ ant jar
$ jruby -S gem install rake rspec
$ jruby -S rake gem
$ jurby -S gem install pkg/ribs-0.0.2.gem
```

The first thing you need to do when connecting to Ribs is to define one or more databases. One of these must be named the default. For example:

databases/ribs_connect.rb
```
require 'rubygems'
require 'ribs'

Ribs::DB.define(:db1) do |db|
  # Basic connectivity:
  db.dialect = 'MySQL'
  db.uri = 'jdbc:mysql://localhost:3306/using_jruby?user=root&password='
  db.driver = 'com.mysql.jdbc.Driver'

  # Extra options:
  db.default = true
  db.properties['hibernate.show_sql'] = 'true'
end
```

---

11. http://www.hibernate.org
12. http://github.com/olabini/ribs

Ola Says...
Ribs vs. Ruby

Since Ribs builds on the strong base of Hibernate, I decided early on to make a few things different from the way Ruby database frameworks generally work with models. Some of these decisions make the usage of Ribs look quite...different.

Making Ruby objects persistent with Hibernate is one side of the coin. One day, I'd like to add the flip side: driving an existing Hibernate domain model (written in Java) with Ribs. This would allow you to very easily use an existing Java model in your Rails application, for example. Other future possibilities include both a migrations framework and some way of handling validations.

There are a few things to notice here. First, in the manner of Hibernate, you specify a dialect, a URI, and a driver class. You can add any kind of extra properties for Hibernate here too. Here, we're using Hibernate's show_sql property to display all the generated SQL code. We're also marking the database explicitly as the default.

The default database is the one Ribs will use for data operations that don't name a specific database. There's an easier way to set the default, which we'll see in a moment.

The next few examples are all designed to build on one another. You'll create a Ruby file with just the connection information and gradually add code to it.

The program should work with little modification on just about any database system. Setting up most commercial servers with Hibernate is not for the faint of heart; it involves finding, installing, and configuring both JDBC drivers and Hibernate dialect classes. Instead, we're going to base our example on the lightweight Apache Derby database, which is much easier to install.[13] Just download a recent build, and copy derby.jar into your project directory.

---

13. http://db.apache.org/derby

As we did with the MySQL example a moment ago, we need to start by connecting to the Derby database:

`databases/ribs_use.rb`

```ruby
require 'rubygems'
require 'ribs'

Ribs::DB.define do |db|
  db.dialect = 'Derby'
  db.uri = 'jdbc:derby:using_jruby;create=true'
  db.driver = 'org.apache.derby.jdbc.EmbeddedDriver'
end
```

Let's do a quick check to make sure Hibernate and Derby can find each other. The following code should produce empty output, with no error messages:

```
$ jruby -J-cp derby.jar ribs_use.rb
```

Now, we'll execute some raw SQL. This practice is not recommended for day-to-day operation but can be useful for creating tables, adding data in batch form, and so on. The following code will create a new table, add some rows, and then print the result of a SELECT:

`databases/ribs_use.rb`

```ruby
Ribs::with_handle do |h|
  h.ddl "DROP TABLE book" rescue nil

  h.ddl <<SQL
CREATE TABLE book (
  id INT NOT NULL GENERATED BY DEFAULT AS IDENTITY (START WITH 1, INCREMENT BY 1),
  title VARCHAR(255) NOT NULL,
  author VARCHAR(255) NOT NULL,
  PRIMARY KEY (id)
)
SQL

  stmt = "INSERT INTO book(title, author) VALUES(?, ?)"
  h.insert(stmt,
           ["To Say Nothing Of The Dog", "Connie Willis"],
           ["A Confederacy Of Dunces", "John Kennedy Toole"],
           ["Ender's Game", "Orson Scott Card"])

  p h.select("SELECT * FROM book")
end
```

This code uses a database handle to manipulate the table structure. (Only low-level Ribs calls require a handle.) We use the handle's ddl method to execute SQL queries. We remove and then create a table of books, and then we use a prepared statement to insert three rows of data. Finally, we extract the data with a simple SELECT statement. So far, this looks more or less the same as the DBI database code. The main difference is that it's Hibernate doing all the work.

Ribs is easiest to use when you follow its conventions. In the simplest case, you don't need to define any mappings at all between SQL and Ruby. With the table of books have sitting in the database, we can define a Ruby class and start using it directly with Ribs:

databases/ribs_use.rb
```ruby
class Book
  attr_accessor :id, :title, :author
end

p R(Book).all
```

This code will create a class called Book and add three accessors for the book's properties. Manually adding these isn't strictly necessary—if Ribs doesn't find any accessors, it just uses the values of instance variables directly instead. There is no need to define a mapping from class fields to table columns here, because we're using the same names for both.

Case doesn't matter at all in this example, but in contrast to Sequel and ActiveRecord, table names need to be singular for models to find them. If you need to define custom behavior for a model, you can do so completely outside the model class if you like—there is no tight coupling between the database and the model.

The actual database call happens when we invoke the R method. This gives us back a *repository*, an object that can be used to find out different information based on the model we passed in. And that's how you work with Ribs: you wrap a plain Ruby object in a call to R and then call methods on whatever you get back. In this case, the all method just returns everything from the database. You can also filter out things by passing arguments to all.

To access and manipulate data, you can do something like this:

databases/ribs_use.rb
```ruby
dog = R(Book).get(1)
dog.title += ": How We Found the Bishop's Bird Stump at Last"
R(dog).save
```

Note that you can get an instance with a specific ID by calling get on the class repository. You use regular Ruby accessors to change data and wrap the instance in a repository to save to the database.

The easiest way to create new instances is through the class repository's create method:

```
R(Book).create :id => 4,
               :title => "Goedel, Escher, Bach",
               :author => "Douglas Hofstadter"
```

This method will first create a new instance of the class, then set all the values you've specified, and finally save it to the database. You don't have to use a repository to create instances, though. You can call new, set up instance methods just like you'd do for any other Ruby object, and involve repositories only when you're ready to touch the database:

```
snow = Book.new
snow.id = 5
snow.title = "Snow Crash"
snow.author = "Neal Stephenson"
R(snow).save
```

To remove a row from the database, you use the destroy! method. This will delete the row and remove any mention of the object in the Hibernate caches.

```
R(snow).destroy!
```

These examples have all shown how you can work with Ribs in a simple case where everything just happens to be named according to the convention. What if that isn't the case, or what if you want to have associations to other model classes?

Ribs allow you to handle these sorts of customizations too, of course—but you need to provide some mappings for the process to work. Over the next few pages, we'll look at a few of the more common relationships you can express.

The definitions for a model class go inside a block attached to the Ribs! method. Before we get to the contents of the block, let's look at the method's options.

```
databases/ribs_mappings.rb
class Blog
  Ribs! :table => 'wp_blog',
        :identity_map => true do |blog|

    # ... mappings go here ...
  end
end
```

The most commonly used option is :table, which specifies the name of
the database table for this model. The other setting shown here, :iden-
tity_map, makes sure that any given row in a database will always be
represented by the same Ruby instance. This makes object comparison easy but can cause surprises in code that expects more traditional
Ruby behavior.

The mappings themselves go inside the block. We describe the database
structure by calling methods on the Rib object that Ribs passes to us.
The first settings we'll change have to do with column names:

```
databases/ribs_mappings.rb
blog.blog_id.primary_key!
blog.title :column => :blog_title
```

Here, we set the blog_id column as the primary key. We also map the
title Ruby attribute to the blog_title SQL column. You can use the same
mapping mechanism to define associations among tables:

```
databases/ribs_mappings.rb
blog.belongs_to    Owner
blog.has_one       Layout, :name => :look
blog.has_n         :posts
```

For this model, we've specified that every blog belongs to an owner. This
code will create an association named owner and will expect the wp_blog
table to have a foreign key called owner_id. You can change the name of
this foreign key by providing a :column parameter.

Next, we've declared that every blog has one layout, accessible through
the look property. Ribs will expect there to be a column named blog_id
on the layout table.

The has_n notation defines one-to-many relationships, such as "A blog
has zero or more posts." You can pass in a Ruby class name or (as
we've done here for readability) a plural noun. These definitions will

give you Hibernate associations between models and will create proxies to simplify working with these objects.

By default, Ribs will just slurp in all your columns. This might not be what you want, especially if you have columns that are large or security-sensitive. The final two declarations in our class show how to deal with these situations:

```
blog.stats.avoid!
blog.auth :avoid, :default => 'abc'
```

Note that the :default parameter allows you specify a default value for any skipped column.

This model has just one mapping. You can define multiple mappings if you want to—for instance, you could have one for each database or let models inherit definitions and mappings from one other. These are quite advanced features, though, and beyond the scope of this chapter.

There are many more things you can do with Ribs, and there are also a couple of interesting alternatives on the horizon if you need behavior that Ribs doesn't provide.[14] But this introduction should at least make it possible for you to start using Ribs to persist your Ruby objects.

6.3 JDBC

We've covered a lot of Ruby database libraries, plus one Java persistence framework, that play well with JRuby. How about other Java libraries? In many cases, you can just fall back on familiar Ruby-to-Java method calls. Say you wanted to work with something like iBatis, for instance. It would be simple to use the techniques from Chapter 2, *Driving Java from Ruby*, on page 15 to call your generated iBatis objects just like any other Java object.

Sometimes, though, you just want to go straight to the database and do one or two queries, without the overhead of a big framework. Thanks to JRuby's outstanding Java integration support, you can work directly with JDBC from your Ruby code. Even without the benefit of abstraction, the code ends up being a bit more tasteful than its Java equivalent would be.

---

14. http://github.com/headius/jibernate

To get a simple connection running with JDBC, you can use something like the following:

databases/jdbc_connect.rb

```ruby
require 'java'

java_import java.sql.DriverManager

DriverManager.register_driver(com.mysql.jdbc.Driver.new)

begin
  url = "jdbc:mysql://localhost/using_jruby"
  conn = DriverManager.get_connection(url, "root", "")
ensure
  conn.close rescue nil
end
```

Even this low-level code looks a bit simpler than the equivalent Java code. The lack of types make it quite readable. The next step would be to get some data out of the database:

databases/jdbc_select.rb

```ruby
require 'java'

java_import java.sql.DriverManager

DriverManager.register_driver(com.mysql.jdbc.Driver.new)

begin
  url = "jdbc:mysql://localhost/using_jruby"
  conn = DriverManager.get_connection(url, "root", "")
  stmt = conn.create_statement
  rs = stmt.execute_query("SELECT * FROM book")

  while rs.next
    p [rs.get_int(1), rs.get_string(2), rs.get_string(3)]
  end

ensure
  rs.close rescue nil
  stmt.close rescue nil
  conn.close rescue nil
end
```

Of course, this little piece of code makes it obvious that it would be nice to have some Ruby sugar on top of the Java ResultSet.

So, let's make a new version:

databases/jdbc_select2.rb

```ruby
require 'java'

java_import java.sql.DriverManager
java_import java.sql.ResultSet

DriverManager.register_driver(com.mysql.jdbc.Driver.new)
module ResultSet
  include Enumerable

  def each
    count = self.meta_data.column_count
    while self.next
      yield((1..count).map { |n| self.get_object(n) })
    end
  end
end

begin
  url = "jdbc:mysql://localhost/using_jruby"
  conn = DriverManager.get_connection(url, "root", "")
  stmt = conn.create_statement

  p stmt.execute_query("SELECT * FROM book").to_a

ensure
  stmt.close rescue nil
  conn.close rescue nil
end
```

This code modifies ResultSet to support Ruby's Enumerable behavior simply by adding an each method. This method is actually quite cute. It fetches the column count from the result set metadata and then uses this information to fetch all the column data on every iteration.

Once we have this method on ResultSet, we can use familiar Ruby idioms like to_a on the result of our SELECT. The full range of Ruby collection operations are available, including map, inject, and sort. In effect, we're building our own framework on top of JDBC, in just a few lines of code. In many cases, you don't need anything more than a little Ruby magic sprinkled on top of a Java library like this.

6.4 Wrapping Up

Databases are in many ways a strange aspect of programming. Some developers treat them as a low-level implementation detail. After all, our customers don't care that we're using SQL under the hood—they care that our programs don't forget their data. And yet, a typical RDBMS is like a high-level programming system in its own right, with its own environments, tools, and languages.

This chapter has provided a whirlwind tour of some of the better choices for working with databases from JRuby. We first spent some time looking at the different parts of ActiveRecord, the most mature Ruby database library, and a good choice for many applications. We also looked at DBI and Sequel to see how some of the existing Ruby libraries solve the task of database connectivity quite differently.

After looking at the pure-Ruby libraries, we moved on to Ribs and JDBC, two options that are available only in JRuby. It can sometimes be hard to pick one framework among all the different choices available, but we hope that this chapter has shown you enough to make an informed decision for your project. Of course, you don't have to just choose one of these and stick with it. Try them to see what fits best. Be sure to reevaluate your choice as your application evolves.

Chapter 7

Building Software for Deployment

Over the previous few chapters, we've journeyed together through the process of writing software in JRuby. We hope you've had the chance to try some of the techniques on programs of your own.

Once you've done the hard part of getting your code working, packaging it up and getting it onto the target computer should be a breeze, right? Well...yes, actually. Both Ruby and Java have established build systems, which developers have been relying on for years. Over the next several pages, we're going to see how these tools—Rake for Ruby, and Ant and Maven for Java—relate to JRuby projects.

7.1 Rake

Rake is Ruby's answer to the venerable UNIX make utility. Jim Weirich began the project in 2003 as a special-purpose language for describing software tasks and their dependencies. Why a new build tool? Consider a simple C-style Makefile for sandwich making:

rake/sandwich/Makefile

```
# Make a tasty lunch
sandwich: bread cheese
        echo "Grilling the sandwich"

# I guess sliced bread really is the greatest thing
bread:
        echo "Slicing the bread"

# Only the finest Emmentaler for our sandwich!
cheese:
        echo "Grating the cheese"
```

The sandwich task depends on the bread and cheese tasks, and so Make will ensure that they run first. This method of building software has stood solidly at the base of software development for decades. But it's not without its drawbacks. Make is fussy about exact indentation, tabs, and spaces. It suffers from subtle variations from vendor to vendor. And for any advanced features—such as making build decisions based on what platform you're using—you're stuck. The result has been a series of horrendous Makefile-makers, each with its own arcane syntax.

Now, let's look at the same set of tasks expressed as a Rakefile:

`rake/sandwich/Rakefile`
```ruby
desc 'Make a tasty lunch'
task :sandwich => [:bread, :cheese] do
  puts 'Grilling the sandwich'
end

desc 'I guess sliced bread really is the greatest thing'
task :bread do
  puts 'Slicing the bread'
end

desc 'Only the finest Emmentaler for our sandwich!'
task :cheese do
  puts 'Grating the cheese'
end
```

Sure, the notation is clearer. But there's much more going on here than just syntax. You have the entire power of the Ruby environment at your disposal, should you need it. Conditional expressions, loops, functions, classes, libraries, you name it. And of course, with JRuby, you have the reach of the Java platform as well.

Getting Started with Rake

If you're coming to JRuby from Java, you'll find that the procedure for kicking off a build with Rake is similar to what you've used with Ant. The rake command looks in the current directory for a *Rakefile*—a description of the tasks that can be performed here. If you name your file Rakefile, Rakefile.rb, or a lowercase version of either of those, Rake will find it automatically.

When you encounter a new Rakefile, it's a good idea to get the lay of the land by running rake first with the -T option. This prints out a list of top-level tasks:

rake/sessions/rake_tasks.txt

```
$ jruby -S rake -T
(in code/rake/sandwich)
rake bread      # I guess sliced bread really is the greatest thing
rake cheese     # Only the finest Emmentaler for our sandwich!
rake sandwich   # Make a tasty lunch
```

Notice how Rake helpfully prints each task's description alongside it. These came from the Rakefile, in the lines beginning with desc.

Rake tasks can perform any actions that you find useful, even things unrelated to building software. Rails uses Rake for all kinds of house-keeping: populating databases, running tests, launching web servers, and so on. To run a task, pass its name to rake on the command line:

rake/sessions/rake_sandwich.txt

```
$ jruby -S rake sandwich
(in code/rake/sandwich)
Slicing the bread
Grating the cheese
Grilling the sandwich
```

If the Rakefile has a task called :default:

rake/sandwich/Rakefile

```
task :default => :sandwich
```

...then you can invoke it by running rake with no arguments.

Like Ant and Make, Rake will run all of a task's dependencies first. You can see this for yourself by invoking Rake with the --trace option:

rake/sessions/rake_trace.txt

```
$ jruby -S rake --trace
(in code/rake/sandwich)
** Invoke default (first_time)
** Invoke sandwich (first_time)
** Invoke bread (first_time)
** Execute bread
Slicing the bread
** Invoke cheese (first_time)
** Execute cheese
Grating the cheese
** Execute sandwich
Grilling the sandwich
** Execute default
```

Here you can see how Rake looks for the :default task, finds and runs its prerequisities, and then ends up back in :default.

Making sandwiches is all well and good, but what does that have to do with Java? Let's look at something more pertinent: using Rake to build a Java program.

Files and Processes

Consider the following Java class:

rake/baseball/Pitcher.java

```
public class Pitcher {
    /**
     * Tosses a pitch across the plate.
     *
     * @return a description of the pitch
     * @see    Catcher
     */
    public String pitch() {
        return "curveball";
    }
}
```

To teach Rake how to compile this code into Pitcher.class, you create a file task:

```
file 'Pitcher.class' => 'Pitcher.java' do
  sh 'javac Pitcher.java'
end
```

Since we've marked the .class file as depending on the .java file, Rake will use the two files' modification times to decide whether the code needs to be recompiled.

If you're used to using Ruby's backtick operator for launching external programs (for example, `rake javac Pitcher.java`), you might wonder why Rake defines its own alternative, sh. The answer is that sh does more than just running programs. It checks exit codes so that the entire build will halt if javac detects a syntax error in the .java file. It also understands Rake's --dry-run option, which prints out what each task *would* do if invoked for real.

Directories

When you're using Rake with external tools such as compilers and documentation generators, you naturally end up juggling files and directories a lot. Rake can help you out here by automatically creating any directory structure you need. For example, consider the following Ruby code that generates Java documentation:

rake/baseball/rakelib/doc.rake

```
sh 'javadoc -d doc *.java'
```

Imagine that this step required the doc directory to be in place before javadoc would run. (It doesn't, but bear with us here.) By wrapping this code up in a Rake task and making it dependent on a directory task, you can ensure that the directory structure will be in place when you need it:

rake/baseball/rakelib/doc.rake

```
directory 'doc'

desc 'Build the documentation'
task :javadoc => 'doc' do
  sh 'javadoc -d doc *.java'
end
```

Rake is smart enough to create just the directories you need. If you have a directory task with foo/bar/baz and some other task requires only foo/bar, then Rake will skip creating baz.

Rules

Now, let's add a second Java class to the mix. Here's the Java code:

rake/baseball/Catcher.java

```java
public class Catcher {
    /**
     * Describes what kind of pitch the {@link Pitcher} tossed.
     */
    public static void main(String args[]) {
        Pitcher pitcher = new Pitcher();
        System.out.println("The pitcher threw a " + pitcher.pitch());
    }
}
```

...and here's the Rake task:

```
file 'Catcher.class' => 'Catcher.java' do
  sh 'javac Catcher.java'
end
```

Notice how similar this is to the task for Pitcher. How can we trim out some of this repetition? By using another Rake feature, the rule task. Think of it as a template for file tasks.

`rake/baseball/rakelib/compile.rake`

```
rule '.class' => '.java' do |t|
  sh "javac #{t.source}"
end
```

Descriptions and Access

As we've seen, you can use the desc function just before defining a Rake task to give a description of that task:

`rake/baseball/rakelib/jar.rake`

```
desc 'Build the application into a .jar file'
task :jar => ['Pitcher.class', 'Catcher.class', 'Manifest'] do
  sh 'jar -cfm baseball.jar Manifest Pitcher.class Catcher.class'
end
```

This serves a couple of different purposes. It documents the Ruby code as a comment would, but it also gives Rake something to report when you use the -T option to ask for a list of available tasks.

If you skip the desc tag and define a task with no description, Rake leaves it out of the -T listing altogether. This comes in handy for distinguishing *public* tasks, which you invoke directly from the command line, from *private* tasks, which are used only by other tasks. For example, the Manifest file is needed only by the :jar task shown previously—it makes sense to leave the Manifest task private:

`rake/baseball/rakelib/manifest.rake`

```
file 'Manifest' do
  File.open 'Manifest', 'w' do |f|
    f.puts 'Main-Class: Catcher'
  end
end
```

Just because your private tasks are left out of the -T report doesn't mean you can't run them. Rake gives you the tools to stay organized but doesn't force organization on you.

Multitasking

Right now, our Java project has two main build targets: :jar for the program and :javadoc for the documentation. Let's put in a top-level :default task to tie these together:

`rake/baseball/Rakefile`

```
task    :default => [:jar, :javadoc]
```

Rake will run the two subtasks, one right after the other. If each one takes six seconds, you can't do any better than twelve seconds total. But these two actions are independent; there's no real reason to make Rake wait for one to finish before starting the next.

So let's create a new task, called :parallel, that runs these two subtasks in separate threads. (In plain Ruby, this wouldn't buy us much, but JRuby uses Java's threads—which are significantly more powerful.) All you have to do to mark a group of tasks as independent of one another is to define it with multitask in place of task:

> rake/baseball/Rakefile

```
multitask :parallel => [:jar, :javadoc]
```

If you run this example with rake parallel on a multicore machine, you should see two of your cores doing work here.

Multiple Files

As a passionate developer, you no doubt care about modularity in your software and want to apply the same principle to your build scripts as well. Breaking a complicated Rakefile into a group of related files makes a lot of sense. But how do you tie them all together?

Since Rake is just Ruby, you could use Ruby's built-in require mechanism to load a file full of subtasks into your main Rakefile. You could also use Rake's alternative, which is called import and has slightly different semantics.

But the simplest thing to do is just dump all the files containing your various Rake tasks into a directory called rakelib, just below the directory where your Rakefile sits. Rake will automatically look for and load all the tasks from there. This is the technique we used for defining the tasks in this example.

Namespaces

As your Rakefile grows, you may start running out of good names for tasks. You end up with either synonym syndrome (tasks named :build, :generate, :create, and so on) or unpalatably long names (generate_class_files, generate_jar_file, generate_docs, and so on).

Fortunately, Rake offers a better way to avoid collisions: namespaces. The idea is to partition your tasks into logical groups—:jar for compilation tasks, :doc for documentation. Then you can have both a jar:create and a doc:create, with no ambiguity.

It's a little bit of overkill to use namespaces for a project as small as this one, but just for fun, let's see what it would look like:

```
jar = namespace :jar do
  # tasks for .class and Manifest go here

  desc 'Compile the Java code'
  task :compile => ['Pitcher.class', 'Catcher.class']

  desc 'Create a .jar file from the compiled code'
  task :create => [:compile, 'Manifest'] do
    sh 'jar -cfm baseball.jar Manifest Pitcher.class Catcher.class'
  end
end

javadoc = namespace :doc do
  directory 'doc'

  desc 'Build the documentation'
  task :create => 'doc' do
    sh 'javadoc -d doc *.java'
  end
end

task :default => [jar[:create], javadoc[:create]]
```

As is the case with any Ruby function, namespace has a return value: a Rake::NameSpace object. We store our namespaces in the jar and javadoc variables so that we can refer to them later when we define our :default task.

Cleanup and File Lists

After our .jar file finishes building, we have no need for the intermediate .class or Manifest files. We could define our own :cleanup task that deletes a bunch of hard-coded filenames. But once again, Rake gives us a handy shortcut for cleanup: the rake/clean add-on.

> rake/baseball/rakelib/clean.rake

```
require 'rake/clean'

CLEAN.include    '*.class', 'Manifest'
CLOBBER.include '*.jar', 'doc'
```

When you load this file, Rake defines two new tasks, clean and clobber—plus two new lists for you to add filenames to. When you run rake clean, Rake will delete anything you've add to the CLEAN list. The even more destructive rake clobber deletes everything on *both* lists.

What's the difference between clean and clobber? The first one is meant for deleting just the intermediate .class and Manifest files and leaving your final .jar intact. clobber, on the other hand, deletes *all* generated files, leaving you with only the source code in your project directory.

Behind the scenes, CLEAN and CLOBBER are Rake::FileList objects. They act like arrays, but they understand wildcards (such as asterisks) and can be expressed with the intuitive include and exclude notation.

So, there you have it: a minimal Java project that has managed to touch on all the important features of Rake. Now, let's see how to integrate Rake more deeply with Java's build systems.

7.2 Ant

No matter what specialized task you need to perform to build your Java project, chances are that it's been done before with Ant. Ant is the oldest, most established Java build tool. It was originally created during the open sourcing of the Tomcat Java web server and was later released as a stand-alone project. Ant solved a lot of make's portability problems by implementing commonly used build tasks in Java.

As Ant continued to mature, it amassed a wide library of portable, reusable functions ("tasks") for every conceivable software development function. These include checking out, compiling, testing, and packaging code; downloading, uploading, and deploying build artifacts; and more.

Of course, Ant is also notorious for the fact that its build scripts are written using verbose XML. With small to medium-sized projects, Ant XML seems fairly innocuous. Let's consider the simplest possible Ant build file:

rake/ant/hello/build.xml

```xml
<?xml version="1.0"?>
<project name="hello" default="hello">
  <target name="hello_from_ant">
    <echo message="Hello from Ant!"/>
  </target>
</project>
```

That's a fair number of pointy angle brackets just to print out some text. At least the intent is fairly clear. When you run ant inside the directory containing build.xml, you get the following:

```
rake/sessions/ant_hello.txt
```

```
$ ant
Buildfile: build.xml

hello:
     [echo] Hello Ant!

BUILD SUCCESSFUL
Total time: 0 seconds
```

Great! Now you have quick, repeatable cross-platform builds. Ant adoption benefits greatly from a shallow learning curve and spreads and multiplies from readily available copy-and-paste examples. However, veterans of Ant build scripts know from experience that they can quickly grow to become unwieldy beyond a few hundred lines of script. Today, JRuby's own build.xml clocks in at almost 1,500 lines!

Of course, code readability suffers in any code project once your files grow too large. With Ant, the problem is compounded because it's not a true programming language. It lacks flow control and abstraction mechanisms, so scripts get verbose and full of duplication more easily.

Just because doing our builds in XML suddenly doesn't feel so comfortable, should we abandon Ant outright? Certainly not! The best part of Ant is its huge library of reusable tasks. Why not put those to use in Ruby code as well? With JRuby's Ant integration, you can run Ant tasks from inside your Rakefile or indeed any Ruby file.

Ruby-Colored Ants

To begin using the Ant integration library, just require it:

```
require 'ant'
```

The main entry point that library provides is a single ant method. This returns a shared instance of an Ant object through which we can invoke Ant tasks. Here's how you'd invoke Ant's built-in echo task. Note the use of a Hash to pass parameters into the task.

Nick Says...

Some Assembly Required

JRuby does not ship with Ant; you still need to have it installed separately. JRuby will detect where Ant is installed by attempting to invoke the ant program, so make sure it's installed and available on your PATH. Modern versions of Mac OS X come with Ant preinstalled, and Ant is available on many flavors of Linux through your distribution's package manager. On Windows, you'll probably have to still download and install Ant and make sure the ant executable is on the PATH.

`rake/ant/examples/echo.rb`

```ruby
require 'ant'

ant.echo :message => "Hello from Ruby!"
```

The ant method also accepts a block, so you can run multiple tasks conveniently:

`rake/ant/examples/setup.rb`

```ruby
require 'ant'

ant do
  echo :message => "Setting up new project"
  echo :message => "Project description goes here.", :file => "README.txt"
  mkdir :dir => "lib"
  mkdir :dir => "test"
end
```

If the Ant task uses nested elements, simply use nested blocks.

`rake/ant/examples/javac.rb`

```ruby
require 'ant'

ant.javac :srcdir => "src", :destdir => "build" do
  classpath do
    fileset :dir => "lib" do
      include :name => "*.jar"
    end
  end
end
```

Nick Says...

Free Your Mind

A fun way to compare the XML and Ruby versions of the build file is to open both in your text editor of choice and quickly cycle back and forth between the two files in a single window, effectively animating the minor differences between the two. If you're like me, watching the angle brackets disappear reinforces the subtle power of omitting extra line noise. That streamlining frees up your mind to be able to see the true intent of the program.

See how the nested pattern of the blocks matches the nested structure of XML elements but without all the angle brackets? This technique is used in several Ruby libraries that manipulate XML, such as Builder and Markaby. Ruby blocks are a natural way to indicate grouping.

So, we have a way to execute chains of Ant tasks, but what about defining build targets? We can do that, too. Here's the equivalent to the build.xml example earlier:

rake/ant/hello/build.rb

```
require 'ant'
ant :name => "hello", :default => "hello" do
  target :name => "hello" do
    echo :message => "Hello Ant!"
  end
end
```

A nice feature of the Ant library is that if you run the file containing your Ant code as a script, it becomes a full-fledged Ant build. Let's run our aptly named build.rb.

rake/sessions/jruby_hello.txt

```
$ jruby build.rb

hello:
Hello Ant!
```

To run a specific target, add it to the end of the command as an argument to the script. If you don't provide an argument, the default target is executed. Of course, if there's no default target and you don't specify one, then nothing gets run.

Rake with Ant

So far, we've had a taste of how easy Rake makes scripting builds, and we've seen the power of calling portable Ant tasks from a Ruby environment. Now, let's bring Rake and Ant together by revisiting our Baseball example. We'll see how mixing in a little Ant can improve the project. If you're unfamiliar with Ant, you might want to have the Ant user manual handy as you put it to use and discover the myriad tasks that are available.[1]

One of the problems with using Make-like rules to compile .java files is that there are many more Java source files in a typical project. Spawning the Java compiler individually on every file is inefficient. So, although our Rake rule for compiling the Pitcher and Catcher classes is clever, it won't scale up well. The Ant javac task is ideally suited for compiling Java sources. Let's put it to use in our Rakefile, in a task called ant:compile.

`rake/baseball/rakelib/ant_compile.rake`

```
require 'ant'

namespace :ant do
  task :compile do
    ant.javac :srcdir -> "."
  end
end
```

As we can see, the javac task has some smart defaults built in to look for .java files. We can compile more files with less code than we did before.

`rake/sessions/ant_compile.txt`

```
$ jruby -S rake ant:compile
(in code/rake/baseball)
Compiling 2 source files
```

The javac task also knows not to recompile files whose source hasn't changed; if we run the task again, no work is done.

---

1. http://ant.apache.org/manual/

```
rake/sessions/ant_compile2.txt
```

```
$ jruby -S rake ant:compile
(in code/rake/baseball)
```

Next, let's take a look at how to generate documentation. Ant also comes with a built-in javadoc task:

```
rake/baseball/rakelib/ant_doc.rake
```

```
namespace :ant do
  task :javadoc do
    ant.javadoc :sourcefiles => FileList["*.java"], :destdir => "doc"
  end
end
```

There are a couple points to be made about this example. One thing you'll notice is that we're starting to use a little bit of Rake where it feels right. In this case, Ant's javadoc task takes a comma-separated list of files in its sourcefiles attribute. JRuby's Ant library treats FileLists specially, by passing them to the underlying Ant task as comma-separated values.

Finally, to complete the Baseball build, we need to create a .jar file. Here we can make use of Ant's jar task, which allows you to specify manifest attributes inline—so we don't need an extra task to create the manifest file, like we did with plain Rake.

```
rake/baseball/rakelib/ant_jar.rake
```

```
namespace :ant do
  task :jar => :compile do
    ant.jar :basedir => ".", :destfile => "baseball.jar", :includes => "*.class"
      manifest do
        attribute :name => "Main-Class", :value => "Catcher"
      end
    end
  end
end
```

Working with Legacy Ant Builds

Another situation where combined Rake/Ant integration can help is by streamlining existing Ant-based builds. Suppose your Ant build has become too heavyweight and full of duplication. Or perhaps you need to do some custom logic that is not manageable with Ant tasks. In many cases, throwing away your build.xml is not feasible. At times like these, making a bridge between Rake and Ant can let each tool do what it's best at.

Importing Ant Tasks into Rake

Ant from Rake—didn't we just cover that? Yes, the ant method can blindly hand a task name off to Ant and say, "Run the task that has this name." But the Ruby side isn't aware of the Ant tasks at all; it's just throwing requests over the wall and waiting for answers. So, you couldn't make a Rake task depend on an Ant task using this technique. If you're using Rake to package a gem that has a .jar dependency, for instance, you wouldn't be able to have a :gem Rake task that depends on a 'compile' Ant task.

Fortunately, there is a way to make Rake more Ant-aware: ant_import. This method parses your build.xml (or any other filename you hand to it) for top-level Ant tasks and gives them names in the Ruby namespace that you can refer to for dependencies. For instance, if you have an Ant task called hello_from_ant, you can use it in Rake like so:

```
require 'ant'

ant_import

task :goodbye_from_rake => :hello_from_ant do
  puts 'Goodbye from Rake!'
end
```

Importing Rake Tasks into Ant

How about going the other direction—making Ant aware of the names and dependencies of your Rake tasks? Piece of cake! Just as Rake has ant_import, JRuby makes a rakeimport task available to Ant. Assuming your Rakefile contains a task called hello_from_rake, here's how you'd call it from Ant:

```
<?xml version="1.0"?>
<project name="hello" default="hello">
  <taskdef name="rakeimport" classname="org.jruby.ant.RakeImport"/>
  <rakeimport/>

  <target name="goodbye_from_ant" depends="hello_from_rake">
    <echo message="Goodbye from Ant!"/>
  </target>
</project>
```

Now that we've discussed the most popular Ruby build system, the most popular Java build system, and how they can work together, it's time to move to other tools.

7.3 Maven

Maven—the popular build, dependency, and release management tool for Java projects—has become a staple in the Java development landscape. Maven is used to build many open source Java projects, and Maven repositories are often the *de facto* place to download and manage library dependencies. Let's look at a few ways that we can interact with Maven with JRuby.

Extending Maven with Rake

Maven is well known to be opinionated and unwieldy if you need your build process to do anything out of the ordinary. Since we've shown how easy it is to manipulate files, execute commands, and invoke arbitrary chains of tasks with Rake, why not extend your Maven project with it? The jruby-rake-plugin for Maven allows you to do just that.

Add the Plug-in to Your POM

Here we need to assume you know a bit about how Maven pom.xml files are structured and are sufficiently vaccinated for angle-bracket syndrome. We'll be adding some plug-in configuration and wiring up Rake tasks to specific phases of the Maven build. If you need some background, you can visit the main Maven website (http://maven.apache.org/pom.html) for details.

To start, ensure your pom.xml has a /project/build/plugins section, and add the jruby-rake-plugin as shown. You can freeze to a specific JRuby release by specifying a value in the <version> tag (as we've done here) or just omit it to pick up the latest release.

rake/maven/pom-outline.xml

```xml
<project>
  ...
  <build>
    ...
    <plugins>
      ...
      <plugin>
        <groupId>org.jruby.plugins</groupId>
        <artifactId>jruby-rake-plugin</artifactId>
        <version>1.5.5</version>
      </plugin>
    </plugins>
  </build>
  ...
</project>
```

Add an Execution

Each Maven plug-in declaration allows for one or more *executions*. Each execution is bound to a build phase. This means we can bind and trigger the rake plug-in to more than one phase of our build. For example, we might want to do some copying or processing of resources to be included in a .jar file during the generate-resources phase, but we might also want to use Rake to launch a custom testing framework during the test phase. We'll write one execution for each phase of the build where we'd like to use Rake.

Each execution declaration should have at least three parts: an ID, a phase, and a goal. Give your execution a unique ID to keep Maven happy, and name the phase of the build where you want to attach the plug-in. A full list of phases appears in the Maven life-cycle reference.[2] Specify rake in the goals/goal section.

rake/maven/pom-simple.xml
```
<plugin>
  <executions>
    <execution>
      <id>my-custom-resource-step</id>
      <phase>generate-resources</phase>
      <goals><goal>rake</goal></goals>
    </execution>
  </executions>
</plugin>
```

This setup assumes you have a companion Rakefile in the same directory as your pom.xml, and it contains a default Rake task. Maven will invoke this task during the generate-resources phase.

OK, that's a pretty good start, but let's say you want to do a little more than rely on defaults. You can add a configuration section, with one or more of these tags inside:

- script: Rather than using an external Rakefile, just embed your Rake tasks right inside pom.xml.
- rakefile: Specify a Rakefile rather than falling back on Rake's standard search mechanism.
- args: Pass arguments to Rake, either task names to execute or NAME=VALUE environment variables.

---

2.   http://maven.apache.org/guides/introduction/introduction-to-the-lifecycle.html#Lifecycle_Reference

As a more extended example, here's some plug-in configuration to test your Java code using the expressive RSpec testing library. (We'll discuss RSpec in Section 8.1, *RSpec*, on page 190.)

```
rake/maven/pom-rspec.xml
<plugin>
  <executions>
    <execution>
      <id>rspec</id>
      <phase>test</phase>
      <goals><goal>rake</goal></goals>
      <configuration>
        <script>
          require 'rspec/core/raketask'
          RSpec::Core::RakeTask.new do |t|
            t.pattern = 'src/spec/ruby/**/*_spec.rb'
          end
          task :default => :spec
        </script>
      </configuration>
    </execution>
  </executions>
</plugin>
```

Maven launches the JRuby process with the appropriate classpath so that any dependencies and Java classes compiled by Maven will be visible to JRuby and RSpcc automatically.

Ensure Gems Are Installed

Sometimes your Rake or Ruby code will need to rely on additional Ruby gems in order to function. The install-gems goal can be used to make sure these gems are present. The jruby-rake-plugin will install these gems into $HOME/.gem/jruby/1.8.

```
rake/maven/pom-gem.xml
<plugin>
  <executions>
    <execution>
      <id>install-gems</id>
      <phase>generate-resources</phase>
      <goals><goal>install-gems</goal></goals>
      <configuration>
        <gems>activerecord activerecord-jdbc-adapter</gems>
      </configuration>
    </execution>
  </executions>
</plugin>
```

That's enough on building software for the moment. Let's now move on to deployment.

7.4 Packaging for Deployment

Conceptually, software deployment in regular Ruby isn't complicated. The general steps go something like this:

1. Install Ruby.

2. Install the required libraries.

3. Copy your .rb files onto the target machine.

Depending on the kind of app, though, things can really break down during steps 1 and 2. The Mac you designed your GUI on may have shipped from the factory with Ruby on it, but your customer's Windows box probably didn't. Your web app might lean on a C-based XML library that your ISP doesn't allow you to compile on their machine.

With JRuby, a lot of these problems go away. Most desktop machines already have a Java runtime on them, so you might get away without asking your users to install any extras. If you're using a Ruby library that contains compiled code, at least it's compiled *Java* code—you won't have to ship multiple DLLs for different platforms. Now, the procedure looks something more like this:

1. Copy jruby-complete.jar and a bunch of .rb files onto the target machine.

So, you can reduce a bunch of hemming and hawing over version numbers and DLLs into a few simple file copies. For desktop programs, this means handing users a .zip file, which they can extract and run with a single command:

```
$ java -jar jruby-complete.jar my_program.rb
```

For web apps, you just scp a directory of source files up to the server or use a tool like Capistrano to do the copying for you.[3]

Java Archives

Although these approaches remove the risk and heartache of Ruby deployment, they still expose Ruby filenames and directory structures

---

3.   http://www.capify.org

to the owner of the target machine. Wouldn't it be nice to use a mechanism Java developers are already familiar with, like .jar files? Fortunately, you can.

The App

We're going to build a tiny program that nonetheless has a couple of the same kinds of dependencies—external Ruby libraries and compiled code—that real-world projects do. Specifically, we're going to do a bit of web scraping with the Hpricot library, which uses a mix of Ruby and Java code.[4] Go ahead and install Hpricot first:

```
$ jruby -S gem install hpricot
```

Now, let's write a small program that uses the library to get a list of recent books published by the Pragmatic Programmers. Create a new project directory, and copy a freshly downloaded or built version of jruby-complete.jar into it (remove any version numbers from the filename). Now, put the following code in scrape.rb:

```
rake/scrape/scrape.rb
```
```ruby
require 'rubygems'
require 'open-uri'
require 'hpricot'

doc = open('http://pragprog.com/categories/upcoming') do |page|
  Hpricot page
end

(doc/'div.book').each do |book|
  title = book.at('div.details/h4').inner_html
  href  = book.at('div.thumbnail/a')['href']

  puts "#{title} is at #{href}"
end
```

We're not going to spend a lot of time dissecting the code here. A quick glance should give you the basic idea: we fetch a specific URL and then search through it for the HTML tags we're interested in.

Before we move on to packaging, make sure the program works:

```
$ jruby scrape.rb
Cocoa Programming is at http://pragprog.com/titles/dscpq/cocoa-programming
ExpressionEngine 2 is at http://pragprog.com/titles/riexen/expressionengine-2
```

---

4. http://github.com/whymirror/hpricot

```
Hello, Android is at http://pragprog.com/titles/eband3/hello-android
iPad Programming is at http://pragprog.com/titles/sfipad/ipad-programming
SQL Antipatterns is at http://pragprog.com/titles/bksqla/sql-antipatterns
The RSpec Book is at http://pragprog.com/titles/achbd/the-rspec-book
```

During development, the line require 'hpricot' loads a library from your system's RubyGems path. Your end user's system is not likely to have Ruby or any gems on it. You'll need to put Hpricot somewhere in the final product where scrape.rb can find it. Following common Ruby practice, we'll install a private copy of Hpricot to a vendor subdirectory of our project for later inclusion in the build.

`rake/scrape/Rakefile`

```
directory 'vendor'

desc 'Install Ruby gems into vendor/'
task :install_gems => 'vendor' do
  sh 'jruby -S gem install -i vendor hpricot'
end
```

With that in place, we're ready to build the .jar.

A Minimal .jar

Recall that a .jar file is basically a renamed .zip file that follows a few conventions. The convention that interests us here is the *Manifest*, which contains (among other things) the name of the Java class to run when the user launches the .jar. Notice that we said "Java class." Alas, there's no direct way to give the name of a Ruby class instead.

If you've been following along with the embedding chapter, you're probably thinking, "Why not just write a tiny Java program that uses the JRuby embedding API to launch the main Ruby class from inside the .jar?" You're right; that's exactly what we're going to do.

`rake/scrape/Launcher.java`

```
import org.jruby.embed.ScriptingContainer;

public class Launcher {
    public static void main(String[] args) {
        ScriptingContainer container = new ScriptingContainer();
        container.runScriptlet("require 'scrape'");
    }
}
```

We've already seen how to create a Rake task to compile this Java code:

rake/scrape/Rakefile
```
desc 'Build Java launcher that will start the Ruby program'
task :build_launcher do
  sh 'javac -cp jruby-complete.jar Launcher.java'
end
```

Now, we just combine the newly built .class file, our Ruby program, and the Hpricot library into a .jar:

rake/scrape/Rakefile
```
desc 'Combine app and launcher into one jar'
task :small_jar => [:install_gems, :build_launcher] do
  sh 'jar -cfm scrape.jar small.manifest Launcher.class scrape.rb -C vendor .'
end
```

The task requires a new file, small.manifest. This is where we provide startup information, which Java uses to find the Launcher class and the supporting JRuby libraries:

rake/scrape/small.manifest
```
Manifest-Version: 1.0
Class-Path: jruby-complete.jar
    .
Main-Class: Launcher
```

With that addition, we can build the .jar file:

```
$ jruby -S rake small_jar
```

Once that's done, you can run the program. You'll need a copy of jruby-complete.jar in the same directory.

```
$ java -jar scrape.jar
Cocoa Programming is at http://pragprog.com/titles/dscpq/cocoa-programming
ExpressionEngine 2 is at http://pragprog.com/titles/riexen/expressionengine-2
Hello, Android is at http://pragprog.com/titles/eband3/hello-android
iPad Programming is at http://pragprog.com/titles/sfipad/ipad-programming
SQL Antipatterns is at http://pragprog.com/titles/bksqla/sql-antipatterns
The RSpec Book is at http://pragprog.com/titles/achbd/the-rspec-book
```

Now, all you have to do to share your program with someone is hand them these two .jar files and tell them what command to run. But why deliver two files when we can deliver one?

One Big Jar

All we have to do to combine the two .jars into one is extract JRuby into a temporary directory:

`rake/scrape/Rakefile`
```
directory 'tmp'

desc 'Extract jruby-complete so we can combine it with the app'
task :extract_jruby => 'tmp' do
  Dir.chdir('tmp') do
    sh 'jar -xf ../jruby-complete.jar'
  end
end
```

...and rerun the jar command, telling it to include the new path as well:

`rake/scrape/Rakefile`
```
desc 'Combine app, launcher, and JRuby into one jar'
task :big_jar => [:install_gems, :build_launcher, :extract_jruby] do
  sh 'jar -cfm scrape.jar big.manifest Launcher.class scrape.rb \
      -C vendor . -C tmp .'
end
```

Since we're just using one .jar now, the manifest is even simpler than the previous one:

`rake/scrape/big.manifest`
```
Manifest-Version: 1.0
Class-Path: .
Main-Class: Launcher
```

And that's it! One deliverable .jar file, containing your app and everything it needs. If you need to repeat this procedure from project to project, you may be interested in the Rawr library, which automates some of these tasks.[5]

Creating Web Archives with Warbler

Now that you have an inkling of how a Ruby application can be easily packaged into a single archive, why not extend that portable goodness to web applications? Warbler is a packaging tool that does just that.

If you're a Java web developer, you're familiar with web archives. Web archives, usually called .war files, are the web application equivalent

---

5. http://rawr.rubyforge.org

of .jar files. .war files are simply .zip-format files with web content (for example, images and style sheets) in addition to application code. Deployment of a .war file usually means simply presenting the file to your Java application server, either by copying it into a "blessed" autodeploy directory or by using a deployment tool specific to the server you're using.

Every .war file has a common structure. The root directory of the archive is the "document root" where you place .html, .css, JavaScript, images, and any other static content that your application requires. The archive has a specially named WEB-INF directory that contains application code, including Java classes, Java .jar libraries, configuration files, and any other content that you don't want to be directly visible to your end users.

Contrast this structure with the one we've already presented for Rails applications. The root of a Rails application contains directories like app and config full of code and configuration, along with a single public directory that represents the document root of the application. It's as if a web archive is the Rails application structure turned inside out.

And so this is the primary function of Warbler—to take a directory containing all the loose files and directories of a Rails application and turn it into a .war file that will run in any Java application server.

Getting Started

The whole point of Warbler is to make it easy to get started—from Rails application to .war file in one command! First, you need to install the warbler gem:

`rake/sessions/gem_install_warbler.txt`

```
$ jruby -S gem install warbler
Successfully installed jruby-jars-1.5.0
Successfully installed jruby-rack-1.0.1
Successfully installed rubyzip-0.9.4
Successfully installed warbler-1.1.0
4 gems installed
```

(You probably noticed the jruby-jars and jruby-rack gems in the list of things that got installed—more on that in a bit.) The warbler gem gives you a warble command. So, now we can go ahead and run it on our rouge application from Section 5.2, *Going Rouge*, on page 92.

rake/sessions/warble_rouge.txt

```
$ jruby -S warble
rm -f rouge.war
Creating rouge.war
```

And within seconds, we've got a stand-alone, dependency-free rouge.war file ready to deploy to a Java application server! Let's peek at some of what's inside:

rake/sessions/rouge_contents.txt

```
$ jar tf introduction_to_rails/rouge/rouge.war
# ...truncated listing...
WEB-INF/
WEB-INF/app/
WEB-INF/config/
WEB-INF/gems/
WEB-INF/lib/
WEB-INF/lib/jruby-core-1.5.0.jar
WEB-INF/lib/jruby-rack-1.0.1.jar
WEB-INF/lib/jruby-stdlib-1.5.0.jar
WEB-INF/log/
WEB-INF/tmp/
WEB-INF/vendor/
images/
javascripts/
stylesheets/
```

As you can see, the Rails application code and directory structure gets stashed below the WEB-INF directory in the archive, and the images, stylesheets, and javascripts directories get promoted to the document root. Warbler also tries to figure out what Ruby gems your application uses and then creates an embedded gem repository for you in WEB-INF/gems.

Most importantly, Warbler bundles a copy of JRuby as .jar libraries, as well as JRuby-Rack, a small bridge from the Java Servlet API to Ruby's Rack API.[6] To the Java server, our Rails application looks just like any other Java Servlet!

Let's go ahead and deploy this file to a Java application server. Two popular open-source servers are Apache Tomcat and GlassFish.[7,8]

---

6. http://github.com/nicksieger/jruby-rack. See also http://java.sun.com/products/servlet and http://rack.rubyforge.org.

7. http://tomcat.apache.org

8. http://glassfish.org

Although we'll leave it as an exercise for you to install and boot one of these servers, we can give you an idea of how to deploy to them.

For Tomcat, you'll simply copy a properly configured rouge.war to the Tomcat webapps directory.[9] Usually, webapps will be found in the Tomcat base directory. If you chose to install Tomcat using your operating system's package manager, it may be elsewhere; for example, Gentoo Linux places it at /var/lib/tomcat-6/webapps.

For Glassfish, use the asadmin command.

```
$ asadmin deploy rouge.war
Application deployed successfully with name rouge.
Command deploy executed successfully.
```

In both cases, once you've deployed rouge.war, you'll be able to access it in a browser at http://localhost:8080/rouge.

How Warbler Packages

We've just seen a simple example of how Warbler looks for application code, static assets, and gem dependencies, and packages them up along with JRuby and JRuby-Rack into a .war file, rearranging the layout of the files to match the standard Java web application structure. This directory shuffling is illustrated in Figure 7.1, on the next page—static content gets moved to the root, while application code is shuffled under the special WEB-INF directory.

So, how did Warbler figure out what to put in the .war file? How can you be sure that it didn't miss something? Much like Rails itself, Warbler is built with some assumptions about typical Ruby web applications that you'd like to package, and it uses that knowledge to discover what needs to be packaged.

If your application doesn't fit those assumptions, that's fine too; Warbler is fully configurable. We'll cover the basics of custom configuration in a moment. But first, let's examine the basic assumptions, so you know where you might need to drop into that configurability to ensure everything your application needs gets packaged.

---

9. Web apps based on recent frameworks like Rails 3 are "properly configured" out of the box. For older systems, you may need to add some extra dependencies; see Section 7.4, *Warbler Configuration*, on page 181.

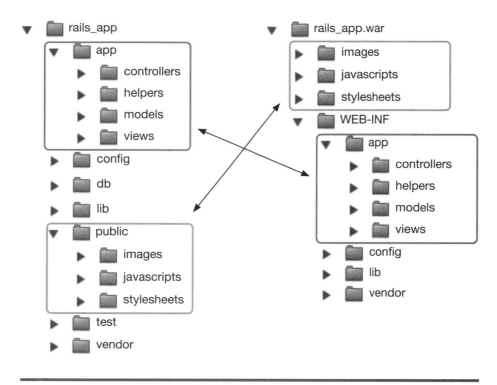

Figure 7.1: RAILS VS. WAR DIRECTORY LAYOUTS

Application Code

Warbler assumes that your application code is found in any of the app, config, lib, and vendor directories. Those directories, if they exist, are copied wholesale into WEB-INF in the .war file.

Warbler also tries to infer what kind of application you're using so that it can set up the application boot process accordingly. JRuby-Rack can boot apps written to almost any Ruby web framework: Rails, Merb, or anything else that uses the Rack API. Warbler autodetects applications by inspecting the local Rake environment and looking on the filesystem:

1. First, Warbler looks for a Rails app by checking for a Rails-specific Rake task named environment.

2. Next, it looks for a Merb app by checking for a Merb-specific task named merb_env.

3. Finally, it looks for a generic Rack-based application by checking for a Rack-specific configuration file named config.ru.

Note that this process sometimes loads the full application environment, which may perform heavyweight actions such as connecting to the database. If you don't want that to happen, you can turn off autodetection; see Section 7.4, *Warbler Configuration*, on the facing page.

Static Assets

Warbler uses Rails' convention of expecting static assets to be in the public directory. It copies these assets to the root of the .war file and strips the public/ prefix from all the filenames.

Ruby Gems

Packaging gems is where it gets a little trickier, since Ruby allows you to require a library without explicitly declaring it as a gem. Warbler only knows of three explicit ways of declaring what gems your application uses:

- Rails 2 applications: Warbler loads the Rails environment and looks at config.gems as specified in the config/environment.rb file. As long as you declare your gem dependencies here, Warbler will be able to find them.

- Rails 3 applications and other projects that use the Bundler gem packaging system: Warbler uses the list of gems from your Gemfile (Bundler configuration file).[10]

- Merb 1.0 applications: Warbler loads the Merb environment and inspects Merb::BootLoader::Dependencies.

For all other applications, you'll need to tell Warbler which gems to package. See the configuration section further on for details.

Miscellany

If you're a Java web developer, you may have encountered web.xml, the configuration file for web applications. Warbler will generate this file for you. We'll get to a few of its gory details in a minute. For now, we'll

---

10. http://gembundler.com/

just mention that Warbler uses this file to feed configuration settings to your app (via JRuby-Rack) at boot time.

The most important of these settings is whether you're using the production, development, or test environment. Warbler provides a configuration setting in case you need something other than the default of production.

You might have noticed that Warbler doesn't include tests or Rakefiles by default, since they are not typically needed in production. This behavior, too, can be overridden in Warbler's config file.

Previously, we pointed out that Warbler packages copies of JRuby and JRuby-Rack for you. These .jar files are sourced from the jruby-jars and jruby-rack gems that get installed alongside Warbler. If you want to upgrade these libraries, you can do so by installing new versions of those gems; Warbler will happily use the latest installed version.

Warbler Configuration

So, you've come across part of your application that Warbler either omitted or didn't package properly; now what? Fortunately, configuring Warbler is almost as easy as building the .war in the first place.

The first thing you'll need to do is generate a configuration file. The warble config command does this:

```
$ jruby -S warble config
cp JRUBY_HOME/lib/ruby/gems/1.8/gems/warbler-1.1.0/warble.rb config/warble.rb
```

As you can see, Warbler copied an example config/warble.rb file for you to modify. The basic contents of the file look like this:

```
Warbler::Config.new do |config|
  # You modify the configuration in here
  # ... lots of settings ...
end
```

We encourage you to have a look at the full config/warble.rb file. It's heavily documented, demonstrates all the available configuration options, and provides reminders about Warbler's default behavior.

Let's consider a few of the more common settings. Say you have some additional files and directories that need to go in your .war file. The config.dirs setting near the top of config/warble.rb contains an array of directories, to which you can easily add your own:

```
config.dirs = %w(app config lib log resources vendor tmp)
```

If you want to include or exclude additional files, you can do that with config.includes and config.excludes. Both take either arrays of filenames or Rake-style FileLists.

```
config.includes << "some/extra/file/you/need"
config.excludes = FileList["lib/super_private/*"]
```

The next area you might want to customize is the set of extra gems that Warbler should include, in case Warbler's discovery process missed one. config.gems provides several different ways to specify gems to include:

```
config.gems += ["activerecord-jdbcmysql-adapter", "jruby-openssl"]
config.gems["rails"] = "2.3.5"
config.gems << Gem::Dependency.new("json_pure", "~> 1.4.0")
```

Warbler usually packages all gems into an embedded gem repository located at WEB-INF/gems inside the .war file. If instead you've "vendored" (copied) your app's required gems into your application's directory tree, you can just tell Warbler to use the appropriate path.

```
config.gem_path = "WEB-INF/vendor/gems"
```

As we saw in the previous section, Warbler tries to autodetect what kind of application you are packaging so that it can set up some reasonable defaults. If you don't want Warbler to do that, there's a line at the top of config/warble.rb that you can uncomment to turn the detection off.

```
# Disable automatic framework detection by uncommenting/setting to false
Warbler.framework_detection = false
```

Just be warned that if you've turned framework detection off, you're probably going to have to specify more details manually in Warbler's configuration. One of those details is the name of the launcher Warbler should use to start your application. You can specify this by setting config.webxml.booter to :rails, :rack, or :merb.

```
config.webxml.booter = :rack
```

Remember that we glossed over the details of web.xml, except to say that it's generated for you? Let's take a slightly closer look now.

web.xml is where Warbler places several key/value pairs to tell JRuby-Rack how to boot the application. The config.webxml object gives you a place to add any other parameters that need to go into this file. For example, setting config.webxml.rails.env = "staging" has the effect of rendering the following fragment inside the .war file's web.xml file:

```
<context-param>
  <param-name>rails.env</param-name>
  <param-value>staging</param-value>
</context-param>
```

One other pair of config.webxml settings you may want to take a look at is jruby.min.runtimes and jruby.max.runtimes. JRuby-Rack uses these to decide how to service requests in a Rails application.

Prior to Rails 2.2, the internals of Rails were not safe for concurrent execution by multiple threads. Rubyists traditionally dealt with this limitation by running several single-threaded Ruby processes at once— the so-called "pack of Mongrels" approach. With JRuby, the Ruby interpreter is just a regular Java object; we can easily create several inside a single JVM. JRuby-Rack can then pool multiple JRuby runtimes, each with its own copy of the application code. When a request comes in, JRuby-Rack selects a free runtime from the pool and hands off the request to it.

The net of all this is that if you need to service concurrent requests in a JRuby-based Rails application, you'll want to measure how much throughput you need and make a trade-off between throughput and available memory. Each runtime takes approximately 20MB of memory after loading the Rails framework code into it, so choose your minimum and maximum number of runtimes carefully!

```
config.webxml.jruby.min.runtimes = 1
config.webxml.jruby.max.runtimes = 1
```

Another approach to concurrency is to write a thread-safe application (one that will run with Rails.configuration.threadsafe! turned on), and set JRuby-Rack's minimum and maximum runtime values to 1.

What if you want even more control over what gets put in web.xml? If you're comfortable with ERB, Ruby's built-in templating language, you can modify the template that Warbler uses to generate this file. Just copy WARBLER_HOME/web.xml.erb to config/web.xml.erb, and make your edits in the copy you just created.

Finally, what if you're using Warbler to package a hybrid Java and Ruby application? If you have additional Java classes or libraries, you can make sure they get packaged by setting the config.java_libs and config.java_classes options. Note that config.java_libs initially contains the JRuby and JRuby-Rack .jar files, so be careful not to remove them unless you know what you're doing.

Warbler Extras

Warbler is built upon Rake internally and draws heavily on lots of Rake features. Even the command line is structured the same as Rake. So in order to receive a list of available "tasks" that Warbler can do for you, you use the -T or --tasks option:

`rake/sessions/warble_t.txt`

```
$ jruby -S warble -T
warble config       # Generate a configuration file to customize your war
warble executable   # Feature: make an executable archive
warble gemjar       # Feature: package gem repository inside a jar
warble pluginize    # Install Warbler tasks in your Rails application
warble version      # Display version of Warbler
warble war          # Create the project .war file
warble war:clean    # Remove the .war file
warble war:debug    # Dump diagnostic information
```

As you can see from the previous list, there are several additional tasks that you can use to extend your .war or integrate Warbler better with your application's build process.

Running warbler pluginize installs a small warbler.rake designed to be used in a Rails project directory:

`rake/sessions/warble_pluginize.txt`

```
$ jruby -S warble pluginize
mkdir -p vendor/plugins/warbler/tasks
```

Looking at warbler.rake, we see the following:

`rake/sessions/warbler.rake`

```
require 'warbler'
Warbler::Task.new
```

You could, of course, just copy those same two lines to any project's Rakefile yourself, but it's nice that Warbler offers this convenient shortcut.

The function of Warbler::Task.new is to define several Rake tasks to perform the packaging work. Of these, Warbler's main task is the war task. If you have other work to do before packaging up your .war file, you can make the war task depend on your other tasks.

As an example, the popular asset_packager plug-in creates single-file, compressed versions of your JavaScript and CSS for production use.[11] To make sure the compressed files are up-to-date before packaging, you might consider putting this in your application's Rakefile:

```
Warbler::Task.new
task :war => "asset:packager:build_all"
```

You can also create multiple Warbler::Task configurations in your Rakefile. You might do this if you wanted to build two different .war files from the same code base. Just pass a different name for the main task in an argument to Warbler::Task.new.

For instance, let's say we wanted to create an extra .war file that had its Rails environment set to staging for use on a staging server. Here's what we'd add to our Rakefile:

```
production_task = Warbler::Task.new
staging_task = Warbler::Task.new("war_staging")
staging_task.config.webxml.rails.env = "staging"
staging_task.config.war_name += "-staging"
```

To build these two .war files, you'd type rake war war_staging, which would create both rouge.war as well as rouge-staging.war.

Another useful feature of Warbler is the executable war command. This adds Winstone, a small (166KB) Java web server, to the resulting .war file.[12] To use it, you run the executable task first and then the war task:

rake/sessions/warble_executable.txt

```
$ jruby -S warble executable war
rm -f rouge.war
Creating rouge.war
```

Now, you can run your web app on its own, without needing a separate Java server:

rake/sessions/war_execute.txt

```
$ java -jar rouge.war
[Winstone 2010/05/19 00:00:07] - Beginning extraction from war file
[Winstone 2010/05/19 00:00:07] - WARNING: The Servlet 2.4/2.5 spec XSD wa...
[Winstone 2010/05/19 00:00:07] - No webapp classes folder found - /privat...
[webapp 2010/05/19 00:00:10] - Info: using runtime pool timeout of 30 seconds
[webapp 2010/05/19 00:00:10] - Warning: no min runtimes specified.
[webapp 2010/05/19 00:00:10] - Warning: no max runtimes specified.
```

---

11. http://github.com/sbecker/asset_packager
12. http://winstone.sourceforge.net/

```
[Winstone 2010/05/19 00:00:10] - HTTP Listener started: port=8080
[Winstone 2010/05/19 00:00:10] - Listener winstone.ajp13.Ajp13Listener no...
[Winstone 2010/05/19 00:00:10] - Listener winstone.ssl.HttpsListener not ...
[Winstone 2010/05/19 00:00:10] - Winstone Servlet Engine v0.9.10 running:...
```

Once that's running, you can visit http://localhost:8080/ to try the application before deploying it. This is a nice all-in-one way to distribute and deploy or run your web application in a single file!

7.5 Wrapping Up

We covered a lot of ground in this chapter. We brought together the strengths of Rake and Ant, the dominant build systems in the Ruby and Java universes. We took a peek at how to deploy JRuby software using Maven, for Java projects that depend on it. Finally, we saw how to deploy Ruby-based web applications (like the Rails app we built in an earlier chapter) onto Java servers.

Earlier in the chapter, we hinted at testing JRuby applications. Let's come back to that now. JRuby provides several great ways to test not only your Ruby code but also your legacy Java code. Join us in the next chapter to find out how.

## Chapter 8

Testing Your Code with JRuby

It turns out that Ruby is a great language for testing both Ruby *and* Java code. And that's where we're going to start our exploration of software testing: at the code level. In this chapter, we'll look at the Ruby tools—test harnesses and mocking libraries—that you're most likely to encounter as you consider how to test individual Java or Ruby classes. For the next chapter, we'll branch out into integration testing, connecting Ruby to Java test frameworks, and other related topics.

 **Ola Says...**

Testing Religion

The Ruby community has had a reputation for being religious about testing for a long time, and there are several extremely good testing frameworks in Ruby. I have personally tried unit testing in most of the popular programming languages and can testify that Ruby frameworks are without doubt the best.

In Ruby, big-picture innovations like Behavior-Driven Development rapidly become frameworks that are practical for everyday development. I don't know why Ruby is the language where many of these things happen, but it might have something to do with the way Ruby programmers naturally seem to embrace metaprogramming and other techniques that take testing to the next level.

If you're specifically interested in testing Java code with Ruby, you might find the JtestR framework helpful. JtestR collects several Ruby frameworks together for use with JRuby and makes the integration with Ant or Maven totally painless. JtestR is described in detail in Section 9.3, *JtestR*, on page 218. Until then, we'll consider each test framework separately. Let's begin with a couple of the more popular tools for organizing and running tests.

8.1 Ruby Test Frameworks

Using JRuby to test Java code is one of the easier ways to get started with JRuby. If you start small and focus on testing, you can overcome the "institutional resistance" to Ruby present in some shops. After all, it's hard for colleagues to object to a quick experiment that's going to be limited to the test suite—especially if the potential payoff is better quality in the shipping product.

Because of Ruby developers' notorious passion for testing and because of programmers' constant temptation to "scratch one's own itch," Ruby boasts an abundance of testing frameworks. Which ones should you investigate? We're going to walk the middle ground between showing you just our favorites and boring you with a laundry list of twenty different choices.

Test::Unit

The first framework most Ruby programmers encounter, Test::Unit, is part of the Ruby standard library. It is quite closely modeled on the original xUnit family of software (including the JUnit framework for Java) and as such doesn't use as many interesting Ruby features as some of the others do.

The main advantage of Test::Unit is that it's available on all Ruby installations. Because it doesn't use as many of Ruby's advanced features, it's also quite straightforward to understand.

JRuby includes Test::Unit, and you can test Java code with it as easily as you can test Ruby.

The following example shows a simple test case that checks some properties of the java.util.HashMap class in the Java core library. We've tried

to use several different parts of Test::Unit to give you a fair idea of the
components in it.

`testing_with_jruby/test_unit/hashmap.rb`

```ruby
require 'test/unit'

require 'java'

java_import java.util.HashMap

class HashMapTestCase < Test::Unit::TestCase
  def setup
    @map = HashMap.new
  end

  def test_new_hashmap_is_empty
    assert @map.isEmpty
  end

  def test_hashmap_with_entry_is_not_empty
    @map.put("hello", "world")
    assert !@map.isEmpty
  end

  def test_value_is_associated_with_added_key
    @map.put("hello", "world")
    assert_equal "world", @map.get("hello")
  end

  def test_entry_set_iterator_next_raises_error_for_empty_hashmap
    assert_raises(NativeException) do
      @map.entrySet.iterator.next
    end
  end
end
```

You can run the code with this command:

```
$ jruby hashmap.rb
Loaded suite hashmap
Started
....
Finished in 0.029 seconds.

4 tests, 4 assertions, 0 failures, 0 errors
```

There are several things going on here; let's look at them one by one.
First, we create a new test case by defining a class that inherits from
Test:Unit::TestCase. Then we define the setup method, which runs before

each test method, much as its counterpart does in JUnit and other frameworks.[1] Finally, we define the tests themselves. Every method whose name begins with test_ will be run as a test by Test::Unit. Each test method is stand-alone and depends only on the setup method for its preconditions and invariants.

Like most frameworks in the xUnit lineage, Test::Unit allows you to test your code using several different assertions. The most common ones are assert, assert_equal, and assert_raises. The general assert method will mark a test as failed if the value passed in is nontrue (in other words, is false or nil). The assert_equal method will compare its arguments using the Ruby == operator. Lastly, assert_raises will make sure that a block of code raises a specific error.[2]

RSpec

RSpec is the tool that managed to bring Behavior-Driven Development to the masses. It continues to challenge us to change the way we think about writing software—to get to the heart of what Test-Driven Development was originally about.

Every test framework has at its core methods to check the truth or falsehood of statements about the code. Test::Unit has the assert_ family of methods. By contrast, RSpec has *expectations,* which are methods added to every Ruby object at test time. These methods are should and should_not.

Expectations take one argument: an expression describing the behavior of some piece of the program. Here are a few examples:

```
(!false).should be_true
'redivider'.reverse.should == 'redivider'
[1,2,3].should include(1)
[].should be_empty
[1].should_not be_empty
'hello'.should match(/ell/)
proc{ Math.sqrt 'a string' }.should raise_error(ArgumentError)
```

---

1. If we had cleanup tasks to run after each test, we could put them in a similar teardown method.
2. Test::Unit also provides an assert_nothing_raised check, but it's usually not necessary—Test::Unit already interprets exceptions thrown by your code as failures.

 **Ola Says...**

A Behavior-Driven Development Primer

Behavior-Driven Development (BDD) is one of the newer buzzwords. It's a technique that extends and builds on Test-Driven Development (TDD). Rather than focusing on a series of pass/fail checks of individual classes, BDD describes the behavior of a system as a whole in terms of specifications or examples. Tests become information that the entire team, even nonprogrammers, can understand and use to make decisions about the project.

The first BDD framework was actually written in Java and was called JBehave. Since then, many BDD frameworks have sprung up, several of them using the language features of Ruby to emphasize clarity in specifications. test/spec and RSpec are the two major frameworks for Ruby, but you can practice BDD even in a standard unit testing framework. It's just a question of style.

RSpec encourages you to think of each expectation as an *example* documenting the behavior of a specific piece of code. An example can be as simple as one low-level method invocation or as far-ranging as a mouse click affecting several classes. You organize groups of related examples into *contexts*. The describe method introduces a context, and the it method wraps each individual example.

Ready to get started with RSpec? First, grab the gem, and then we'll talk code.

```
$ jruby -S gem install rspec
...
Successfully installed rspec-core-2.0.1
Successfully installed diff-lcs-1.1.2
Successfully installed rspec-expectations-2.0.1
Successfully installed rspec-mocks-2.0.1
Successfully installed rspec-2.0.1
5 gems installed
```

In the following snippet, we describe "an empty", HashMap given to us by the setup code, using specific statements about its behavior: it "should have size zero", and so on:

`testing_with_jruby/rspec/hashmap_spec.rb`

```ruby
require 'java'

java_import java.util.HashMap

describe "An empty", HashMap do
  before :each do
    @map = HashMap.new
  end

  it "should be empty" do
    @map.should be_empty
  end

  it "should have size zero" do
    @map.size.should == 0
  end

  it "should allow elements to be added"
end
```

You can run the code like this:

```
$ jruby -S rspec hashmap_spec.rb
..*

Pending:
  An empty Java::JavaUtil::HashMap should allow elements to be added
    # Not Yet Implemented
    # ./hashmap_spec.rb:18

Finished in 0.046 seconds
3 examples, 0 failures, 1 pending
```

As you can see, the text passed to the describe method explains what goes on in the before :each block. In other words, it gives the context of the examples.

One thing you've no doubt noticed is that the third example has no implementation. Presumably, the next thing we're going to do is write that test. In the meantime, RSpec will report it as pending and will print its description to jog our memory with what we need to add. You can take this "code as documentation" mind-set one step further and use the -fs flag to document the *entire* specification, rather than just the failed or pending steps:

```
$ jruby -S rspec -fs hashmap_spec.rb

An empty Java::JavaUtil::HashMap
  should be empty
  should have size zero
  should allow elements to be added (PENDING: Not Yet Implemented)

Pending:
  An empty Java::JavaUtil::HashMap should allow elements to be added
    # Not Yet Implemented
    # ./hashmap_spec.rb:18

Finished in 0.13 seconds
3 examples, 0 failures, 1 pending
```

Examples and expectations are the core of RSpec. Even using just these two features will bring a lot of clarity to your tests. Once you're comfortable, you'll likely want to explore its more advanced features. Later in the chapter, we'll look at one such feature: support for mock objects. But first, there are a couple more unit test framework we'd like you to see.

test/spec

The test/spec framework combines the simplicity of Test::Unit with the clear syntax of RSpec.[3] So, you can use your existing knowledge of Test::Unit, while adopting the advantages of BDD at a pace you choose. To try these examples, install the test-spec gem (note the hyphen):

```
$ jruby -S gem install test-spec
```

Using test/spec, our HashMap example would look like this:

> testing_with_jruby/test_unit/hashmap_test_spec.rb

```
require 'rubygems'
require 'test/spec'

require 'java'

java_import java.util.HashMap

describe "an empty HashMap" do
```

---

3. There's actually a slight difference of syntax. RSpec expectations favor spaces and underscores, while test/unit uses dots everywhere.

```ruby
  before :each do
    @map = HashMap.new
  end

  it "should be empty" do
    @map.isEmpty.should.be true
  end

  it "with an added entry should not be empty" do
    @map.put("hello", "world")
    @map.isEmpty.should.not.be true
  end

  it "should associate a value with a key" do
    @map.put("hello", "world")
    @map.get("hello").should.equal "world"
  end

  it "should raise error on entryset iterator next" do
    proc do
      @map.entrySet.iterator.next
    end.should.raise NativeException
  end
end
```

...and running would look the same as in Test::Unit:

```
$ jruby hashmap_test_spec.rb
Loaded suite hashmap_test_spec
Started
....
Finished in 0.02 seconds.

4 tests, 4 assertions, 0 failures, 0 errors
```

There is nothing really revolutionary here, but that's kind of the point. Readability is noticeably better than in Test::Unit, particularly when we have a failure. Let's see what happens if we force one of the tests in hashmap_test_spec.rb to fail:

```
$ jruby hashmap_test_spec.rb
Loaded suite hashmap_test_spec
Started
..F.
Finished in 0.117 seconds.

1) Failure:
test_spec {an empty HashMap} 003 [should associate a value with a key](an empty...
[hashmap_test_spec.rb:28:in `test_spec {an empty HashMap} 003 [should associate...
hashmap_test_spec.rb:26:in `run']:
```

```
<"world"> expected to be != to
<"world">.
```

```
4 tests, 4 assertions, 1 failures, 0 errors
```

We now get an explanation based on the context and description of the test case, rather than just a method name. With test/spec, you can sneak these nice RSpec-like features into established projects that are already using the Test::Unit infrastructure.

shoulda

Both RSpec and test/spec are significant departures from the style of Test::Unit. What if you'd rather stay on familiar ground and use the Test-Case class to group your tests but still gain some flexibility? Like nesting groups of tests or writing test methods with nicer-looking names?

Shoulda is a small framework that gives you exactly these benefits, plus the ability to add test macros.[4] This last feature has made it one of the main testing frameworks for Rails applications. When the most common kinds of tests are already written for you, your own tests end up communicating your intent quite concisely.

The main difference between Test::Unit and Shoulda is in the way you write tests. Instead of defining new methods for tests, you provide blocks that include the test code. You still use the assertions that Test::Unit provides and whichever mocking framework you like.

Now that we know what Shoulda is, let's look at another version of our HashMap test:

testing_with_jruby/shoulda/hashmap_shoulda.rb

```ruby
require 'rubygems'
require 'shoulda'
require 'java'

java_import java.util.HashMap

class HashMapTestCase < Test::Unit::TestCase
  context "New hashmap" do
    setup do
      @map = HashMap.new
    end
```

---

4. In Shoulda, *macros* are reusable, customizable tests. The name evokes the more powerful Lisp macros that inspired them.

Ola Says...

Shoulda at ThoughtWorks

ThoughtWorks has written several of the largest Rails applications in the world, and for a number of these, the developers chose Shoulda over RSpec. Why? They felt that extending the framework with custom tests and assertions was much more complicated in RSpec. Since that time, RSpec has improved its support for writing matchers—but Shoulda is still held in high regard.

```ruby
  should "be empty" do
    assert @map.isEmpty
  end

  should "raise error on entryset iterator next" do
    assert_raises(NativeException) do
      @map.entrySet.iterator.next
    end
  end

  context "with one entry" do
    setup do
      @map.put("hello", "world")
    end

    should "not be empty" do
      assert !@map.isEmpty
    end

    should "have size one" do
      assert_equal 1, @map.size
    end

    should "associate a value with a key" do
      assert_equal "world", @map.get("hello")
    end
  end
end
end
```

To run the example, install the gem:

```
$ jruby -S gem install shoulda
```

...and then run the Ruby file directly:

```
$ jruby hashmap_shoulda.rb
Loaded suite hashmap_shoulda
Started
.....
Finished in 0.267 seconds.

5 tests, 5 assertions, 5 failures, 0 errors
```

The output of running this code looks exactly the same as with Test::
Unit; only the style of writing tests has changed. Each individual test is
a block passed to should, rather than a method beginning with test_. And
we've used the context method to gather our tests into logical groups,
which can be nested. The contexts lend their names to the generated
test methods, as you can see when you run the test suite with the -v
option:

```
$ jruby hashmap_shoulda.rb -v
Loaded suite hashmap_shoulda
Started
test: New hashmap should be empty. (HashMapTestCase): .
test: New hashmap should raise error on entryset iterator next. (...): .
test: New hashmap with one entry should associate a value with a key. (...): .
test: New hashmap with one entry should have size one. (HashMapTestCase): .
test: New hashmap with one entry should not be empty. (HashMapTestCase): .

Finished in 0.264 seconds.

5 tests, 5 assertions, 0 failures, 0 errors
```

One feature of Shoulda we're really fond of is the ease with which you
can create custom macros—reusable chunks of test code. Imagine we
wanted to test some of the other Map implementations in java.util. Since
all of these classes share a common interface and even some common
behavior with HashMap, it would be nice to exercise them all with the
test code we've already written.

Extracting our code into a macro is easy. First, we define a new Ruby
module and drop all our test code into a single method inside that
module.

```
testing_with_jruby/shoulda/map_shoulda.rb
```
```ruby
require 'rubygems'
require 'shoulda'
require 'java'

java_import java.util.HashMap
java_import java.util.TreeMap
java_import java.util.concurrent.ConcurrentHashMap

module MapMacros
  def should_behave_as_a_map
    # Everything inside the "New hashmap" context from before,
    # *except* the first "setup" block and the outermost pair of
    # "context ... end" lines
  end

  def self.included(type)
    type.extend self
  end
end
```

What's the self.included method there for? This is a bit of Ruby book-keeping to ensure that any Ruby class using this module has access to the should_behave_as_a_map method. In particular, we want to drop this module into our TestCase-derived class, so we can use our macro in several different contexts:

```
testing_with_jruby/shoulda/map_shoulda.rb
```
```ruby
class MapTestCase < Test::Unit::TestCase
  include MapMacros

  context "new HashMap" do
    setup { @map = HashMap.new }
    should_behave_as_a_map
  end

  context "new TreeMap" do
    setup { @map = TreeMap.new }
    should_behave_as_a_map
  end

  context "new ConcurrentHashMap" do
    setup { @map = ConcurrentHashMap.new }
    should_behave_as_a_map
  end
end
```

This will allow us to test the common behavior of all three Map implementations, without repeating ourselves.

```
$ jruby map_shoulda.rb -v
Loaded suite map_shoulda
Started
test: new ConcurrentHashMap should be empty. (MapTestCase): .
test: new ConcurrentHashMap should raise error on entryset iterator next...
test: new ConcurrentHashMap with one entry should associate a value with a key...
test: new ConcurrentHashMap with one entry should have size one. (MapTestCase): .
test: new ConcurrentHashMap with one entry should not be empty. (MapTestCase): .
test: new HashMap should be empty. (MapTestCase): .
test: new HashMap should raise error on entryset iterator next. (MapTestCase): .
test: new HashMap with one entry should associate a value with a key. (...): .
test: new HashMap with one entry should have size one. (MapTestCase): .
test: new HashMap with one entry should not be empty. (MapTestCase): .
test: new TreeMap should be empty. (MapTestCase): .
test: new TreeMap should raise error on entryset iterator next. (MapTestCase): .
test: new TreeMap with one entry should associate a value with a key. (...): .
test: new TreeMap with one entry should have size one. (MapTestCase): .
test: new TreeMap with one entry should not be empty. (MapTestCase): .

Finished in 1.021 seconds.

15 tests, 15 assertions, 0 failures, 0 errors
```

Large Ruby applications use metaprogramming—code that writes code —to tame complexity. Shoulda is a great fit for testing all kinds of programs, because macros give your tests the same level of expressive power. For example, if somewhere in your Rails code you have an association like this:

```
has_many :fubars
```

...you can test it like this, using the Rails helpers that come with Shoulda:

```
should_have_many :fubars
```

Many of these features are present to some degree in other frameworks. But where Shoulda really shines is in its simplicity. We've covered most of its core usage here. All that's left are a few specific conveniences for Rails developers. There's no "hazing period" on the learning curve, and even the source code makes for good reading.

8.2 Going to the Next Level with ZenTest

ZenTest is a collection of useful tools written by Ryan Davis and others for simplifying Ruby testing. The ones most applicable to JRuby are unit_diff, autotest, and multiruby. You can get them all in one fell swoop by installing the ZenTest gem (note the capitalization):

```
$ jruby -S gem install ZenTest
```

unit_diff reformats test logs, so you can eyeball a printout and see exactly what went wrong—Java developers will recognize this feature from JUnit. All you have to do is pipe your test output to the unit_diff command, like this:

```
$ jruby test/your_test_case.rb | jruby -S unit_diff
```

This will give you output similar to what you'd normally see, but with the error messages conveniently compressed. You're left with just the parts you need to read in order to understand what failed.

autotest makes continuous testing easy. If you follow a few simple naming conventions, it will figure out which tests it needs to run for each file. Every time you save a modification to your class, autotest will run the corresponding tests. This smoothes your workflow dramatically; you can continue coding functionality, with the assurance that you will be notified as soon as something fails.

multiruby allows you to run code against multiple Ruby implementations, including JRuby. This capability is a life-saver for library writers, who must wrestle with compatibility across some ten different Ruby implementations.

All of these tools are documented on Ryan Davis's blog.[5] We encourage you to give them a try once you have a growing body of test code to maintain.

Now we're going to move on to one more crucial facet of unit testing: test doubles.

8.3 Mocking and Stubbing

In most projects, you'll eventually end up needing to test code that relies on external libraries or services. Your unit tests should minimize

---

5. http://blog.zenspider.com

 **Ian Says...**

__Mocks vs. Stubs__

What's the difference between mocks and stubs? They can both be used in place of a real object, but mocks are pickier: they care *how* they're called. Therefore, only mocks are allowed to cause a test failure. For more complete explanation, see Martin Fowler's article "Mocks Aren't Stubs."*

*.   http://martinfowler.com/articles/mocksArentStubs.html

their dependencies on outside software. The conventional way of solving this problem is to use *test doubles*, which are stand-ins for external code.[6] In Java, this process usually requires designing your application around interfaces and then providing fake implementations—*mocks and stubs*—that return canned values.

Ruby's "open classes" make it easy to replace an object's methods at runtime. This capability is useful for creating mocking frameworks, since we don't have to rely on Java interfaces. We can just replace individual methods that would normally talk to an external service.

Since Java doesn't support Ruby's level of metaprogramming, some of our favorite mocking and stubbing techniques aren't available in JRuby. For instance, you can modify a Java class in Ruby, but those modifications will be visible only on the Ruby side—Java won't be able to see them.

Fortunately, there are still plenty of things that *do* work fine with Java. Let's take a look at a couple.

RSpec Mocks

RSpec comes with its own mocking and stubbing framework, which works well in JRuby. You'll run into some limits when you're testing Java code, though—we'll see what those limits are in a minute.

---

6.   http://xunitpatterns.com/Test%20Double.html

The basic idea is that you start with a mock object, add some canned behavior to it, and finally pass it into the code you're testing. RSpec can create an empty object for you via the mock method, but you can actually mock or stub methods on *any* Ruby object (including classes!). For Java to be able to call your canned methods, the mock object will need to implement a Java interface.

Since java.util.HashMap has been our guinea pig in this chapter, let's see how we'd use RSpec's mock objects to check one of its constructors: the one that takes an existing Map. What we expect is that the Java code will do the following:

1. Call size() on the Map.
2. Ask for its entries.
3. Get an Iterator from that entry set.
4. Call hasNext() on the Iterator until we get a false result.

Documenting these expectations is easy. First, we bring in the Java classes we need:

`testing_with_jruby/rspec_mock/hashmap_spec.rb`

```
require 'java'

java_import java.util.Map
java_import java.util.HashMap
java_import java.util.Iterator
java_import java.util.Set
```

Now, we create a Ruby object implementing the java.util.Map interface and use the should_receive method to document our expectations:

`testing_with_jruby/rspec_mock/hashmap_spec.rb`

```
describe HashMap do
  it 'can be created from an empty Map' do
    map = Map.new
    map.should_receive(:size).and_return(0)

    iter = Iterator.new
    iter.should_receive(:hasNext).and_return(false)

    set = Set.new
    set.should_receive(:iterator).and_return(iter)

    map.should_receive(:entrySet).and_return(set)

    HashMap.new(map).size.should == 0
  end
end
```

What's going on with those lines that say Map.new, Iterator.new, and Set.new? Shouldn't it be illegal to create instances of those, since they're just interfaces?

Behind the scenes, JRuby is creating anonymous Java classes that implement the interfaces. That connection is actually the key to how Java mocking works in JRuby.

Go ahead and run the test with RSpec:

```
$ jruby -S rspec hashmap_spec.rb
.

Finished in 0.574 seconds

1 example, 0 failures
```

If the Java code fails to make the sequence of calls we've specified, RSpec will print a failure message. Add the following incorrect expectation just after the line containing :hasNext:

```
iter.should_receive(:next)
```

Now, try to run the test again:

```
$ jruby -S rspec hashmap_spec.rb
F

Failures:
1) Java::JavaUtil::HashMap can be created from an empty Map
  Failure/Error: iter.should_receive(:next)
  (org.jruby.gen.InterfaceImpl639549753@a00a64).next(any args)
      expected: 1 time
      received: 0 times
  # ./bad_hashmap_spec.rb:17
  # :1

Finished in 0.377 seconds
1 example, 1 failure
```

See the bit in the error message about expecting :next with "any args"? For this example, we didn't care about what arguments Java passed into our mock Map. Some situations may call for more exactness. Both RSpec and its competitors have various constraints you can apply to passed-in arguments.[7]

---

7. http://rspec.info/documentation/mocks/message_expectations.html

RSpec mocks are available everywhere you can write examples. They're also available in Cucumber step definitions, which are described in Section 9.1, *Writing High-Level Tests with Cucumber*, on page 207—but this use is less common.

The mocking techniques we have seen so far rely on Java interfaces. RSpec isn't able to add mock implementations to a concrete Java class. For that, we'll need to turn to another mocking tool.

Mocha

Mocha is one of the top Ruby mocking/stubbing frameworks, designed to work in several different testing frameworks, including most of the ones we've seen so far. Its API is less chatty than RSpec's (for example, expects instead of should_receive) but still reads somewhat like English.

Let's see how the previous example would look with Mocha. First, we need to install the framework:

```
$ jruby -S gem install mocha
```

Second, we need to configure RSpec to use Mocha. The following code can go before or after the java_import directives from last time:

testing_with_jruby/mocha/hashmap_spec.rb

```
require 'mocha'

RSpec.configure do |config|
  config.mock_with :mocha
end
```

Finally, we can use Mocha-style mocks inside the test:

testing_with_jruby/mocha/hashmap_spec.rb

```
describe HashMap do
  it 'can be created from an empty Map' do
    map = Map.new
    map.expects(:size).returns(0)

    iter = Iterator.new
    iter.expects(:hasNext).returns(false)

    set = Set.new
    set.expects(:iterator).returns(iter)

    map.expects(:entrySet).returns(set)

    HashMap.new(map).size.should == 0
  end
end
```

What have we gained, apart from a syntax that's less likely to overflow our right margin? For one thing, Mocha isn't tied to one test framework, so you can reuse your knowledge in other frameworks. Though it's beyond the scope of this example, Mocha also has really sophisticated argument-checking tests. Finally, if you use JtestR (discussed in Section 9.3, *JtestR*, on page 218), Mocha allows you to mock concrete classes, instead of just interfaces.

It's tempting to discuss how some of our other favorites, like Schmock and FlexMock, play in JRuby.[8],[9] But doing so wouldn't get us any further along in this book's mission, which is to shed light on how Java and Ruby interact. So, let's break camp here and move on to wider testing topics.

8.4 Wrapping Up

In this chapter, we've seen how Ruby's top-notch unit test frameworks can seamlessly test Java code. Since isolating the code under test is a key part of this process, we've also looked at a couple of mocking and stubbing libraries. Amazingly, we've been able to redirect Java calls into our waiting Ruby surrogates—even though the Java code in question had no knowledge of Ruby!

Our charge to you is to start testing with JRuby today. Scour your Java projects for some class whose test coverage is less than you'd like, install RSpec or one of its cousins, and add one or two simple tests. Odds are, you'll see enough of a benefit at the code level to wonder what JRuby can do for your project-wide test efforts.

In the next chapter, we're going to zoom out from individual unit tests and consider ways to drive an application as a whole from JRuby. We'll also see how to fit your JRuby tests into the universe of Java tools and libraries.

---

8. http://rubyforge.org/projects/schmock
9. http://flexmock.rubyforge.org

## Chapter 9

Beyond Unit Tests

Over the past several pages, we've tested individual chunks of Ruby and Java code using Ruby's delightful test frameworks. But what about applications as a whole? Can JRuby be pressed into service for functional testing? That's the question we're going to lead off with. First, we'll see how JRuby can turn your user stories into live tests. Next, we'll take on the most popular class of acceptance testing in Ruby: web automation.

Once we've completed our tour of Automation-ville, we'll turn back to the Java universe. There are a few aspects of integrating Ruby testing tools into Java projects that we should discuss before leaving the topic of testing.

9.1 Writing High-Level Tests with Cucumber

The first logical step upward from checking individual classes is wiring up several classes together and testing them as a group. This is the focus of integration testing.

We've seen how the RSpec framework and its cousins make it easy to write tests for Ruby and Java classes in a clear Ruby notation. But even the most lucid programming language is still a programming language. When you're writing about broader parts of the program, your audience may include people outside your close-knit circle of developers. With that in mind, the RSpec team created the Story Runner, which allows you to write your tests in plain English. This component has since spun off into a stand-alone project, Cucumber.

You might say that stories are the purest embodiment of BDD; they help you focus on the app's behavior as a whole. Cucumber separates the writing of a story from the implementations of the individual steps. Programmers implement the steps in Ruby or Java, and the whole team—including nontechnical people—can participate in writing and critiquing the overall stories.

To show you the flavor of Cucumber, we'll write a small story about searching the Web. In subsequent sections, we'll hook this code up to a real browser and breathe life into this test.

beyond_unit_tests/selenium/search.feature

```
Feature: Web search

  In order to tell my searches apart
  As a person who browses in multiple tabs
  I want to see the term I searched for

  Scenario: Page title
    Given I am on the search home page
    When I search for "hello world"
    Then the page title should begin with "hello world"
```

Cucumber stories tend to follow a certain rhythm. They begin with some optional documentation about the feature you're testing. The important parts are the clauses that begin with Given, When, and Then, which define the different parts of the story. The actual implementations are in a Ruby "step definition" file. We'll get to that in a second, but first let's run the story as is. Save the story as search.feature, and run the following commands:

```
$ jruby -S gem install cucumber rspec
$ jruby -S cucumber search.feature
```

You'll get a report that contains a copy of the original test script, followed by the pass/fail results:

```
Feature: Web search
  In order to tell my searches apart
  As a person who browses in multiple tabs
  I want to see the term I searched for

Scenario: Page title                                      # search.feature:7
  Given I am on the search home page                      # search.feature:8
  When I search for "hello world"                         # search.feature:9
  Then the page title should begin with "hello world" # search.feature:10

1 scenario (1 undefined)
3 steps (3 undefined)
0m0.238s
```

Ola Says...

The History of Cucumber

Cucumber, and the RSpec Story Runner before it, started out as the project RBehave, which in turn owes its heritage to JBehave. Both of these were created by Dan North, a coder at ThoughtWorks and one of the fathers of BDD. JBehave and the projects it inspired did much to define and spread the BDD way of developing software to the world.

All three steps are listed as "undefined," because we haven't yet told Cucumber *how* to visit the home page, search for a term, or look at the page title. We'll eventually fill in that behavior. The end of the test report gives us a starting point—three Ruby snippets we can paste into a text editor:

```
Given /^I am on the search home page$/ do
  pending # express the regexp above with the code you wish you had
end

When /^I search for "([^"]*)"$/ do |arg1|
  pending # express the regexp above with the code you wish you had
end

Then /^the page title should begin with "([^"]*)"$/ do |arg1|
  pending # express the regexp above with the code you wish you had
end
```

What goes inside those three blocks? If you're using Cucumber for integration testing, the job might be as simple as creating a couple of Ruby objects, gluing them together, and seeing how they interact. You had probably lean fairly heavily on mocks to stand in for other parts of the system.

On the other hand, functional and acceptance tests typically drive the full app instead of just a few pieces. The method by which you do that is highly context-dependent. Some applications have their own custom scripting interfaces. Others run on web servers and can be driven through HTTP. And if all else fails, you can grit your teeth and code to a full-on GUI automation framework.

9.2 Acceptance Testing

If you're testing a program through its user interface, you'll need some kind of automation library tailored to the GUI technology you're using. There are libraries out there for Swing, SWT, Flash, HTML, and more. Once you've seen how to hook one or two of these up to Cucumber, you should be able to do so for any of them. So, we're going to go for "bang for the buck" here and just look at web testing frameworks. After all, there's a fair chance you're coming to this book from the web development world.

Your approach to writing your scripts should suit the type of web application you're testing. Some apps are really simple: they wait for a network request and then reply to it with HTML. You don't need a real web browser to drive these, just a Ruby script that knows how to send a request and what kind of reply to expect. Other web applications may involve multiple requests, authentication, cookies, JavaScript, and so on. Rather than teaching Ruby to understand all of these concepts, you may find it simpler to launch a regular web browser and use its scripting interface to visit the site.

In this section, we're going to write a few different styles of test. We'll begin with the browser-based approach, because despite its complexity, it's actually easier to get started with.

Selenium and Watir are two different tools that share the same purpose: taking control of a real web browser in order to help you test your application. Selenium is language- and browser-independent. By contrast, Watir is Ruby-only (it's right there in the name: Web Application Testing in Ruby) and was originally specific to Internet Explorer. To target a different browser, you install a flavor of Watir made for that browser: FireWatir, SafariWatir, ChromeWatir, and so on.

Both libraries have their uses, and in fact either one would do fine for implementing the steps of the Cucumber test we saw earlier. So, we're going to look at both.

Selenium

Selenium is available in a Ruby-friendly format consisting of two gems: the remote control server (which does the dirty work of driving the browser) and the Ruby client interface. Here's how to install the gems and start the server:

```
$ jruby -S gem install selenium-rc selenium-client
$ jruby -S selenium-rc
```

Keep that server running in the background as you turn your attention to the more interesting part: the step definitions. These should go into step_definitions/search_steps.rb:

```
Given /^I am on the search home page$/ do
  $browser.open 'http://www.yahoo.com'
end

When /^I search for "([^\"]*)"$/ do |term|
  $browser.type 'p', term
  $browser.click 'search-submit'
  $browser.wait_for_page_to_load 10
end

Then /^the page title should begin with "([^\"]*)"$/ do |title|
  $browser.get_title[0...title.length].should == title
end
```

Behind the scenes, calls like click or wait_for_browser_to_load are sending instructions to the selenium server, which is in turn controlling Firefox. The $browser global is an instance of Selenium::SeleniumDriver. It represents a connection we need to set up before the first test step runs and tear down after the last one completes. In Cucumber, this kind of setup code goes in a file called support/env.rb.

```
require 'selenium'

$browser = Selenium::SeleniumDriver.new("localhost",
                                        4444,
                                        "*firefox",
                                        "http://www.yahoo.com",
                                        15000)

$browser.start

at_exit {$browser.stop}
```

To run a stand-alone Cucumber test, just pass the feature name to the cucumber command:

```
$ jruby -S cucumber search.feature
```

Selenium's API calls are easy to write, if not quite idiomatic Ruby. They're also fairly easy to run, though they do require the extra step of starting a separate server.

Watir

Since it was created just for Ruby, writing Watir code feels more natural in a Ruby project. Watir also uses a more direct technique for controlling the browser. Not only is there no background server, but there are also fewer security restrictions on the kind of scripts you can run.

The user story for the web search looks exactly the same for Watir as it did for Selenium; the only things that need to change are the step definitions and the setup/teardown code. Here are the new step definitions:

beyond_unit_tests/watir/step_definitions/search_steps.rb

```
Given /^I am on the search home page$/ do
  $browser.goto 'http://www.yahoo.com'
end

When /^I search for "([^\"]*)"$/ do |term|
  $browser.text_field(:name, 'p').set term
  $browser.button(:id, 'search-submit').click
  $browser.wait
end

Then /^the page title should begin with "([^\"]*)"$/ do |title|
  $browser.title[0...title.length].should == title
end
```

...and here's the new setup/teardown code:

beyond_unit_tests/watir/support/env.rb

```
require 'firewatir'

$browser = Watir::Browser.new

at_exit {$browser.close}
```

As you can see, the API is similar to Selenium's but has a certain Ruby *je ne sais quoi*. The trade-off for this elegance is compatibility. As we mentioned, Watir comes in several browser-specific flavors. As of this writing, only FireWatir, the Firefox version, is known to work well with JRuby. To install it, run the following:

```
$ jruby -S gem install firewatir
```

> ### Ian Says...
> #### Webrat Family Reunion
>
> Webrat is part of a family of related web testing libraries that have similar APIs but different trade-offs. For instance, Celerity is geared toward JavaScript-heavy pages.* Capybara supports several browser back ends but leaves out some features in the name of portability.† If you like this style of API but need something specific that Webrat doesn't offer, you may want to take a look at one of these other toolkits.
>
> ---
>
> *. http://celerity.rubyforge.org
> †. http://github.com/jnicklas/capybara

Then, install the JSSh plug-in for Firefox, which adds the testability hooks that Watir uses.[1] Once that's done, you can run the Cucumber story the same as before.

Now that we've seen two different libraries that drive a live browser, let's look at a different approach: talking directly to a web application from Ruby.

Webrat

Webrat is a Ruby library that provides a simple API for web testing.[2] With it, you write calls like visit_link '/blog/new' or click_button 'Create' to drive your site.

In addition to making tests easy to write, Webrat aims to make them easy to *run*. Your test code will call straight into your application code, as long as it's written in one of the Ruby frameworks Webrat knows about. Not only do you not need a web browser, but you don't even need to launch your application in a web *server*.[3]

Let's see what one test case might look like in Webrat. Since we need a Ruby app to test, let's use the Rouge restaurant guide from Chapter 5,

---

1. http://wiki.openqa.org/display/WTR/FireWatir+Installation
2. http://github.com/brynary/webrat
3. If Webrat isn't aware of your particular web framework, you can go back to running your own server and use the simple Webrat API on top of Selenium or other back ends.

Introduction to Rails, on page 85. From the rouge directory you created in that chapter, make a subdirectory called features and a file called features/manage_restaurants.feature with the following text:

```
introduction_to_rails/rouge/features/manage_restaurants.feature

Feature: Manage restaurants
  In order to provide up-to-the-minute listings
  As a guidebook author
  I want to add, remove, and modify restaurants

  Background:
    Given I am logged in as an admin

  Scenario: Add a restaurant
    Given the following restaurants:
      | name            |
      | Kenny and Zuke's |
      | Horse Brass Pub |
    When I add the following restaurant:
      | name           |
      | New Old Lompoc |
    Then I should see the following restaurants:
      | name            |
      | Kenny and Zuke's |
      | Horse Brass Pub |
      | New Old Lompoc  |
```

This format should feel familiar from the previous Cucumber examples. We've added a couple of new twists, though. The Background section adds a step that will run at the beginning of each Scenario. It doesn't really save you any typing if you have only one test case. But it spares the linguistic awkwardness of Given I am logged in... / And the following restaurants.

Also, note that you can define tables of test code as ASCII art. Table-driven testing is a tremendously expressive way to show several examples in a compact space.

How does Cucumber pass that chunk of tabular data into your test code? It constructs an instance of a class called Cucumber::Ast::Table, which provides several convenient methods for getting at the information inside. Let's see how to use one of these methods. Put the following code into a file called features/step_definitions/restaurant_steps.rb:

```
introduction_to_rails/rouge/features/step_definitions/restaurant_steps.rb

Given /^the following restaurants:$/ do |restaurants|
  Restaurant.create!(restaurants.hashes)
end
```

The table's hashes method returns the cells of the table converted to an array of Hash objects:

```
[{"name" => "Kenny and Zuke's"},
 {"name" => "Horse Brass Pub"}]
```

By a lovely coincidence, this happens to be the same format that Active-Record's create! method takes. Yes, we're creating the database record directly behind the scenes, rather than going through the GUI.[4] You wouldn't want to do this in the heart of the test (the When and Then steps), where we're actually checking the GUI. But it's sometimes OK during the Given step, which is really just the setup.

Now we can move on to the When step:

```
introduction_to_rails/rouge/features/step_definitions/restaurant_steps.rb
When /^I add the following restaurants?:$/ do |restaurants|
  restaurants.hashes.each do |r|
    visit new_restaurant_path
    fill_in 'restaurant[name]', :with => r[:name]
    click_button 'Create'
  end
end
```

Those three lines in the middle are Webrat calls. See how fluidly it reads? "Visit this URL. Fill in this field. Click this button." Let's go through those line by line.

We could have written the URL directly as visit '/restaurants/new'. But our code will be a little more future-proof if we use new_restaurant_path, a name that Rails defined for us while we were building Rouge.

Webrat identifies the text field to fill in by its name property. In other words, this code is expecting to see a chunk of HTML that looks something like <text name="restaurant[name]">. Similarly, the call to click_button looks for a submit button whose value is Create.

To check the results, we go back to the list of restaurants and make sure the newly added one shows up.

---

4. In *The RSpec Book* [CAD+09], David Chelimsky refers to this technique as "Direct Model Access."

```
introduction_to_rails/rouge/features/step_definitions/restaurant_steps.rb
Then /^I should see the following restaurants:$/ do |expected|
  visit restaurants_path

  actual = table(tableish('table:nth-of-type(2) tr', 'td,th'))
  actual.map_headers! { |h| h.downcase }

  expected.diff! actual
end
```

Just like the other two steps, this one takes a table as input—in this case, a table listing the restaurants we expect to see. We need to make a similar table of the actual restaurants on the page. Cucumber's Rails integration provides the tableish method for this purpose.

tableish takes as parameters the kinds of HTML tags we're looking for (the hairy details of CSS3 selectors are a topic for another day) and uses them to slice the document up into an array of Hash objects:

```
[{"Name" => "Kenny and Zuke's", "Phone" => "", "Address" => ""},
 {"Name" => "Horse Brass Pub", "Phone" => "", "Address" => ""},
 {"Name" => "New Old Lompoc", "Phone" => "", "Address" => ""}]
```

Did you notice the hash keys are all capitalized? The ASCII-art table in our scenario spelled the columns in all lowercase letters. Do we rewrite the test or do some kind of translation? We recommend the latter, because it's easier to keep things up-to-date when the web designer changes the page.

The translation code is simple. First, we get the array of hashes into one of those powerful Cucumber table objects; that's what the table method does. Next, we call map_headers! to do the translation.

Finally, we can compare the two tables via their diff! method. By default, this comparison is forgiving of the extra Phone and Address columns that appear on the page but not in our test. (We don't care about them for this particular scenario.)

One last thing: we need to take care of the login step from the scenario background.

```
introduction_to_rails/rouge/features/step_definitions/restaurant_steps.rb
Given /^I am logged in as an admin$/ do
  Administrator.create! :username => 'admin', :password => 'admin'
  basic_auth 'admin', 'admin'
end
```

Because Rouge users (including administrators) are stored in the database, we have to create a new account before we can log in. Then, we can use Webrat's basic_auth method to specify the login credentials.

We're almost ready to run the tests. We just have a bit of housekeeping to do first. Add the following to the end of your Gemfile:

introduction_to_rails/rouge/Gemfile

```
group :development, :test do
  gem 'webrat'
  gem 'cucumber-rails'
  gem 'cucumber'
  gem 'rspec-rails', '~> 2.0'
end
```

Now, run the following commands in the project directory:

```
$ jruby -S bundle install
$ jruby script/rails generate cucumber:install --rspec --webrat
$ jruby -S rake db:migrate
```

This will install the pieces Webrat needs to talk to your Rails app and generate a few Cucumber-specific configuration files in the project directory. We'll need to make a couple of customizations on top of this configuration. Create a file in features/support called webrat_config.rb, and put the following code in it:

introduction_to_rails/rouge/features/support/webrat_config.rb

```
Webrat.configure do |config|
  config.mode = :rack
end

require 'webrat/core/methods'

World Webrat::Methods
World Rack::Test::Methods
```

Once that's done, you can run an all-in-one Rake task that takes care of setting up the database and running the test:

```
$ jruby -S rake cucumber
```

Because this test doesn't require a browser or server, it's easy to run on a variety of machines, from your development team's PCs to the continuous integration server. But Webrat doesn't try to be a full browser, and you may have some tests that require one. Many projects successfully use a mix of both styles.

9.3 Plugging Into Java

By this point, we've seen several compelling Ruby test frameworks. Some of them are only of tangential interest to Java users, but others can provide inspiration for real Java projects. In this section, we'll talk about which ones are good candidates for your Java project. We'll finish up with a discussion of how JRuby and the existing Java test frameworks play together.

JtestR

JtestR is a new framework that simplifies using Ruby for testing Java projects. It doesn't include much original code; instead, it collects several state-of-the-art Ruby libraries together with some glue code geared toward Java testing. Why use Ruby to test Java? Because the ease of writing tests in Ruby will encourage you to write more and better tests.

With JtestR, you don't have to hook up any of the plumbing that would normally be necessary to integrate JRuby with your Java infrastructure. You just download a .jar file, add a few lines to your Ant build file, and then start writing tests. Here's what you get when you install the latest version of JtestR (0.6 as of this writing):

- JRuby 1.5+

- Test::Unit

- RSpec

- Expectations (another test framework)

- dust (yet another test framework)

- Mocha

- ActiveSupport

We've already been through most of these libraries. So, we'll just take you on a tour through JtestR's capabilities and show you how to get started with it.

Fast Startup

One of the problems with using JRuby for testing is the long startup time. You want your tests to run instantaneously so that nothing gets in the way of constant testing. JtestR speeds up testing by providing a background server with a pool of ready-to-use runtimes. When a client wants to run a test, the server assigns it a runtime and prepares another one.

Build Tools

Anything intended to be part of the Java ecosystem needs to have extremely good integration with the currently available tools. JtestR ties in with the two most popular Java build tools, Ant and Maven. This integration requires only a simple one-time setup. Here's what an Ant build file would look like, assuming you've saved JtestR to lib/jtestr.jar:

beyond_unit_tests/jtestr/build.xml

```
<?xml version="1.0" encoding="utf-8"?>

<project basedir="." default="test" name="simple_ant_test">
  <description>
    Simple example Ant project for jtestr
  </description>

  <taskdef
      name="jtestr"
      classname="org.jtestr.ant.JtestRAntRunner"
      classpath="lib/jtestr.jar"/>

  <taskdef
      name="jtestr-server"
      classname="org.jtestr.ant.JtestRAntServer"
      classpath="lib/jtestr.jar"/>

  <target name="test" description="Runs all tests">
    <jtestr/>
  </target>

  <target name="test-server" description="Starts test server">
    <jtestr-server runtimes="3"/>
  </target>
</project>
```

This file gives you two new build targets, test and test-server. To use them, first open a new console window, and run ant test-server there. Leave that running, and then use the test target as usual. By default, JtestR assumes your tests are in the test directory, but you can adapt this setting to your project.

A minimal Maven 2 POM for JtestR would look like this:

```
beyond_unit_tests/jtestr/pom.xml
<?xml version="1.0" encoding="utf-8"?>

<project>
  <modelVersion>4.0.0</modelVersion>
  <groupId>org.jtestr</groupId>
  <artifactId>jtestr-maven-example</artifactId>
  <packaging>jar</packaging>
  <version>0.1</version>
  <name>JtestR Maven Example</name>

  <build>
    <directory>target</directory>
    <outputDirectory>target/classes</outputDirectory>
    <sourceDirectory>src</sourceDirectory>

    <plugins>
      <plugin>
        <groupId>org.jtestr</groupId>
        <artifactId>jtestr</artifactId>
        <version>0.6</version>
        <configuration>
          <port>20333</port>
        </configuration>
        <executions>
          <execution>
            <goals>
              <goal>test</goal>
            </goals>
          </execution>
        </executions>
      </plugin>
    </plugins>
  </build>
</project>
```

To use the background server with this configuration file, execute the jtestr:server goal.

JtestR can be made to work with IDEs as well. For an example of Eclipse integration, see http://www.evalcode.com/2008/08/jruby-jtestr-in-eclipse.

Reusing Java Tests

With JtestR, you can take your existing Java tests written for the JUnit or TestNG framework and run them right alongside your new Ruby tests. All you have to do is add the names of your Java test classes to JtestR's config file, which is called jtestr_config.rb by default:

```
junit ['com.example.SomeTest',
       'com.example.SomeOtherTest']
```

(You can also go the other direction and let JUnit drive your Ruby tests, as we'll see in a moment.)

JtestR includes many smaller, but still useful, features. For instance, as we discussed in Section 8.3, *Mocha*, on page 204, the version of Mocha that ships with JtestR contains a few tweaks to enable mocking both Java interfaces and Java classes. A full catalog of these little niceties is beyond the scope of this chapter. For more information, see the JtestR documentation.[5] This is the short, short version: if you're just getting started adding Ruby tests to a Java project, we strongly recommend using JtestR.

JUnit, TestNG, and Other Java Frameworks

Of course, there are lots of great Java testing frameworks around, and in some cases you might want to supplement your chosen Ruby framework with a few Java tests. You'll usually find that you need to do a few extra steps in these situations. For instance, once you've written the actual test code in Ruby, you'll need to manually register your test classes with Java.

Most of the current Java test frameworks rely on static type annotations to find test suites and test cases. This system doesn't mesh well with Ruby's dynamic classes. The easiest way to reconcile the two is to write a thin Ruby wrapper around your tests. The wrapper will implement a Java testing interface, call the real Ruby test code, and report the results back to JUnit or TestNG.

The JRuby project has used this technique with some success—see the test directory of the JRuby source. The tests are a mixture of Java and Ruby code, and they use several different frameworks. One overarching JUnit test suite churns through this motley collection of test steps and then assembles the results for JUnit.

---

5. http://jtestr.codehaus.org

Driving any of these frameworks from Ruby is as easy as any other Java integration. You just call into the Java classes and methods using the same techniques we've been discussing throughout this book. That's all JtestR does when it runs JUnit and TestNG tests.

A JUnit Example

To make this section a bit more concrete, we'll take a quick look at how you can run Test::Unit tests from JUnit. Most of the code will be in Ruby; the Java side will consist of a small JUnit adapter. This general pattern—a Ruby project with a thin Java wrapper—pops up frequently in JRuby projects.

The first thing we need is a class that will present itself to JUnit as a test case. We'll be using the older, nonannotation JUnit API here; this will work fine with either JUnit 3 or 4. The code looks like this:

beyond_unit_tests/junit_integration/TestUnitSuite.java

```java
import org.jruby.embed.ScriptingContainer;

import junit.framework.Test;
import junit.framework.TestCase;
import junit.framework.TestResult;

public class TestUnitSuite implements Test {
    private void runTestCasesIn(ScriptingContainer runtime, TestResult result) {
        Object junit_adapter = runtime.runScriptlet("JUnitAdapter");
        Object instance = runtime.callMethod(junit_adapter, "new", result);
        runtime.callMethod(instance, "run_tests");
    }

    public int countTestCases() {
        return -1;
    }

    public void run(TestResult result) {
        ScriptingContainer runtime = new ScriptingContainer();
        runtime.runScriptlet("require 'test_unit_junit'");

        Object junit_class    = runtime.runScriptlet("JUnitAdapter");
        Object junit_instance = runtime.callMethod(junit_class, "new", result);
        runtime.callMethod(junit_instance, "run_tests");
    }

    public static Test suite() {
        return new TestUnitSuite();
    }
}
```

This class's three methods provide the interface that JUnit expects to see. The interesting bits are all in the run() method. Using the techniques from Chapter 3, *Ruby from Java: Embedding JRuby*, on page 45, we load our Ruby code into a new ScriptingContainer object, create an instance of a Ruby class, and call its run_tests method.

To build this Java code, you can add something like the following fragment to your Ant build file:

beyond_unit_tests/junit_integration/build.xml

```
<target name="compile"
        description="Compile the source files for the project.">
  <javac destdir="." debug="true" source="1.5" target="1.5">
    <classpath refid="build.classpath"/>
    <src path="."/>
  </javac>
</target>
```

Provided that you have both jruby-complete.jar and junit-4.8.1 in your build. classpath, you should get a clean build with ant compile at this point.

The Ruby Adapter

The Ruby code is a lot more involved, so let's take it in segments. First, we need to bring in both the Ruby Test::Unit libraries and the Java JUnit ones:

beyond_unit_tests/junit_integration/test_unit_junit.rb

```
require 'test/unit'
require 'test/unit/collector'
require 'test/unit/ui/testrunnermediator'

require 'java'
java_import 'junit.framework.TestCase'
java_import 'junit.framework.AssertionFailedError'
```

Now, we can define the JUnitAdapter class, whose run_tests method we just called from Java:

beyond_unit_tests/junit_integration/test_unit_junit.rb

```
class JUnitAdapter
  def initialize(test_result)
    @test_result = test_result
  end

  def run_tests
    Dir["test/**/*_test.rb"].each do |f|
      load f
    end
```

```
      Test::Unit::AutoRunner.new(false) do |runner|
        runner.collector = collect_all_test_unit_classes
        runner.runner   = report_results_to_junit
      end.run
    end
  end
```

The main method, run_tests(), will first load all relevant files from the test directory, and then we hand them off to Test::Unit's AutoRunner class to run. This class uses a common Ruby idiom for customization: its new method can take a block containing additional options. In this case, we're specifying how Test::Unit should search Ruby's memory for tests and how it should report results while the tests are running.

You'll notice we're leaning on a couple of helper methods, collect_all_test_ unit_classes and report_results_to_junit. Their details belong firmly in the "things needed only by the maintainers of Test::Unit" category, so just gloss over the gnarly bits and focus on the class names:

`beyond_unit_tests/junit_integration/test_unit_junit.rb`

```
class JUnitAdapter
  private

  def collect_all_test_unit_classes
    proc do |runner|
      c = TestUnitClassCollector.new
      c.filter = runner.filters
      c.collect("Tests", test_unit_classes)
    end
  end

  def report_results_to_junit
    proc do |runner|
      TestUnitResultHandler.instance_variable_set :@result_handler, @test_result
      TestUnitResultHandler
    end
  end

  def test_unit_classes
    all = []
    ObjectSpace.each_object(Class) do |klass|
      if Test::Unit::TestCase > klass
        all << klass
      end
    end
    all
  end
end
```

This code references two new classes we'll need to define, TestUnitClass-Collector and TestUnitResultHandler. First, let's look at the collector. Its job is to collect a bunch of separate Ruby classes into a single test suite. Test::Unit calls into it before running the tests. Alas, the details are a piece of necessary, but uninteresting, boilerplate:

`beyond_unit_tests/junit_integration/test_unit_junit.rb`

```ruby
class TestUnitClassCollector
  include Test::Unit::Collector

  def collect(name, klasses)
    suite = Test::Unit::TestSuite.new(name)
    sub_suites = []
    klasses.each do |klass|
      add_suite(sub_suites, klass.suite)
    end
    sort(sub_suites).each{|s| suite << s}
    suite
  end
end
```

And now, we'll see the TestUnitResultHandler class that's tasked with handing Test::Unit results back to JUnit:

`beyond_unit_tests/junit_integration/test_unit_junit.rb`

```ruby
class TestUnitResultHandler
  def self.run(suite, ignored=nil)
    runner = new suite
    runner.instance_variable_set :@result_handler, @result_handler
    runner.start
  end

  def initialize(suite, io=STDOUT)
    if suite.respond_to? :suite
      @suite = suite.suite
    else
      @suite = suite
    end
  end

  def start
    @mediator = Test::Unit::UI::TestRunnerMediator.new @suite

    @mediator.add_listener Test::Unit::TestResult::FAULT,
                           &method(:add_fault)
    @mediator.add_listener Test::Unit::TestCase::STARTED,
                           &method(:test_started)
    @mediator.add_listener Test::Unit::TestCase::FINISHED,
                           &method(:test_finished)

    @mediator.run_suite
  end
end
```

This code is the public interface to the class. Test::Unit will call the static run method and expect us to create and launch an instance of the class. You'll see that we're adding callbacks to something called a *mediator*, which you can think of as a test step watcher. Each time something interesting happens, like a step failing or a test suite completing, Test::Unit will notify the mediator—which will in turn notify us. Inside the three callbacks, we just need to hand the results off to JUnit:

`beyond_unit_tests/junit_integration/test_unit_junit.rb`

```ruby
class TestUnitResultHandler
  private

  def add_fault(fault)
    case fault.single_character_display
    when 'F': @result_handler.add_failure(@current_test,
                                  AssertionFailedError.new(fault.to_s))
    when 'E': @result_handler.add_error(@current_test,
                                  java.lang.Throwable.new(fault.to_s))
    end
  end

  def test_started(name)
    @current_test = RubyTest.new(name)
    @result_handler.start_test(@current_test)
  end

  def test_finished(name)
    @result_handler.end_test(@current_test)
  end
end
```

What's that RubyTest object we're creating inside test_started? It's just a tiny Ruby class that implements the required methods from JUnit's org.junit.TestCase interface:

`beyond_unit_tests/junit_integration/test_unit_junit.rb`

```ruby
class RubyTest < TestCase
  def countTestCases; 1; end
  def run(result); end
  def toString; name; end
end
```

Whew! That's a lot of detailed API work to tie these two test frameworks together. The good news is that it needs to be written only once. You should be able to drop these two files into any JRuby project, add some tests, and run them with Ant. Let's do that now.

The Actual Tests

Go ahead and drop a couple of ..._test.rb files into the test directory. For this example, we've copied the HashMap tests from the previous chapter into a file called test/hashmap_test.rb:

`beyond_unit_tests/junit_integration/test/hashmap_test.rb`

```ruby
require 'test/unit'

require 'java'

java_import java.util.HashMap

class HashMapTestCase < Test::Unit::TestCase
  def setup
    @map = HashMap.new
  end

  def test_new_hashmap_is empty
    assert @map.isEmpty
  end

  def test_hashmap_with_entry_is_not_empty
    @map.put("hello", "world")
    assert !@map.isEmpty
  end

  def test_value_is_associated_with_added_key
    @map.put("hello", "world")
    assert_equal "world", @map.get("hello")
  end

  def test_entry_set_iterator_next_raises_error_for_empty_hashmap
    assert_raises(NativeException) do
      @map.entrySet.iterator.next
    end
  end
end
```

Here's a fragment you can add to your Ant build file to run these tests:

`beyond_unit_tests/junit_integration/build.xml`

```xml
<target name="test" depends="compile"
        description="Compile the source files for the project.">
  <junit haltonfailure="false" fork="yes">
    <classpath refid="run.classpath"/>
    <formatter type="plain" usefile="false"/>
    <test name="TestUnitSuite"/>
  </junit>
</target>
```

Ready to run some tests?

```
$ ant test
Buildfile: build.xml

compile:

test:
    [junit] Testsuite: TestUnitSuite
    [junit] Tests run: 4, Failures: 0, Errors: 0, Time elapsed: 8.615 sec
    [junit]
    [junit] Testcase: test_entry_set_iterator_next_raises_error_for_empty_hashmap...
    [junit] Testcase: test_hashmap_with_entry_is_not_empty(HashMapTestCase) took...
    [junit] Testcase: test_new_hashmap_is_empty(HashMapTestCase) took 0.005 sec
    [junit] Testcase: test_value_is_associated_with_added_key(HashMapTestCase)...

BUILD SUCCESSFUL
Total time: 10 seconds
```

From here, we leave the tests in your capable hands.

9.4 Wrapping Up

This chapter began by showing how to use Ruby frameworks for higher-level testing of Java programs. We saw a tiny sampling of the web UI automation libraries available for acceptance testing. Finally, we talked about how to bring your elegant Ruby-based tests into the world of sophisticated Java tools.

Don't wait to introduce great testing to your Java project. Download JtestR today, and tie it into your existing Java tests. As you add new tests, add them in Ruby using one of the expressive frameworks we've seen. If you're feeling really ambitious, you might finish off by plugging everything into a continuous integration server.[6] We think you'll find that Ruby is the best language for testing Java code—no matter whether you prefer JtestR, an ad hoc collection of libraries, or some new and awesome tool that you're about to write and unleash on the world. Now get testing!

---

6. http://wiki.jruby.org/JRubyAndContinuousIntegration

Chapter 10

Building GUIs with Swing

You've heard it before: "write once, run anywhere," or *WORA* for short. The term has been used (and overused) by Java developers over the past decade and a half to refer to the Holy Grail of portability. Reality never quite lives up to the hype, and indeed WORA's early waves of promise crashed against the familiar rocks of platform-specific quirks.

The story is more hopeful today, especially in the area of GUI development. If you write a Java GUI application on Windows, it can also run on Mac OS, Linux, or any other platform where Java runs—while taking on a native look and feel.

However, for Java language developers, this comeback has been hard-earned. Swing, the primary GUI API for Java, is a byzantine framework. It works great once you've invested your blood and sweat into making a robust application. But the amount of effort needed to learn the ins and outs of Swing often frustrates developers into abandoning the framework altogether.

10.1 JRuby to the Rescue!

There has been an explosion of GUI frameworks for JRuby. Most of these work by papering over some of Swing's more puzzling complexities. They also reduce the amount of boilerplate code you have to write, by leaning on powerful Ruby features like blocks.

Why is there so much interest in JRuby GUI development? As you might have guessed, Java is part of the answer. In Java shops, enterprising coders[1] have used Ruby frameworks to ease the pain of supporting their company's chosen platform.

There's another factor, too: mainstream Ruby. The C version of Ruby has no widely used cross-platform GUI toolkit. Yes, some builds of Ruby ship with support for the Tk graphical widget set. But it's no exaggeration on our part to say that Tk is not universally beloved by Ruby developers. JRuby and Swing can provide just the sort of happy ending to the Ruby GUI development story we've all been waiting for.

To give you an idea of the feel of GUI development on JRuby, we're going to write one application using four different frameworks. What sort of application, you ask? It needs to be something short enough to fit in a chapter but complicated enough to show you some of the trade-offs you'll need to make in your own projects.

As we were putting this book together, the answer came to us: how about an application to write and organize the chapters for a book? We're going to build a glorified text editor that lets you write a series of chapters in a simplified markup language and then preview the final pages. Ready? Let's get started!

10.2 Swing

The first Ruby framework is...no framework at all. We're going to just use the Java integration features we talked about in Chapter 2, *Driving Java from Ruby*, on page 15 and script a solution using the Swing APIs directly. Seeing the Swing solution first will be a great base to build on for understanding the benefits and trade-offs of the other frameworks.

Before we get into the code, let's take a look at where we're headed. We want to end up with something like Figure 10.1, on the facing page.

On the left side is a list of chapters. We have two so far and can add a third one at the end by clicking Add Chapter. The right side of the window is for content. In the Edit pane, we can write plain text with a little basic markup (for example, asterisks for *bold* text). The Preview pane shows what the end result will look like after we apply all the formatting.

---

1. No pun intended

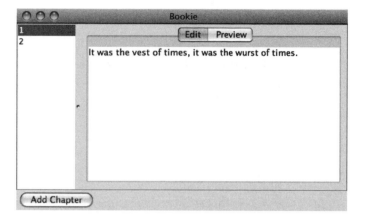

Figure 10.1: Swing Interface

Ready to see the code? Let's start by bringing in a few libraries and classes we'll need:

guis/swing/bookie.rb

```
require 'java'
require 'rubygems'
require 'redcloth'

classes = %w(JFrame JButton JList
             JEditorPane JSplitPane JTabbedPane JTextPane
             DefaultListModel ListSelectionModel BoxLayout
             text.html.HTMLEditorKit)

classes.each do |c|
  java_import "javax.swing.#{c}"
end

java_import java.awt.Dimension
```

First, we load the java library. This lets us java_import a few Swing classes for convenience. Notice that we're also loading a gem called redcloth. RedCloth is an implementation of Textile, a wiki-like markup language.[2]

Go ahead and install that now, while we're on the subject:

```
$ jruby -S gem install RedCloth
```

From this point on, the majority of the code is just laying out the GUI and spelling out behavior. We'll be using stock Swing techniques here.

---

2. http://redcloth.org

You'll see plenty of places where a Ruby framework could have saved us some effort.

We'll start by creating the Edit and Preview windows as a JTextPane and JEditorPane, respectively:

guis/swing/bookie.rb

```
edit    = JTextPane.new
preview = JEditorPane.new

preview.editable   = false
preview.editor_kit = HTMLEditorKit.new
preview.document   = preview.editor_kit.create_default_document
```

This should be fairly self-explanatory. We've marked the Preview pane as noneditable, because it's, well, a preview.[3] We also need to designate it as an HTML-capable window, since RedCloth renders Textile down to HTML.

Next, we'll create a list box to contain the names of the chapters:

guis/swing/bookie.rb

```
chapters = JList.new(DefaultListModel.new)
chapters.selection_mode = ListSelectionModel::SINGLE_SELECTION

class << chapters
  def add_chapter
    count = model.size
    model.add_element count + 1
    selection_model.set_selection_interval count, count
  end
end

chapters.add_chapter
```

The first line creates a new JList and specifies two *models*—one for the contents of the list and one for the selection. Swing applies Model-View-Controller (MVC) concepts everywhere, sometimes to an annoying degree. Moreover, it seldom offers sensible defaults. Mastering Swing requires both writing new models and crawling through the API docs to find existing models.

The Add Chapter button (which we haven't defined yet) will need a way to append chapters to our list. We could add an add_chapter method

---

3. Recall that the syntax editable = false is shorthand for setting a Java property, as in setEditable(false).

to the JList class. But it's safer to confine our changes to just this one instance. That's what the class << chapters line does.[4]

Inside add_chapter, we find out how many chapters are currently on the list and then add a new item at the end. We then make the new chapter the selected item. Now, let's move on to GUI events.

`guis/swing/bookie.rb`
```
contents = Hash.new('')

chapters.add_list_selection_listener do |e|
  unless e.value_is_adjusting
    new_index = e.source.get_selected_index
    old_index = [e.first_index, e.last_index].find { |i| i != new_index }

    contents[old_index], edit.text = edit.text, contents[new_index]
    preview.text = RedCloth.new(edit.text).to_html
  end
end
```

This code creates a table to hold our chapters (indexed by number) and then gives the JList an *event listener* to update the text in the window when the user selects a new chapter. The event listener is a bit of a mouthful, but it's easy to understand if we break it down a piece at a time.

```
chapters.add_list_selection_listener do |e|
  # ...
end
```

Each time the end user selects a chapter, Swing will call all the listeners registered to that control. In Java, you'd put your event code in a ListSelectionListener. But since this interface has only one method, you can just pass a Ruby block to add_list_selection_listener instead. JRuby will take care of creating a listener class for you.

```
unless e.value_is_adjusting
  # ...
end
```

When the user changes the selection, Swing may actually fire a stream of several events. We have to test the event to make sure it's not in the middle of one of these streams. If you feel surprised that Swing requires this kind of arcane knowledge just for a simple app, you're not alone.

---

4. For an explanation of adding methods to Ruby objects and classes at runtime, see http://ola-bini.blogspot.com/2006/09/ruby-singleton-class.html.

`guis/swing/bookie.rb`

```
new_index = e.source.get_selected_index
old_index = [e.first_index, e.last_index].find { |i| i != new_index }
```

The event object, e, has a first_index and a last_index field. One of them represents the previous selection and one the new selection—but we can't know in advance which one is which. We actually have to test them both against the result of get_selected_index.

`guis/swing/bookie.rb`

```
contents[old_index], edit.text = edit.text, contents[new_index]
preview.text = RedCloth.new(edit.text).to_html
```

This last bit saves away the old text and replaces the Edit pane with the new text. It also updates the Preview pane with the HTML generated from RedCloth.

Now, let's make a tab control for the Edit and Preview windows so that the user can toggle between them. We do this by creating a JTabbedPane and adding the two windows to it:

`guis/swing/bookie.rb`

```
tabbed_pane = JTabbedPane.new JTabbedPane::TOP, JTabbedPane::SCROLL_TAB_LAYOUT
tabbed_pane.add_tab 'Edit', edit
tabbed_pane.add_tab 'Preview', preview

tabbed_pane.add_change_listener do |event|
  if tabbed_pane.selected_component == preview
    preview.text = RedCloth.new(edit.text).to_html
  end
end
```

Notice that this control also gets an event listener. When the user switches to the Preview window, we want to regenerate the HTML in case they've modified the chapter.

`guis/swing/bookie.rb`

```
split_pane = JSplitPane.new JSplitPane::HORIZONTAL_SPLIT
split_pane.add chapters
split_pane.add tabbed_pane
```

The previous code creates a split pane, with the chapter list on one side and the Edit/Preview windows on the other.

`guis/swing/bookie.rb`

```
button = javax.swing.JButton.new 'Add Chapter'
button.size = Dimension.new 40, 40
button.add_action_listener { chapters.add_chapter }
```

When the user clicks the Add Chapter button, the block we supply here gets called. Like the other listeners, this block has access to the chapters list control, which is a local variable that we defined *outside* the block.

The final step is to create a top-level window, or JFrame, to hold everything else.

`guis/swing/bookie.rb`

```
frame = JFrame.new 'Bookie'
frame.size   = Dimension.new 500, 300
frame.layout = BoxLayout.new frame.content_pane, BoxLayout::Y_AXIS
frame.add split_pane
frame.add button
frame.visible = true
```

The frame uses a *layout manager*, Swing's way of specifying where controls will appear relative to one another (both initially and when the window is resized). Layout managers are a rich topic in their own right and worth reading up on if you plan on doing a lot of Swing work.

There we have it. In the worst-case scenario of using raw Swing without the help of any Ruby frameworks, we spent about 60 lines of code. Not too bad, actually. You could add another 60 lines to deal with loading, saving, and printing documents. But before you go write the next great text editor, let's look at some JRuby-based GUI frameworks built on top of Swing. Maybe we'll find ways to remove some of the Swing esoterica from our top-level GUI code.

10.3 Rubeus

Rubeus is a GUI framework whose developers think that completely eliminating the details of Swing may not be possible.[5] No matter how good an abstract framework is, some of Swing's details will leak into your code. With that in mind, they decided to concentrate on removing the worst of Swing's pain points, without ever hiding the fact that you're still coding to the Swing API. You can think of Rubeus as Swing with a Ruby friendly-syntax.

This pragmatic approach has a few advantages:

- You can still read Swing documentation and training materials and apply what you've learned to your Rubeus project.

---

5. http://code.google.com/p/rubeus

- People who already know Swing will experience a quick learning curve and improved productivity.
- Rubeus's underlying code base is smaller than other frameworks. This simplicity leads to easier maintenance.

Are you convinced this idea could work or at least willing to indulge us for a few pages? Let's look at some code:

```
guis/rubeus/bookie.rb
require 'java'
require 'rubygems'
require 'rubeus'
require 'redcloth'

java_import javax.swing.DefaultListModel
java_import javax.swing.text.html.HTMLEditorKit

Rubeus::Swing.irb
```

The top of the file looks similar to the straight Swing example, with the addition of the rubeus gem to the mix. But where did all our java_imports go? They've been almost completely replaced with one line: the call to Rubeus::Swing.irb. This method makes the most commonly used Swing classes available to us.

You'll find much that's familiar in the rest of the application, too. As we said, Rubeus is a short step away from raw Swing. One difference that should pop out, though, is that all the constructors take a block. This means you can lay your Ruby code out according to the structure of your GUI. Here's the skeleton of the code you'll be writing:

```
JFrame.new('Bookie') do |frame|
  frame.layout = BoxLayout.new(:Y_AXIS)

  JSplitPane.new(JSplitPane::HORIZONTAL_SPLIT) do
    JList.new
    JScrollPane.new(:preferred_size => [400, 250]) do
      JTabbedPane.new(:TOP, :SCROLL_TAB_LAYOUT) do
        JTextPane.new
        JEditorPane.new
      end
    end
  end

  JButton.new('Add Chapter')
  frame.visible = true
end
```

Note that the JSplitFrame gets added to the JFrame, without our having to call the add method ourselves. Also, take a second look at this line:

```
frame.layout = BoxLayout.new(:Y_AXIS)
```

In pure Swing code, we would have had to say something like this instead:

```
frame.layout = BoxLayout.new(frame.content_pane, BoxLayout::Y_AXIS)
```

Rubeus knows that a layout manager always needs its frame's content_pane to be passed in, so it takes care of that detail for us. It also provides :Y_AXIS as a shortcut to BoxLayout::Y_AXIS. Less ceremony, more readability. The next piece of code goes just *inside* the JSplitPane block:

guis/rubeus/bookie.rb
```
@chapters = JList.new(DefaultListModel.new)
@chapters.selection_mode = ListSelectionModel::SINGLE_SELECTION

class << @chapters
  def add_chapter
    count = model.size
    model.add_element count + 1
    selection_model.set_selection_interval count, count
  end
end

@chapters.add_chapter
```

This looks just like the chapters section from before, with one difference. We're defining @chapters as an instance variable now, rather than as a local variable. This is because the chapter list belongs to a very deeply nested block but needs to be visible from a higher-level block later.

The internal table of chapters, along with the event listener that manipulates it, is nearly the same as in pure Swing. Again, we are using instance variables instead of local variables. The following code goes right after the previous excerpt (still inside the split pane):

guis/rubeus/bookie.rb
```
@contents = Hash.new('')

@chapters.add_list_selection_listener do |e|
  unless e.value_is_adjusting
    new_index = e.source.get_selected_index
    old_index = [e.first_index, e.last_index].find { |i| i != new_index }
    @contents[old_index], @edit.text = @edit.text, @contents[new_index]
    @preview.text = RedCloth.new(@edit.text).to_html
  end
end
```

Now for a few containers to carry all this stuff. Because the JTabbedPane lives inside a JScrollPane, their constructors follow the same nesting. This is the last piece of code inside the split pane:

guis/rubeus/bookie.rb

```ruby
JScrollPane.new(:preferred_size => [400, 250]) do |scroll|
  JTabbedPane.new(:TOP, :SCROLL_TAB_LAYOUT) do |tab|
    tab.add_change_listener do |event|
      if tab.selected_component == @preview
        @preview.text = RedCloth.new(@edit.text).to_html
      end
    end

    @edit    = JTextPane.new
    @preview = JEditorPane.new

    @preview.editable = false
    @preview.editor_kit = HTMLEditorKit.new
    @preview.document = @preview.editor_kit.create_default_document

    tab.set_titles ['Edit', 'Preview']
  end
end
```

Another shorthand that Rubeus allows is passing in common options to a component's constructor. In the previous excerpt, notice how we set the scroll pane's preferred size:

```ruby
JScrollPane.new(:preferred_size => [400, 250]) do |scroll|
```

This code replaces a wordier line from the previous example:

```ruby
scroll_pane.setPreferredSize(java.awt.Dimension.new(400, 250))
```

The final cool shortcut is the ability to pass your event-handling code as a block to the constructor for the component. This code goes inside the overall JFrame block, just *above* the final end:

guis/rubeus/bookie.rb

```ruby
JButton.new('Add Chapter', :size => [40, 40]) { @chapters.add_chapter }
frame.visible = true
```

In Rubeus, a block passed into a constructor can mean one of two things. For a container, a block is for setting up properties and laying out child components. For an actual GUI control, a block is for event handling. What about containers that happen to be controls as well? For those, you'd use a block for layout and good ol'-fashioned add_event_listener for events.

Using Rubeus is definitely a big improvement over writing your Swing application with just JRuby's basic Java scripting. If you're comfortable with Swing, you'll probably find Rubeus easy to use. If not, you might prefer a framework that's a bit further removed from the Swing API. Let's take a look now at two such frameworks.

10.4 Monkeybars

Monkeybars is an opinionated Model-View-Controller (MVC) framework that sits on top of Swing. Although it knows about Swing, it tries to shield you from it as much as possible. In this sense, Monkeybars feels more like a framework in its own right than just a Swing add-on. This abstraction has its pluses and minuses, as we'll see.

Part of Monkeybars' appeal is that it plays nicely with Matisse, the GUI editor built into the NetBeans IDE. While you can certainly write a Monkeybars program without Matisse, we'd like to show you how much rote layout code you can skip by using a graphical editor.

One thing we'd like you to keep in mind while you're writing code in this section is the emphasis on separating concerns. The data at the heart of the application, the user interface, and the logic connecting them are three separate entities. This kind of design lends itself well to scalable, testable GUIs.

Project Structure

To get started, make sure you have a version of NetBeans installed that has both Ruby and Java support. The easiest way to do this is to download the Full edition, but you can also add either language to your existing installation through the Tools → Plugins menu item. Next, install the Monkeybars gem, plus a packaging helper called Rawr:

```
$ jruby -S gem install monkeybars rawr
```

Now, create the overall structure for your project. Run the following commands in order (some may take a few minutes to finish):

```
$ jruby -S monkeybars bookie
$ cd bookie
$ jruby -S rawr install
$ jruby -S rake generate ALL=src/bookie
```

The word ALL in the final command indicates that Monkeybars should generate a model, view, and controller.

If you look at the new top-level bookie directory, you'll find a structure that may remind you of a Ruby on Rails application. Since all Monkeybars applications share this layout, learning the conventions once means you'll know your way around any new project. Here are the more important files and directories:

- lib/java: Location of .jar files for JRuby and Monkeybars

- lib/ruby: External Ruby libraries such as RedCloth

- src/application_controller.rb and src/application_view.rb: Code shared across all user-defined controllers and views

- src/manifest.rb: Where you'll specify external dependencies

- src/bookie: Your custom model, view, and controller

Once you have the project structure in place, it's time to hook it up to NetBeans. Launch the IDE, and then select New Project from the File menu. In the dialog box that appears, choose Java in the left pane and Java Project with Existing Sources in the right pane. Hit Next, and browse to the bookie directory. Type *Bookie* for the project name. Hit Next again. Add the src subdirectory to the list of project source directories.

When you click Finish, you should see the Bookie project in the list on the left side of the screen. Right-click the project icon, and choose Properties.... Click the Libraries category, and then select Add Library.... Choose Swing Layout Extensions (the GUI editor needs these extensions). Now click Add JAR/Folder, and select both jruby-complete.jar and monkeybars.jar from within your lib/java directory. Whew! Quite a bit of setup, but it will pay off when we sketch out our GUI in Matisse. Let's do that now.

User Interface

Expand the Source Packages list under the project name. Right-click the bookie package and choose New → JFrame Form.... Type *Bookie* for the form name, and then click Finish. NetBeans will open a layout screen that should look something like Figure 10.2, on the next page.

The gray rectangle in the middle of main screen is the new GUI layout. This is where you'll drag controls from the palette. Let's start with the Split Pane, since it will contain most of the other components. Drag a Split Pane from the palette into the layout area. Resize it until it fills up

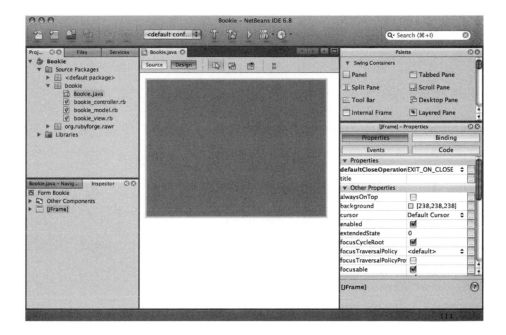

Figure 10.2: THE MATISSE GUI EDITOR

almost the entire rectangle, leaving only a thin strip along the bottom big enough for a button. As you do this, notice that Matisse helps you snap the component to the nearest edge of the window.

At this point, you have two huge buttons with a splitter between them. Don't panic—the buttons are just placeholders, which we'll soon fill in with real controls. The first of these will be the chapter list. Drag a List from the palette onto the left button. Matisse will replace the button with the new control.

Filling in the other half of the layout follows a similar process. Drag a Tabbed Pane onto the right button. It won't have any tabs at first; these will get created automatically as you drag controls into the middle of it. Go ahead and do that now. You'll need a Text Pane for the first tab and an Editor Pane for the second. (You may need to scroll down in the palette to find these controls.)

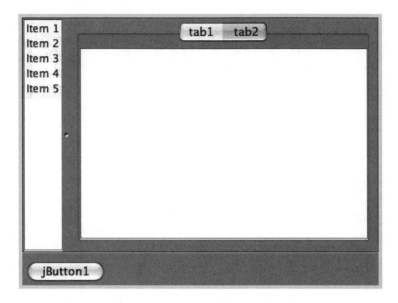

Figure 10.3: THE GUI LAYOUT

You're almost done with the GUI. Drag a Button into the lower-left cor-
ner of the layout. You should now have something that looks like Figure 10.3.

At this point, we have nearly the same layout as our previous incarna-
tions of Bookie. The controls don't have the right labels, though, and
we need a little plumbing to connect to Ruby. Before we get to that, let's
take a peek behind the veil and see what Matisse has done for us.

Click the Source button above the layout, and you'll see a file of Java
code. Inside the listing, click the + just to the left of the words Generated
Code. The text will expand to show you the generated Swing layout
code. This is what Matisse has saved you the drudgery of writing.

One thing you may notice in the generated code is that the variable
names are pretty generic: jSplitPane1, jScrollPane1, and so on. Let's change
those to something a little more developer-friendly.

Click the Design button to get back to the layout view. Select the list
control you created a minute ago. In the bottom-right area of the Net-
Beans window, you should see a Properties pane for the list. Inside this
pane, click the Code button. You should see a property called Variable

Name. Double-click its value (jList1), and change it to chapters. If you then go back and view the generated source, you'll see that the variable name has now changed.

Using the same method, change the variable names for the following GUI components:

- jTabbedPane1 (click the gray area just above the tabs): Change to tabs.
- jTextArea1 (click the first tab and then the white area underneath): Change to edit.
- jEditPane1 (click the second tab and then the white area underneath): Change to preview.
- jButton1: Change to add_chapter.

While we're at it, let's change the tab names. Click the first tab, wait for a second, and click it again. Change the name to *Edit*. Do the same for the second tab, which you'll call *Preview*, and for the button, which you'll call *Add Chapter*. You're in the home stretch now—just a few more properties to set.

In the previous sections, we had to pass certain parameters into our controls when we created them. For example, we had to pass a Default-ListController into the JList constructor. We'll need to wire up the same kinds of code-related properties in Matisse.

Select the chapter list inside the layout, and then in the Properties window click the Properties button. In the row containing the model property, click the ... button to the right of the value. A dialog will appear; choose Custom code, and enter the following:

```
new javax.swing.DefaultListModel()
```

Once you've closed the dialog box, look right below the model property to find selectionMode. Change it to SINGLE. Now, you'll need to make a similar round of changes to the Preview window (the white area in the second tab):

- document: Custom code, preview.getEditorKit().createDefaultDocument().
- editable: Uncheck this option.
- editorKit: Custom code, new javax.swing.text.html.HTMLEditorKit().

With those changes, we're done with the layout and can finally add some Ruby code. Before we do, though, let's go back over a couple of key observations about this process. First, using the graphical editor has made it easy to get our layout drawn clearly. But once the initial sketch was done, the baroque details of Swing API started to rear their heads again.

For this project, the speed of creating a nice interface was worth the few extra seconds ferreting around in the property dialogs. This may not be the case for all projects, though. Fortunately, the method for hooking Monkeybars up to a GUI is the same, no matter whether that GUI was generated from Matisse or written by hand.

Kicking the Tires

Before we give life to all these controls, let's add just enough Ruby code to get the app running. The first thing Monkeybars needs is the name of the GUI class you drew in NetBeans. Open src/bookie/bookie_view.rb, and change the set_java_class line so that the contents of the file look like this:

```
class BookieView < ApplicationView
  set_java_class 'bookie.Bookie'

  # The rest of your view code will go here.
end
```

Now, in src/main.rb, search for the line that says Your application code goes here. Replace that line with the following:

guis/monkeybars/src/main.rb

```
BookieController.instance.open
```

The program needs to know where to find the definition of BookieController. By convention, Monkeybars apps keep this information in src/manifest.rb. Open this file, and add the following lines to the end:

guis/monkeybars/src/manifest.rb

```
add_to_load_path '../src/bookie'
require 'bookie_controller'
```

That's all you need to run the app. Click the Run button in the toolbar. If NetBeans asks you to select a main class, choose org.rubyforge.rawr.Main. You should see something resembling the other two versions of this app you've written. If you get an error message, retrace your earlier steps to make sure all the variables and properties are set correctly.

Everything up and running? Great! Let's get to the code.

Model, View, and Controller

As we mentioned, Monkeybars is an MVC framework. Over the next few pages, we'll look at each of these components in turn.

Model

Let's look at the model first, since it contains no dependencies on Monkeybars. It's just a Plain Ol' Ruby Object (PORO). Replace the contents of src/bookie/bookie_model.rb with the following:

guis/monkeybars/src/bookie/bookie_model.rb

```ruby
class BookieModel
  attr_reader    :chapters
  attr_accessor :text, :index

  def initialize
    @chapters = ['']
    @text = ''
    @index = 0
  end

  def add_chapter
    @chapters << ''
    switch_to_chapter @chapters.size - 1
  end

  def switch_to_chapter(new_index)
    @chapters[@index], @text = @text, @chapters[new_index]
    @index = new_index
  end
end
```

This code is similar to what you've written in the previous exercises. But notice one key difference: there is no reference of any kind to the GUI or to Monkeybars. This is just a simple class that holds a list of chapters, plus an index and text denoting the currently selected chapter. All the knowledge of the GUI is in the view and the controller.

View

Let's turn to the view. All the modifications you'll make to src/bookie/bookie_view.rb will go inside the BookieView class you edited a moment ago. Go ahead and add the first connection to the GUI:

guis/monkeybars/src/bookie/bookie_view.rb

```ruby
map :view  => 'edit.text',
    :model => 'text'
```

This code tells Monkeybars how to set the contents of the Edit window from the model. Whenever it's time to update the view in response to some action from the user, Monkeybars will run the equivalent of this:

```
edit.text = model.text
```

The Preview window takes its content from the model's text property as well. But we need to process it to HTML before sending it to the control. The :using option in Monkeybars is meant for exactly this kind of filtering:

guis/monkeybars/src/bookie/bookie_view.rb

```
map :view  => 'preview.text',
    :model => 'text',
    :using => ['redcloth', nil]

def redcloth(text)
  RedCloth.new(text).to_html
end
```

The nil parameter, by the way, refers to data going the other direction: from the GUI back into the model. Since this is not an editable window, we don't care about fetching data from the GUI.

For the view to find the RedCloth library, we're going to have to copy some code into the project directory. The easiest way to do this is with the gem unpack command, followed by a rename. We'll just show the UNIX version of this, because the Windows version is similar (move instead of mv):

```
$ jruby -S gem unpack RedCloth --target=lib/ruby
$ mv lib/ruby/RedCloth-4.2.3-universal-java lib/ruby/redcloth
```

Then you'll need to add these lines at the end of src/manifest.rb to tell it to load the library:

guis/monkeybars/src/manifest.rb

```
add_to_load_path '../lib/ruby/redcloth/lib'
require 'redcloth'
```

Now, here's the code to connect the currently selected chapter in the GUI (chapters.selection_model.single_index) to the currently selected chapter in the model (index):

guis/monkeybars/src/bookie/bookie_view.rb

```
map :view  => 'chapters.selection_model.single_index',
    :model => 'index'
```

Swing list selections don't really have a single_index property. But thanks to Ruby's on-the-fly programmability, we can add one. Put the following code in src/swing_ext.rb:

guis/monkeybars/src/swing_ext.rb

```ruby
java_import javax.swing.DefaultListModel
java_import javax.swing.DefaultListSelectionModel

class DefaultListSelectionModel
  def single_index
    get_min_selection_index
  end

  def single_index=(i)
    set_selection_interval i, i
  end
end
```

...and add this line to the end of manifest.rb:

guis/monkeybars/src/manifest.rb

```ruby
require 'swing_ext'
```

We've just connected the model's and the view's notions of the currently selected chapter. But what about the array of chapter names that populate the list? That's a separate connection. Like the HTML preview, this new connection needs an intermediary layer to translate between Ruby arrays and Swing DefaultListModels:

guis/monkeybars/src/bookie/bookie_view.rb

```ruby
map :view  => 'chapters.model',
    :model => 'chapters',
    :using => ['list_items', nil]

def list_items(chapters)
  items = DefaultListModel.new
  1.upto(chapters.size).each { |n| items.add_element n }
  items
end
```

The trinity is nearly complete. We just need to teach Bookie how to react to mouse clicks from the user. This behavior will go into the controller.

Controller

The BookieController class inside src/bookie/bookie_controller.rb defines the controller. The code generator placed a nearly empty class in that file

Tom Says...

Why Do We Have to Update the View Explicitly?

Relying on update_view is an intentional design decision of the Monkeybars team. In traditional MVC applications, views would automatically get updated whenever a model would change. Once an application gets really large, these updates can be frequent and unpredictable—especially if one model has complex relationships with another model. Giving the developer control makes updates easier to manage. There is, however, a shortcut for the cases when you know it's OK for Monkeybars to call update_view automatically: just append ! to the method name.

for you. All the mods you'll make will go inside that existing class definition. Let's start with the handler for the Add Chapter button:

`guis/monkeybars/src/bookie/bookie_controller.rb`

```
def add_chapter_action_performed
  model.text = view_model.text
  model.add_chapter
  update_view
end
```

This snippet highlights one of the most convenient aspects of Monkeybars programming. The act of defining a function with this exact name means that Monkeybars will automatically call add_event_listener on the add_chapter button for us. This shortcut follows a "convention over configuration" philosophy similar to the Ruby on Rails framework.

In the body of the event handler, we save the contents of the Edit window into the current chapter and then tell the model to add a new one. All of our event handlers will call update_view when they're done with their work.

The next event handler is for when the user selects a different chapter:

`guis/monkeybars/src/bookie/bookie_controller.rb`

```
def chapters_value_changed(e)
  unless e.value_is_adjusting
    new_index = e.source.get_selected_index
    old_index = [e.first_index, e.last_index].find { |i| i != new_index }
```

```
    if new_index >= 0 && old_index
      model.text = view_model.text
      model.switch_to_chapter new_index
      update_view
    end
  end
end
```

After making sure we're actually switching chapters and not just receiving one of those extra Swing notifications, we follow a similar flow to what we did before. We grab the text of the Edit window, update the model, and tell the view to update the controls.

We need just one more event handler. When the user switches from one tab to another, we need to update the Preview window.

guis/monkeybars/src/bookie/bookie_controller.rb

```
def tabs_state_changed(e)
  model.text = view_model.text
  update_view
end
```

Technically, we need to update only if we're switching *to* the Preview window. Feel free to add that optimization, if you want.

There's a lot more to Monkeybars than we have time for here. But you've at least had a chance to see how it helps you split up the responsibilities of your code in an MVC-like fashion. In particular, the business logic in your Ruby domain models can be kept separate from the GUI.

10.5 Limelight

And now for something completely different. Up to this point, we've considered frameworks of varying levels of abstraction. But even the most helpful frameworks still expose us to some of Swing's gory details.

Limelight is a radical departure from the other frameworks. Although it uses a few Swing classes for things like menus, most of the drawing is done directly onto a canvas object. The result is that Limelight has only a minimal connection to Swing.

Limelight uses a theater metaphor for the various parts of your program. Here are its main concepts:

Production: Your application

Stage: A top-level window (what Swing would call a *frame*)

Theater: A collection of stages

Prop: Any visible component of the UI

Player: A prop that also has behavior[6]

Scene: A collection of props that can be loaded into a stage

Cute, huh? Even if you're not normally a fan of these kinds of extended metaphors, we'd like you to suspend your disbelief (hey, another theater expression!) for a few pages. Consider how these concepts might apply to a program. Imagine you're writing a hardware configuration wizard. You'd use one theater with a single stage, because wizards are typically single-window programs. Each time the user advances through a step, you'd cycle to the next scene, which would have its own props and players. During development, you'll spend most of your time in scenes, laying out props and players.

Limelight's other big feature is its style system, which is influenced by the Cascading Style Sheets (CSS) used on web pages. When you construct a prop, you change colors, borders, gradients, and other visual properties by editing a style file. Warning: this can lead to addictive hacking sessions where you spend hours tinkering with your app's appearance. But it also gives you a huge level of customization. We'll be counting on that as we try to make the Limelight version of Bookie look like the other versions.

Like Monkeybars, Limelight is an opinionated software framework with a "convention over configuration" aspect inspired by Rails. When you create a new production (or join someone else's), the code will have a familiar directory layout and naming convention.

Before we get to writing apps, we'd like to show you how to launch Playbills, the gallery of demo productions that ships with Limelight:

```
$ jruby -S gem install limelight
$ jruby -S limelight open
```

One of the more compelling demos in the gallery is Limelight Docs, the API browser/interactive tutorial. This is more than just a collection of passive code snippets; you can edit and rerun the examples right there in the app. Of course, both Playbills and Limelight Docs were written using Limelight.

---

6. Is that what directors think of their actors?

Production

Normally, you'd create a new Limelight app by creating a production and populating it with a scene:

```
$ jruby -S limelight create production bookie
$ cd bookie
$ jruby -S limelight create scene bookie
```

But like the cooking-show parody in the abridged version of *Titus Andronicus*, we're going to haul a fully baked pie out from under the counter instead.[7] Why are we taking a shortcut? Because Limelight programs tend to be quite a bit longer than their counterparts in other frameworks. That's the downside of all that customizability. You can still see the full source code by thumbing ahead to Appendix F, on page 315 or by downloading it from the book's web page.[8]

Once you have a bookie directory containing the entire project, you can launch the app from inside that directory by using the open command:

```
$ jruby -S limelight open .
```

A screenshot of the finished app appears in Figure 10.4, on the following page. The colors and styles are reminiscent of a more conventional Swing app, but this version definitely has its own distinctive look.

To see how we arrived at that look, let's go through some of the more prominent files in the project structure. First, peek inside production.rb. In a new Limelight project, this would contain lots of commented-out examples of how to attach Ruby code to various phases of the application's life cycle.

We've edited it down to the one hook Bookie needs:

guis/limelight/bookie/production.rb
```ruby
module Production
  attr_reader :chapter_contents

  def production_opening
    require 'redcloth'
    @chapter_contents = [{:title => '1', :text => ''}]
  end
end
```

---

7. See *The Compleat Works Of Wllm Shkspr (Abridged)* [BLS94].
8. http://pragprog.com/titles/jruby/source_code

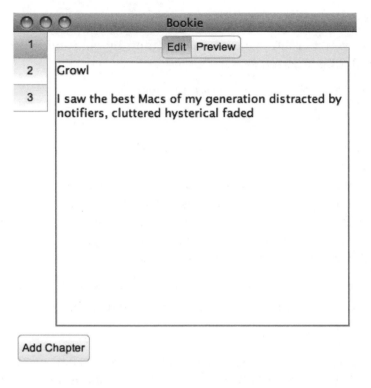

Figure 10.4: BOOKIE IN LIMELIGHT

The production_opening hook runs at startup, which gives us the chance to bring in the libraries we need and do some initialization. Notice that we've also added an attr_accessor to make the list of chapters visible from our players and props.

The second file to look at is stages.rb. Limelight has defined a default scene for us. We need to make our bookie scene the default instead:

guis/limelight/bookie/stages.rb

```
stage 'default' do
  default_scene 'bookie'
  title 'Bookie'
  location [200, 25]
  size [400, 400]
end
```

Notice that this file uses a concise, readable syntax to describe the stage. You'll find nice touches like this throughout Limelight.

Scene and Props

Now let's go through the various props and players in the bookie scene. First, there is the props.rb file:

guis/limelight/bookie/bookie/props.rb

```ruby
root do
  center do
    chapter_list :id => 'chapter_list'
    dual_pane :id => 'dual_pane' do
      tabs do
        tabs_shadow
        tabs_holder do
          tab_button :text           => 'Edit',
                     :id             => 'edit_tab',
                     :on_mouse_clicked => 'scene.dual_pane.edit!',
                     :styles         => 'left_tab'
          tab_button :text           => 'Preview',
                     :id             => 'preview_tab',
                     :on_mouse_clicked => 'scene.dual_pane.preview!',
                     :styles         => 'right_tab'
        end
      end
      preview_pane :id => 'preview_pane'
      edit_pane :players => 'text_area',
      :id => 'edit_pane'
    end
  end
  add_chapter :text => 'Add Chapter'
end
```

This file spells out the GUI controls in the app. The structure of the code mirrors the nested relationships among all the props in the scene. Props can have attributes, either stock ones that come with Limelight (such as :on_mouse_clicked) or custom ones we define (such as :id). You'll notice there's no information on size, location, or color. How does Limelight know where and how to draw these? It uses information from styles.rb.

The style file is typically a scene's largest file. It's also the one you'll spend most of your time in. We're not going to do a line-by-line explication here. Instead, we'll just take a close look at the tab control.

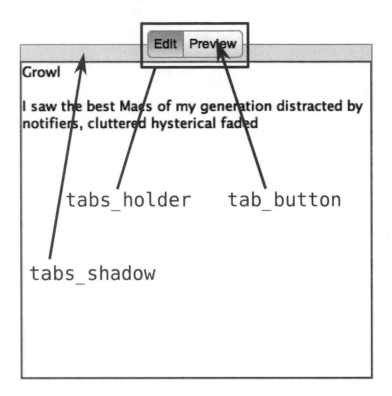

Figure 10.5: BOOKIE IN LIMELIGHT

The following code is an excerpt from the props.rb file we saw a moment ago, stripped down to just the structure of the tabs:

```
tabs do
  tabs_shadow
  tabs_holder do
    tab_button # Edit button
    tab_button # Preview button
  end
  edit_pane
  preview_pane
end
```

Compare this code with Figure 10.5. Each object corresponds to a graphical element in the screenshot. Most of these connections are obvious, but what about tabs and tabs_holder? Well, tabs is just the whole screenshot. tabs_holder is a container that wraps the two tab buttons. We've added this prop to make layout easier.

Let's look at its style code:

guis/limelight/bookie/bookie/styles.rb

```
tabs_holder {
  extends :fill_parent
  float :on
  y '15%'
  x '37%'
}
```

This is one of the more intricate styles in the project, so we'll go over it line by line. Starting at the bottom and working our way up, we see a relative x and y position that will keep the buttons nicely centered no matter the window size.

The next line up, float :on, resembles the CSS property of the same name. It allows the tab holder to overlap other controls. Here, we want to overlap the tab shadow to make the entire section look like a cohesive unit.

Finally, we come to extends :fill_parent. This notation is Limelight's way of sharing common styles. Several of Bookie's props need to expand to fill their containers. So, we've defined a common fill_parent style at the top of the file:

guis/limelight/bookie/bookie/styles.rb

```
fill_parent {
  width '100%'
  height '100%'
}
```

We'll show just one more style example before moving on: the rounded corners of the right tab button.

guis/limelight/bookie/bookie/styles.rb

```
right_tab {
  top_right_rounded_corner_radius 4
  top_right_border_width 1
  bottom_right_rounded_corner_radius 4
  bottom_right_border_width 1
  left_border_width 0
  right_border_width 1
  top_border_width 1
  bottom_border_width 1
}
```

You can see how the right side of the button has a rounded border on both corners, while the left side has no border at all (because that's where the left tab button is). The code is straightforward but verbose. Unlike the CSS syntax that inspired it, Limelight requires you to put each style on its own line.

We encourage you to look through the rest of the styles file to see how the scene is laid out. When you're ready to move on, catch the debut of our scene's players in the next section.

Players

Players are just props that happen to contain behavior. There are in fact two different types of players: built-in and user-defined. The built-in types are the usual suspects: buttons, text areas, and so on. The user-defined ones are for things like tab controls, where we've had to write custom code to show and hide each tab. Let's just look at a simple control for now: the Add Chapter button.

The button's definition in props.rb is spartan, and its code in styles.rb only defines its look. Where is its behavior? Limelight organizes player behavior in a scene's players directory. The convention is one file per player, with one Ruby module inside it—both of them named after the player. For instance, the behavior for the Add Chapter player goes into the AddChapter module defined in players/add_chapter.rb.

guis/limelight/bookie/bookie/players/add_chapter.rb

```ruby
module AddChapter
  def mouse_clicked(e)
    contents    = production.chapter_contents
    title       = (contents.length + 1).to_s
    new_content = {:title => title, :text => ''}
    contents << new_content

    scene.chapter_list.repopulate
  end
end
```

There is only one method in here, mouse_clicked. You don't have to do anything special to hook this code up to the mouse; Limelight knows to look for it by name. These kinds of implicit callbacks make reacting to user input a snap, even for custom components.[9]

---

9. Limelight supports this style for several other events, including mouse_clicked, mouse_entered, mouse_exited, mouse_pressed, mouse_released, mouse_dragged, mouse_moved,

At the end of the callback, we find the bookie scene and tell its chapter_list prop to repopulate itself with the updated chapter contents.

Sometimes you have behavior that is common to more than one prop. For example, both the Edit and Preview buttons need to tell the tab control to switch tabs. For this case, we've put the common code into a prop type called DualPane and specified a couple of its method names directly in props.rb:

guis/limelight/bookie/bookie/props.rb

```
tab_button :text              => 'Edit',
           :id                => 'edit_tab',
           :on_mouse_clicked  => 'scene.dual_pane.edit!',
           :styles            => 'left_tab'
tab_button :text              => 'Preview',
           :id                => 'preview_tab',
           :on_mouse_clicked  => 'scene.dual_pane.preview!',
           :styles            => 'right_tab'
```

Each of these two buttons asks the dual_pane prop to execute a different method. Note that props can find one another through the scene attribute. You may be wondering whether you can put any arbitrary code into props.rb. Indeed, you can. You could put all your styles and behavior into this file, but we don't recommend it. We suggest using this kind of inlining for the simplest cases only.

In truth, we have only scratched the surface of Limelight, but we hope you have a foothold in understanding how its parts fit together.

10.6 Wrapping Up

GUI development is an area of JRuby programming that grows more exciting daily as new toolkits pop up. Mainstream Ruby's lack of a strong cross-platform GUI is one reason people are migrating to JRuby.

Once you've decided to use Swing, you still have find the right Ruby framework to use with it. Let's consider the frameworks we've looked at and try to identify why you might find each one appealing.

Raw Swing is for the programmers from Java-land who prefer not to use any fancy Rubyisms beyond the ones they supply. They are perfectly

---

key_typed, key_pressed, key_released, focus_gained, focus_lost, button_pressed, and value_changed.

Tom Says...

A Time-Saving Scene

In our complete Bookie example, we have an additional scene called devtool, with a single button labeled Refresh. We used this scene as we wrote the example code. Every time we tweaked our layout or styling, we'd click the button to update the bookie scene with the latest changes. This was much faster than exiting and restarting the app.

To run Bookie with this debug helper enabled, set the BOOKIE_DEV environment variable before launching:

```
$ BOOKIE_DEV=1 jruby -S limelight open .
```

Adapting this tool to your own Limelight productions is easy; just copy the code and point it at the scene you're developing. It's a huge time-saver.

happy developing their own ad hoc frameworks to suit their needs. After all, "not invented here" is a valid critique if the alternative is staring at an error log, wondering which incantation will pacify a framework.

Rubeus is for those who want a little of Ruby's brevity to help cut out Swing boilerplate but who still feel comfortable with the Swing APIs. They're fine with organizing the components and code for large projects on their own—just as they did in Java.

Monkeybars provides answers for a lot of code structure questions but still requires a healthy amount of Swing knowledge. Like Rails, it emphasizes strict boundaries between the model, view, and controller—which makes it especially appealing for large UI applications. Its easy integration with RAD tools like NetBeans Matisse is another compelling point.

Limelight is the least Swing-like of the frameworks. The easy organization and offbeat metaphors are reminiscent of Shoes, the beloved GUI toolkit from the C Ruby world.[10] This independence is a double-edged

10. http://github.com/shoes/shoes

sword. On the plus side, you might not need to crack open a single Swing reference manual while you're writing your app. On the minus side, you're going to have a hard time integrating existing Swing components like the Flying Saucer HTML renderer or the WorldWind map viewer.

We hope you've enjoyed touring the JRuby universe with us. We've been through a lot together, from tentative first steps with the language through the best of Ruby and Java. Please visit the forums to let us know how your journey went and what you're building with JRuby.[11] Happy coding!

---

11. http://forums.pragprog.com/forums/125

Part III

Reference

Ruby 101

Remember that JRuby at its heart is just Ruby, so you'll get the most out of JRuby by having a little knowledge of the language. That's our aim for this chapter: to give a quick overview of Ruby from a Java programmer's perspective. For a much more detailed look, see a dedicated book on Ruby such as the "Pickaxe" (*Programming Ruby: The Pragmatic Programmers' Guide* [TFH08]).

A.1   Meet Ruby

We're going to start with the high-level view as we answer the question "What is Ruby like?"

Ruby Is Dynamic and Strong

Ruby is often described as being a member of the family of dynamic languages. What do we mean by *dynamic*? Computer-language enthusiasts use the term to explain type systems. A statically typed language like Java knows the types of a program's variables at compile time, long before the program runs. With a dynamic language, a variable's type can't usually be known until runtime. Consider the following similar-looking snippets:

```
// Java:
int price;
price = 10;            // OK
price = "a chicken";  // compile-time error

# Ruby:
price = 10          # OK
price = "a chicken" # OK
```

The main difference that immediately sticks out is that the Java variable has a declared type, and the compiler forces assignments to conform to that type. By contrast, you don't declare variables in Ruby; you just start using them.

It may be tempting to think that Ruby has no types at all, but nothing could be further from the truth. Even though *variables* don't have types in Ruby, *values* most certainly do! In both Ruby and Java, you can find out a value's type easily:

```
// Java:
"Fred".getClass().getName(); // => java.lang.String
```

```
# Ruby:
"Fred".class.name # => String
```

As you can see, the "Fred" object has a type called String in both Java and Ruby. Each type supports a specific list of operations; for strings, that'd include combining, searching, capitalizing, and so on. In both languages, trying to take the square root of a string would cause an error; you'd have to convert it to a different type first. For this reason, both Java and Ruby are known as strongly typed languages.

We should mention one other thing about variable declarations. In Ruby, there's no need to ever declare a variable without giving it a value, as is sometimes done in Java. Instead, a variable is implicitly declared the first time it is given a value. What happens if you refer to a variable before it has been assigned a value?

```
a = 1
puts a
# >> 1
puts b
# >> undefined local variable or method `b' for main:Object (NameError)
```

While we're on the subject of variable visibility, Ruby's if statement has the curious property that variables inside it are visible from outside. In programming-language parlance, it doesn't introduce a new scope.

```
cat = 'The cat lives outdoors'

if 2 + 2 == 4
  cat += ' but can be seen indoors'
  dog = 'The dog lives indoors'
end

dog += ' but can be seen outdoors'
```

```
puts cat
# >> The cat lives outdoors but can be seen indoors

puts dog
# >> The dog lives indoors but can be seen outdoors
```

One consequence of Ruby's dynamic nature is that many errors that would be considered compile errors in Java code are not revealed until you run your program.

Everything Is an Object

You'll recognize many of Ruby's object-oriented features from your experience with Java. Objects are instances of classes, which can be built-in or user-defined. Objects embody both state (instance variables) and behavior (methods). A program manipulates objects by calling methods —which Ruby also refers to as *sending messages*.

However, Ruby takes this notion further than other object-oriented languages, including Java. How? Well, it's common to hear that in Ruby "Everything is an object." That includes the primitive, built-in types that come with the language:

```
"123".to_i # => 123
123.to_s   # => "123"
true.to_s  # => "true"
nil.to_s   # => ""

"123".nil? # => false
nil.nil?   # => true
```

Have you ever tried calling a method on null in Java?

Everything Has a Value

As we saw in the previous section, everything in Ruby is an object. You can call methods on anything—even things such as numbers, booleans, and class definitions. Another "universal Ruby law" is that everything you do in Ruby returns a value.

Java makes the distinction between expressions (which return values) and statements (which don't). In Ruby, there is no such distinction. Everything returns a value—not always a terribly useful one but definitely something. Even a class definition has a return value!

This feature of Ruby comes in handy with conditional expressions. Consider the following Java fragment:

```java
// Java:
String result = "";

switch (getNumberFromSomewhere()) {
case 2:  result = "twins";        break;
case 3:  result = "triplets";     break;
case 4:  result = "quadruplets";  break;
default: result = "unknown";      break;
}

System.out.println(result);
```

...and its Ruby equivalent:

```ruby
# Ruby:
puts case get_number_from_somewhere
     when 2 then 'twins'
     when 3 then 'triplets'
     when 4 then 'quadruplets'
     else         'unknown'
     end
```

Since a switch statement in Java can't return a value, the Java example has to set aside a variable to store the result so we can print it. In Ruby, cases are expressions and will return the last value mentioned in whichever branch got taken. Since we don't need to save away a value in a variable, it's actually possible to just pass the entire case expression as an argument to puts. This looks really weird if you haven't seen it before but will soon become second nature.

A.2 A Closer Look

Now, let's take a closer look at the Ruby language. We'll cover how to accomplish the most common programming tasks. Along the way, we'll look for both similarities and differences from Java.

Defining Classes

Ruby is a class-based object-oriented language. This means that all objects must be of exactly one class. Unlike Java, you can create classes and add or remove methods at any time—even while your program is running.

Ruby is also a single-inheritance language (although that is not the full story). In Ruby, just like in Java, every class has exactly one parent class, or superclass. If you don't specify one, it will be Object.

So, everything is an object, and all objects must have a class. Does that mean classes have a class too? Yes, and (as you might have guessed) it's called Class. And like all classes, Class has a superclass—it's called Module, and we'll encounter it in a little while.

Have we tied you in a knot with all this abstract talk? Let's breathe some life into these lofty concepts with some real code. Imagine you want to keep track of all the various ways to reach your authors: by phone, mail, and so on. In this admittedly contrived example, you might define a class called Locator that could represent a phone number or street address:

```ruby
class Locator
  def initialize(location)
    @location = location
  end
end
```

Any Ruby method named initialize acts like a Java constructor: Ruby calls this method automatically for each new object. Unlike Java constructors, Ruby initializers are inherited. When we get around to defining PhoneNumber and Address classes, we won't need to write initializers for them—they'll use Locator's version automatically, unless we tell them otherwise.

There is only one line of code in this method, but it's an important one. It creates a new instance variable called @location and assigns the value of the incoming location argument to it. As with the other variables we've seen so far in this appendix, you don't need to declare Ruby instance variables. They just spring into being the first time you assign something to them, as we're doing here. We are making sure that every Locator that gets created will have an instance variable called @location.

By itself, Locator isn't terribly useful. Let's define a couple of kinds of locators:

```ruby
class PhoneNumber < Locator
  def valid?
    @location =~ /^\d{3}-\d{3}-\d{4}$/
  end
end
```

```
class Address < Locator
  def valid?
    @location =~ /^\d+ .+$/
  end
end
```

Both PhoneNumber and Address are defined to be subclasses of Locator, which we indicate with the left angle bracket after the class name. The next line of each class defines a method called valid?. The trailing question mark is a Ruby convention that says this method is intended to be used as a boolean.

The body of each valid? method checks whether the contents of the @location variable match a particular pattern. The pattern, given in a regular-expression syntax similar to java.util.regex.Pattern, does some extremely basic verification. Phone numbers will match if they conform to the typical U.S. format (DDD-DDD-DDDD). Addresses are expected to contain one or more digits, a space, and then one or more characters.

The =~ operator (also called the *match* operator) returns a number if it finds a match and returns nil if it doesn't. Because Ruby treats all numbers (even zero!) as true and nil as false, we just return the match result from the function.

Finally, we can get to the definition of a Person:

```
class Person
  def initialize
    @locators = []
  end

  def add_phone_number string
    number = PhoneNumber.new(string)
    @locators << number if number.valid?
  end

  def add_address string
    address = Address.new(string)
    @locators << address if address.valid?
  end
end
```

To be sure that we have somewhere to store all the locators for a person, we use an initialize method to create an @locators instance variable and set it to an empty array.

This class also has a couple of methods to add phone numbers and addresses. Let's look at the first of those, add_phone_number. Inside it, we create a new PhoneNumber object by calling new. Recall that this will cause Ruby to call the new object's inherited initialize method for us, with the same parameters we pass to new.

We store the freshly created object in a new local variable called number, which, like an instance variable, springs into being the first time we set it to something. We use the << operator to append the new object to our list—but only if it's valid (note the trailing if expression).

Here's how you might use the code from this project:

```
ola = Person.new

# The following locators get added,
# because they're in the right format:
ola.add_phone_number '555-231-4555'
ola.add_address("1 Did It My Way")

# The following locator gets ignored,
# because it's not a valid US phone number:
ola.add_phone_number '42'
```

We have deliberately written this code with a variety of punctuation choices. Some method definitions or calls have parentheses, and some don't. Some strings use single quotes, and others use double quotes. Ruby's flexible syntax allows you to use whichever style suits your program best.

Defining and Calling Methods

We've seen a couple of method definitions already. Let's dive a little deeper into the subject.

Class Methods

So far, we've only seen instance methods: methods that act on a single instance of an object. What about static methods, which belong to the entire class instead of one object? Doesn't Ruby have those?

Yes and no. Ruby has something that looks and acts similar to Java's static methods. It's called a *class method*. There are multiple ways to define one, but the most popular ways are to name it self.method_name or ClassName.method_name.

Here's how those two styles would look for defining something like a factory method for our Person class:

`ruby_101/class_method.rb`

```
class Person
  def self.with_address_and_phone_number(addr, ph)
    p = Person.new
    p.add_address(addr)
    p.add_phone_number(ph)
    p
  end
end

# The following can appear between "class Person ..." and "end",
# or it can stand alone, outside the class definition.
#
def Person.with_address_and_phone_number(addr, ph)
  # ...
end
```

As you can see, this looks just like a static method. But really, it's just a regular method. Instead of belonging to an individual Person, it belongs to the Person class. Remember, classes are objects, too—that means they can have methods attached to them.

While we're on the subject of method definition, note that you can redefine methods in Ruby if you want. Both of the previous definitions could be placed in the same program, and Ruby wouldn't complain. You can also modify class definitions. For instance, you could have multiple class Person ... end sections in your program, even some that might or might not execute based on a runtime condition. That isn't something you'd do in a typical program, but it can be a big help if you're trying to extend Ruby itself.

Method Arguments

Ruby methods can take zero or more arguments. Instead of overloading methods, Ruby allows methods to take optional arguments (with a default value). You can also create methods that take an arbitrary number of arguments. An argument like that is usually called a *rest argument*.

Regular arguments are separated by commas, as you've already seen. To create a method that takes optional arguments, you use the equal sign:

```ruby
def you_gave_me(present = nil)
  present
end

you_gave_me            # => nil
you_gave_me "a pony" # => "a pony"
```

This method takes one optional argument. If the argument is not supplied, present will contain nil. You can have several optional arguments and even default values that are calculated. In the following example, we use the first argument to calculate the default value for the second one.

```ruby
def area(width = 10, height = 2 * width)
  width * height
end

area        # => 200
area 5      # => 50
area 5, 20 # => 100
```

Ruby also has a way of taking an arbitrary amount of arguments, like Java's varargs. You define a rest argument using the asterisk:

```ruby
def quote(person, *words)
  person + ' says: "' + words.join(' ') + '"'
end

quote 'Ola'                      # => "Ola says: \"\""
quote 'Ola', 'keep', 'coding!' # => "Ola says: \"keep coding!\""
```

As you can see, the asterisk takes all the remaining arguments and squishes them into an array called words. The asterisk can also perform the opposite action: expanding an array into individual arguments for a method. Consider the following function that requires three arguments:

```ruby
def something(needs, three, arguments)
  'Yay!'
end

my_array = ['one', 'two', 'three']

something(my_array)  # ~> ArgumentError
something(*my_array) # => 'Yay'
```

This feature is called *splatting*, after the asterisk's nickname. It's very handy, so you'll see it used all over the place.

Common Ruby Types

Just as you would expect, the Ruby language and core library include a large number of built-in types. We're just going to take a look at the core data types that you'll need to understand to get going with Ruby.

Numbers

Ruby uses three main classes to represent numbers: Float, Fixnum, and Bignum. As you've no doubt guessed from its name, Float is for standard IEEE floating-point numbers. The other two are for integer types: fixed-size (for example, 32-bit) and arbitrarily large, respectively. Ruby will automatically use the "right size" type for each integer value.

Strings

Matz took a great deal of inspiration from Perl when he created Ruby. In particular, Ruby shares Perl's excellent text-manipulation abilities. Many of these powers are vested in the String class. Have a peek at the official documentation for this class, and you'll see a lot of operations with useful, self-explanatory names: reverse, capitalize, and so on.[1]

You can create a Ruby string using several different literal syntaxes:

```
one = "hello world"

two = 'is this right?'

three = %["This is a Ruby string, isn't it?" he asked.]

four = <<ARBITRARY_END_MARKER
Here, you can use layout,
white space, "quotes," etc.
ARBITRARY_END_MARKER
```

Notice that you can enclose Ruby strings in either single quotes or double quotes. Double quotes have a few more bells and whistles, such as the simple backslash escape sequences common to many languages (\r, \n, ...).

Ruby supports two more kinds of string literals that can save you a lot of extra backslashes and quote marks. The first is the %-style quote, which lets you in effect choose your own quote marks. The second is a multiline string called a *heredoc*. It includes everything between the two occurrences of your ARBITRARY_END_MARKER.

---

1. http://ruby-doc.org/core/classes/String.html

Symbols

Ruby's Symbols are a heritage from Lisp. They're a bit like read-only Strings. The difference goes deeper than that, though. When you create a Symbol (by typing a name that begins with a colon), there will exist only one instance of that symbol—no matter how many times you use that name in your program.

```ruby
def exact_same_object?(a, b)
  a.id == b.id
end

# All occurrences of the same Symbol
# share the same instance:

a_class      = :String
another_class = :String

exact_same_object?(a_class, another_class) # => true

# Each string literal creates its own
# separate instance of String:

fake_cheese = "String"
cat_toy     = "String"

exact_same_object?(fake_cheese, cat_toy)   # => false
```

You'll typically use Strings for things that your user will see and Symbols for things that the rest of your Ruby program will see: class names, method names, database columns, and so on.

Regular Expressions

Another part of Ruby's Perl heritage is its extremely good support for regular expressions. These allow you to succinctly describe the structure of a piece of text and then see whether some string has that structure. You create a Regexp by enclosing your pattern in slashes:

```ruby
pattern = /([^,]+), ([A-Z]{2}) (\d{5})/

if "Portland, OR 97201" =~ pattern
  puts 'Yay, it matches!'
  puts 'City  ' + $1
  puts 'State ' + $2
  puts 'ZIP   ' + $3
end
```

Regular expression syntax is a language all its own. The previous example shows a few common operations. You use square braces to match a single character of a certain kind, plus signs or braces to denote repetition and parentheses to say, "Store this partial match in a variable for later."

Booleans

In Ruby, booleans are just like any other values. They have a class, you can call methods on them, and you can even add your own methods to them.

In Ruby, true is the sole instance of a class called TrueClass, and false is the only instance of FalseClass. The equivalent of Java's null is called nil, and it is the only instance of NilClass.

One important thing to note is that Ruby considers nearly any value "true enough" to satisfy conditional expressions like if. Only false and nil count as false-like values. Rubyists sometimes colloquially refer to this loose definition of truth as "truthiness," in a nod to comedian Steven Colbert.[2]

Just to hammer the point home, consider the following exploration of truthiness in Ruby:

```ruby
def truthy?(value)
  if value then true else false end
end

truthy? true  # => true
truthy? false # => false
truthy? nil   # => false
```

So far, so good. Let's look at a few more surprising cases:

```ruby
truthy? ""   # => true
truthy? []   # => true
truthy? 0    # => true
```

As you can see, even empty strings, empty arrays, and the number zero are truthy in Ruby.

---

2. http://en.wikipedia.org/wiki/Truthiness

Operators and Assignment

Most Ruby operators are just methods with weird names. For example, if an object has a method named +, then that object can participate in expressions like a + b. The only operators that aren't methods are those that are deeply woven into the syntax of Ruby, such as the assignment operator (a single equal sign).

You will recognize many of Java's operators in Ruby, but there are a fair number that may be unfamiliar or at least slightly different from their Java equivalents. They are as follows:

Operator	Description
[], []=	These methods read and write values in collections.
<=>	This method, affectionately called the *spaceship operator*, compares values during searching and sorting—much like the compareTo( ) method of Java's Comparable class does.
===	Ruby's case statement calls this operator to see which branch matches the argument. It's sometimes called the *relationship operator*, because it's more general than equality.
=~, !~	You have already seen the first of these operators. It's used to match a regular expression against a string. The second version is just its inversion; it will return false if it the regular expression matches.
.., ...	These two operators create ranges (usually ranges of numbers). With two dots, the range includes the final element, and with three dots it doesn't.

While we're at it, it's worth mentioning that Ruby does not have the ++ or -- operators that some languages do. Why not? It doesn't fit into the "everything is an object" model. If Ruby allowed these operators, then nonsensical expressions like 4++ would be possible.

Fortunately, that doesn't mean you're stuck typing x = x + 1 all the time. Most binary Ruby operators can be combined with an equal sign and thus become an assignment operator. So, something like x = x * 5 can be more succinctly written as x *= 5.

This ability to combine with = isn't just limited to arithmetic. A very common idiom in Ruby is to use the ||= operator to say, "Assign a value to this variable, but only if it doesn't already have a value."

```
# Assume @foo doesn't exist yet.

@foo ||= 42

puts @foo # >> 42

# The next line will not do anything,
# since @foo already has a true value.

@foo ||= 25

puts @foo # >> 42
```

The &&= operator works much the same, except that it sets the value only if the variable already exists.

Ruby has left-shift and right-shift operators (that's << and >>), just like Java. However, these operators are quite commonly overloaded for other types to mean "append." Both String and Array have versions of << for appending a new value.

Collections

Ruby sports a number of useful collection classes: arrays, hash tables, and so on. Arrays are more or less like java.util.ArrayLists. They support the same kinds of operations: indexing, inserting/removing elements, and so on. Hashes are the equivalent of Java's java.util.HashMap. They represent mappings from keys (of any type) to values.

Arrays are created with square brackets, and hashes are created with curly braces. Both are indexed using square brackets:

```
primes     = [1, 3, 5, 'seven']
composites = [2, 4, 6, 9, 10]
misc       = [0]

# Oops.  We should store 7 as a prime.  Let's fix that:
primes[3] = 7

numbers = {:primes => primes, :composites => misc}

# Oops.  We gave the wrong list for composites.  Let's fix that:
numbers[:composites] = composites
```

You can leave off the curly braces when you're passing a hash in a method call. This lets you get some of the benefits of Python-style keyword arguments:

```ruby
def bio(details)
  for key, value in details
    puts "My #{key} is #{value}."
  end
end

bio :name     => "Nick",
    :location => "Minneapolis",
    :drink    => "tea",
    :quest    => "JRuby"

# Prints:
#   My name is Nick.
#   My location is Minneapolis.
#   My drink is tea.
#   My quest is JRuby.
```

The loop in this example leads us naturally to our next topic: program flow.

Control Structures

You've already seen a few simple examples of Ruby's if expression. In its more complicated incarnation, an if can be followed by any number of elsif clauses and, optionally, one final else. Ruby also has unless, which is the opposite of if. (For clarity's sake, please don't use elsif or else with unless.)

Most Ruby programs don't use lots of elsif conditions. Once you are beyond a couple of conditions, you'll usually want to get the extra flexibility of Ruby's case:

```ruby
def tell_me_about(value)
  case value
  when 0..9
    puts "It's a one-digit number"
  when Fixnum
    puts "It's an integer"
  when /[A-Z]{2}/
    puts "It's two capital letters"
  when String
    puts "It's a string"
  else
    puts "Don't know what it is"
  end
end
```

A case expression checks its argument against each of the when clauses, in the order they're listed. As you can see, you can compare Ruby objects by numeric range, regular-expression match, class name, and more.

Ruby has while loops like Java does. It also has a for loop, but you'll almost never see it in real programs. Instead, Ruby offers something much more powerful: blocks.

Blocks

Blocks are a huge part of Ruby. Basically, they're little chunks of code that you can pass around your program as arguments. You define them by wrapping some code in curly braces or the words do and end. Most people prefer braces for single-line blocks and do/end for multiline blocks (but use your own judgment!):

```
list = [1, 2, 3, 4]

list.each { |n| puts n }

list.each do |n|
  puts n
end
```

This code calls an Array method called each; this method takes a block. each calls the block (also known as *yielding* to it) once for each item in the array.

Like functions, blocks can take arguments. That's the |n| you see in between pipe characters.

It's easy to write your own method that takes a block. You can either explicitly name the final argument as a block by spelling it with a leading ampersand or just call yield from within your method:

```
def yield_thrice(value)
  yield value + 10
  yield value + 20
  yield value + 30
end

def call_thrice(value, &block)
  block.call value + 10
  block.call value + 20
  block.call value + 30
end
```

```
# Both of these will print the numbers 110, 120, and 130:
yield_thrice(100) { |n| puts n }
call_thrice(100)  { |n| puts n }
```

Every time the method yields to the block (via yield or call), the block runs with whichever parameters were passed to it.

Blocks are used all over the place in Ruby, and you will see many of them in this book. If this syntax is new to you, it's worth taking a minute to type in the previous examples and make a few experimental changes to the code to see how blocks work.

Exceptions

Like Java, Ruby has exceptions. Unlike Java, Ruby's exceptions are all unchecked.

The Ruby equivalent of Java's try/catch/finally is begin/rescue/ensure. (Curiously, Ruby also has keywords named try and catch, but they are not related to exceptions at all.)

The following code raises an exception and then rescues it:

```
begin
  puts "Everything's fine so far"
  raise "I'm raising an exception right now"
  puts "Ruby will never run this line"
rescue => e
  puts "My exception says: #{e}"
end
```

This example raises a string, which Ruby is kind enough to wrap up in a RuntimeError object for us. You can define your own exception types if you like. Here's a more advanced example with our own exception class and multiple rescue clauses (Ruby examines these from top to bottom, so make sure you order them from specific to general):

```
class ImCold < RuntimeError
end

begin
  raise ImCold, "Brrr, it's chilly in here!"
rescue ImCold => e
  puts "I'm cold. #{e}"
rescue Exception => e
  puts "Some exception other than ImCold was thrown."
ensure
  puts "This will _always_ print, kinda like Java's finally"
end
```

As you can see, we also used an ensure clause, which Ruby will run no matter what exceptions are raised or rescued.

A.3 Getting the Job Done

You'll eventually come into contact with most of the previous concepts as a natural part of working with Ruby. But you may be wondering about specific getting-started tasks—such as writing text to the screen or loading code from another library. So, let's end this chapter on a light note and talk about these uses.

There are two methods that are most often used to display information in Ruby. The first one is called puts. It calls to_s on its arguments (effectively telling them, "Convert yourself to a string") and then prints the resulting strings to standard output—with each one followed by a newline. puts' slightly more verbose cousin, p, calls inspect on each argument ("Give me some details about yourself") and prints the results to standard error.

Based on these definitions, you've probably deduced that puts is more useful for regular program output and p is more useful for debugging.

That covers a bare minimum of output; how about input? Ruby provides a method called gets, which is the inverse of puts. It waits until the user types in something ending in a newline and then returns the result.

Here's a small example of Ruby I/O:

```
puts "Welcome to my program. What's your name?"
name = gets

p name
puts "Hello #{name}"
```

At some point, that brilliant input/output program you're writing is going to outgrow a single file. Say you've decided to put the main program in main.rb and some helper functions in helper.rb. In main.rb, you can just say require 'helper' (no trailing .rb extension) or load 'helper.rb' (with extension). The difference between these two is that require will only load a file once; load will reload a file as many times as you call it.

And there you have it—a whirlwind tour of Ruby in less than twenty pages.

Appendix B

Ruby/Java Interoperability

JRuby takes great pains to "do what you mean" when you're passing data between Ruby and Java. The situations we saw in Chapter 2, *Driving Java from Ruby*, on page 15 should get you through most of your everyday use of JRuby. For those times when you need fine-grained control over how JRuby is copying your data or which overload you're calling, you can refer to the details in this appendix.

B.1 How Method Selection Works

JRuby tries to choose the Java methods and parameters that best fit what you're passing in from Ruby. The upside is that things "just work" when you're calling Java from Ruby. The downside is that describing how this process works requires a bit of detail. Most of the time, you won't need to worry about what JRuby is doing under the covers. But in case you're curious...

There are two forces at play for method selection:

• Selecting the right Java method, aka "target method"

• Coercing, casting, or otherwise converting arguments to appropriate types

Let's say you're attempting to call the foo() method on class X. First, JRuby will use Java reflection to search for all public and protected methods named foo() for X and its superclasses. Child classes' methods override their parents', just as in pure Java. Next, JRuby narrows down the list to just the methods that match the number of arguments you're passing in, including methods with variable argument lists.

Ruby Type	Java Type	Notes
NilClass (nil)	A null reference	Use SomeJavaClass.null to call a specific overload with a null reference.
TrueClass (true), FalseClass (false)	A primitive or boxed boolean value	
Fixnum	Any primitive or boxed numeric: int, java.lang.Float, etc.	Matches the widest type available; force to a specific type if you need a different overload.
Float	Any primitive or boxed floating-point value: float, java.lang.Double, etc.	Matches the widest type available; force to a specific type if you need a different overload.
Bignum	java.math.BigInteger	
String	java.lang.String	Requires converting character-by-character, which is slow. Consider pre-converting, or just using Java Strings.

Figure B.1: BASIC TYPES

When there's more than one matching overload, JRuby looks for the best fit based on the passed-in parameters. Types that map directly between Ruby and Java get preferential treatment. For instance, Ruby Fixnums match Java integer types (both primitive and boxed), Ruby strings match Java strings, and so on.

If no direct mappings exist, JRuby tries a looser fit by converting between different numeric types. For a Ruby Integer with no corresponding Java int or Integer argument, JRuby will look for a Java Numeric. As a last resort, JRuby looks for parameters that are Java interfaces and attempts to implement those interfaces on the fly.

B.2 Parameter Types

For a number of basic types, JRuby performs automatic conversions in both directions across the Java/Ruby boundary. JRuby uses the mapping in Figure B.1 for selecting among overloaded methods and for converting parameters.

Ruby Type	Java Type	Notes
Array	`java.util.List`, `java.util.Collection`, or a primitive array.	Similar precision guarantees to `Float` and `Fixnum` conversion.
Any type	Any interface type	Applies only to the last parameter. If a target method takes an interface type, JRuby will attempt to implement the interface around the passed-in Ruby object.
Java `Class` objects imported into Ruby	`java.lang.Class`	
Everything else	Actual type or `java.lang.Object` (i.e., no conversion).	

Figure B.2: OTHER TYPES

Java Type	Differences from Parameter Passing
`java.lang.String`	Kept as a Java object (not converted to Ruby), but gains some Ruby methods. If you need a true Ruby `String`, call `to_s`.
`java.util.List` or `java.util.Collection`	Kept as a Java collection (not converted to Ruby), but gains some Ruby methods. If you need a true Ruby `Array`, call `to_a`.
Primitive array	Kept as a Java array (not converted to Ruby), but supports basic indexing. If you need a true Ruby `Array`, call `to_a`.

Figure B.3: RETURN TYPE EDGE CASES

When no simple mapping between Ruby and Java types exists, JRuby uses the conversions in Figure B.2.

B.3 Return Values

What about returning values back to the Ruby world? Most of the conversions we've discussed in this appendix work the same in the other direction, from Java to Ruby. The exceptions are discussed in Figure B.3.

There's no need to carry these tables around on little laminated cards or anything. The conversions we've seen are designed to stay out of your way and call the right overload with a minimum of typing on your part. For that 1 percent of the time when you need to specify an overload, you can use java_send, java_alias, and java_method.

Configuring JRuby

This chapter is a reference to the most common command-line arguments and runtime properties for JRuby. We've chosen not to inundate you with an uncurated alphabetical listing. Too many options depend on one another for such an order to make any sense. Instead, we've broken down the settings by category.

C.1 Command-Line Options

First, let's look at arguments you pass to the jruby executable on the command line.

Getting Information About JRuby

The first few options are the ones you'd likely reach for first when learning your way around a new environment.

--copyright and --version

These do what you'd expect: they display the copyright and version information for JRuby. The version information also includes the exact Ruby language version on which your JRuby installation is based. This can come in handy for reporting bugs in libraries.

--properties

This option prints out a huge list of settings that affect how JRuby finds, loads, interprets, compiles, and runs code. A short description and default value accompany each property.

If you're interested in tuning JRuby's performance under the hood, keep reading this chapter for information on how to change these properties. Make sure you pay attention to the ones marked as experimental or dangerous!

-h or --help

We were wondering whether to even mention the --help option. Doesn't every program support this? Still, we're bringing it up because it really is a good idea for you to take a minute and explore some of the various options JRuby offers you.

Running Ruby Code

The options in this section control how JRuby executes Ruby code. Most of these are also present in the C implementations of Ruby.

-v, --verbose, and -w

The -v and --verbose flags set the global variable $VERBOSE to true, print JRuby's version information, and then proceed to execute the provided script. (If no script is provided, JRuby will only print its version.) This variable directs Ruby programs, and the JRuby environment itself, to enable extra logging. Specifically, the Kernel object's warn method produces output only if $VERBOSE is true.

The -w is the same as -v, except the former does not print any version information when JRuby launches.

-K code

Ruby 1.8 and JRuby in 1.8 mode normally default to ASCII as the expected character encoding. With -K, you can specify a different encoding, such as UTF-8. Acceptable encodings are UTF8, SJIS, EUC, or ASCII (aka NORMAL).[1] The values are case-insensitive, and only the first character matters.

--1.8 and --1.9

JRuby currently starts up in Ruby 1.8 compatibility mode by default, but you can force it to run in 1.9 mode by specifying the --1.9 flag. In the future, 1.9 mode may become the default; at that point, you'll use --1.8 to specify compatibility with Ruby 1.8 instead.

---

1. As of this writing, JRuby's support for UTF-8 and ASCII is more complete than for the other encodings.

-S *script*

The -S flag is for running shell scripts using JRuby. It comes in handy if you need to run a script that's in your PATH but isn't marked as executable. It's also useful if you have multiple scripts with the same name. When you use this flag, JRuby searches for your program in the following places:

- The current directory
- The JRuby bin directory ($JRUBY_HOME/bin)
- The directories in the PATH environment variable, in order

The -S flag is especially helpful if you have multiple Ruby or JRuby instances on the system. With it, you can specify that you want to run JRuby's version of, say, the gem command, rather than your system Ruby's version.

-e *command*

As an alternative to specifying a script file, you can use the -e flag to pass a snippet of actual Ruby code on the command line. You've probably seen this flag in action already (and we use it liberally throughout this chapter). Once you've gotten used to having -e around, you'll wonder how you ever got along without it!

-I *directory*

Ruby searches for files to require or load on the load path, provided in the $: (or $LOAD_PATH) global variable. The -I flag adds the specified directory—or directories, separated by your platform's path separator character—to the load path, so they will be searched as well.[2]

-r *script*

The -r option directs JRuby to load the specified file at launch time, just as though your Ruby program loaded it with the require method on the first line. You'll often use this flag for loading Ruby standard libraries, especially in one-liner scripts passed to -e.

-C *directory*

With this flag, JRuby will switch to the specified directory before beginning execution.

---

2. The path separator is a semicolon on Windows and a colon basically everywhere else.

Charlie Says...

Enabling Shebang

UNIX-style shebang lines work with JRuby only if you've installed the native launcher. You can do this by using one of the official JRuby installer packages or by running jruby -S gem install jruby-launcher.

-c

During development, you may want to check that a script is syntactically correct without actually running it. The -c flag does exactly that, checking the syntax of the provided script and either reporting errors or printing the text "Syntax ok" and exiting.

-y or --yydebug

These flags turn on verbose parser debugging in JRuby's parser. It might be helpful if you have a really peculiar syntax error and can't figure out why, but otherwise you'll probably never need them.

-s

The simplest way to process command-line parameters may be to use the -s flag. The -s flag turns on basic argument processing, doing the following for you:

- Simple flags (like -foo) set the same-named global variable to true (the equivalent of $foo = true, in this case).

- Name/value flags (like -foo=bar) set the same-named global to the string value specified (the equivalent of $foo = 'bar', in this case).

The -s flag is normally used in a script's "shebang" line, as in the following example:

```
#! /usr/local/bin/jruby -s
# Greets the person named by the -name=... option
print "Hello, " + $name
```

Charlie Says...

On Defaults

Why isn't set_trace_func enabled by default? Because it requires that JRuby check for an installed function before and after every call, on every exception raised, at every line, and on entry into every class body. The majority of scripts never use this functionality, so we avoid this performance hit by default.

If you use -s on the command line (instead of a shell script), you need to use two dashes to separate the arguments meant for JRuby from the ones meant for your Ruby code:

```
$ jruby -s -e 'puts $foo, $bar' -- -foo -bar=baz
true
baz
```

In the previous example, -s and -e are options for JRuby, and -foo and -bar are specific options for this program.

-d or --debug

This option turns on debug mode, both by enabling additional internal logging for JRuby and by setting the $DEBUG global variable for use by your program. Optional logging like this is useful at development time to get a bit more information out of JRuby or third-party libraries. It's also a great way to add debug logging to your own programs (you never know when it might save you).

The same flag also sets up JRuby for debugging or profiling scripts that use Kernel#set_trace_func to track execution events like calls and exceptions. If you want to use set_trace_func at all, you should pass --debug.

--ng and --ng-server

Running any JRuby program means waiting for the JVM to start. For long-running processes like web servers, this brief delay doesn't matter. But for quick shell scripts that you run over and over again, even the shortest pause becomes annoying.

The Nailgun project is designed to let any Java-based project take an end run around the JVM startup time.[3] It works by starting one instance of the JVM in the background and then using a fast C client to connect to it.

JRuby comes with Nailgun. To use it, just start a server and leave it running:

```
$ jruby --ng-server
```

Then pass the --ng flag to JRuby:

```
$ jruby --ng -e "puts 'Hello from Nailgun!'"
```

Before using Nailgun for the first time, you'll have to compile the C client (except on Windows, where JRuby comes with a precompiled client). Fortunately, this step takes only a few seconds. From JRuby's tool/nailgun subdirectory, type the following:

```
$ ./configure && make
```

There are a few interesting interactions between Nailgun and long-running JRuby programs. So, we recommend you stick with the traditional launcher for servers, daemons, and GUI programs and use Nailgun just for quick shell scripts.

-x (optional directory)

Like the same Perl parameter that inspired it, -x tells JRuby to ignore the beginning of the file containing your program until it hits a ruby shebang line. You can use it to run a Ruby program that's embedded inside a larger, non-Ruby file (such as an email message).

Interacting With the JVM

Now we'll move from the Ruby language to the Java platform, as we consider options that affect how the JVM runs.

--jdb

If you're coming to JRuby from a Java background, you may have used the command-line jdb debugger to investigate problems with your programs or third-party code. When you supply the --jdb argument, JRuby runs with jdb instead of just java. This allows you to set breakpoints and step through code. We recommend you pair this option with the

---

3. http://martiansoftware.com/nailgun/index.html

-X+C flag (which we'll get to in a moment) so that you can step through compiled Ruby code instead of being stuck in JRuby's interpreter.

--sample

JRuby ships with its own profiler, which you can enable by passing the --sample option. As an example of how it can come in handy, consider the Ackerizer example from Chapter 2, *Driving Java from Ruby*, on page 15. You'll recall that we replaced a Ruby method with a Java one and saw a big speed increase.

This program was simple enough to be able to see by inspection where the slow code was. In real-world projects, the answers are never so obvious. Slowdowns are revealed only by careful profiling. Here's how we might have profiled the Ackerizer program:

```
$ jruby --sample -J-Xss128m ackerizer.rb
```

Here are the relevant lines of the output, trimmed a bit to fit on the page:

```
29.6% org.jruby.RubyFixnum$i_method_1_0$RUBYINVOKER$op_equal.call
24.5% org.jruby.internal.runtime.methods.CallConfiguration$3.pre
14.0% org.jruby.internal.runtime.methods.JittedMethod.call
11.1% org.jruby.RubyFixnum$i_method_1_0$RUBYINVOKER$op_minus.call
5.8% org.jruby.RubyFixnum$i_method_1_0$RUBYINVOKER$op_plus.call
5.0% ruby.jit.ruby.Users.username.ackermann.ack3178554_3306611.__file__
4.2% org.jruby.runtime.callsite.CachingCallSite.call
4.1% ruby.jit.ruby.Users.username.ackermann.ack3178554_3306611.__file__
```

The program spends 98.3 percent of its calculation time either in ack itself or in the basic math operations that underlie it. It's a small wonder that fixing this one function made the program so much more responsive!

-J

Sometimes, you need fine-grained control over the performance of the Java runtime. The java command has its own set of parameters for this purpose, and you can use any of them from JRuby. Just prepend -J to the Java option you want (with no spaces).

For example, you may want to specify how much memory to allocate to the JVM. In Java, you'd pass the -Xmx option to the runtime, like this:

```
$ java -Xmx512m com.example.someJavaProgram
```

Charlie Says...
More on Profiling

When we say we ship our own profiler, we're actually saying "Since all JVMs ship with their own basic profilers, we get one for free!" Here, --sample is actually the same as passing the -Xprof flag to the underlying JVM (for example, by using the -J flag described in this chapter).

The stock JVM sampling profiler is a good tool of first resort for investigating bottlenecks. But for large-scale profiling, we recommend either using one of the larger Java tools (such as NetBeans, VisualVM, or YourKit) or using Ruby-specific profiling libraries (such as jruby-prof).

Since JRuby is just another Java library, you could pass this parameter the same way by using just the plain java binary and referencing jruby.jar, like this:

```
$ java -Xmx512m -jar /path/to/jruby.jar some_jruby_program.rb
```

But as soon as you try to do anything nontrivial like using the Ruby libraries that come with JRuby, you'll run into path issues and have to type in even more command-line options. JRuby's -J option offers a much better way:

```
$ jruby -J-Xmx512m some_jruby_program.rb
```

When you combine -J with Java's -D*name=value* flag, you can tweak Java's many runtime parameters—including the ones you read from JRuby's --properties argument.

For example, you might pass the -Xdock:name option to make a Swing app look a little more at home on a Mac:

```
$ jruby -J-Xdock:name="My Program" some_jruby_program.rb
```

If you launch your program with this extra flag, the Dock icon will carry the name you specify instead of just "org.jruby.Main."

--server and --client

Even though the -J gives you access to the full range of command-line parameters for the JVM, a few settings are common enough to warrant their own dedicated JRuby arguments. Such is the case with --server and --client, which launch the Java runtime in "server" or "client" mode—for JVMs that support this choice.

Server mode optimizes for long-running processes, at the cost of longer startup times. So, don't go crazy and use it on every single JRuby program you write. But keep it in mind for things such as websites and message queues.

Client mode optimizes less but does so sooner and with less impact to startup time and "cold" performance. JRuby usually will default to client mode, except of course on JVMs that don't have a client mode (like 64-bit Hotspot-based JVMs).

--manage

All standard Java SE runtimes ship with support for the Java Management Extensions (JMX), which allow you to manage a running JVM remotely. Many distributions of Java do not have remote JMX enabled by default, so JRuby provides the --manage flag to turn it on. On Hotspot (Sun's VM or OpenJDK), this simply sets the Java property com.sun.management.jmxremote.

--headless

Many of Java's standard libraries have dependencies on the GUI/graphics subsystem, and the JVM "helpfully" starts up a GUI window for you when these libraries are loaded. The --headless flag (and the java.awt.headless it sets to true behind the scenes) suppresses this behavior, so you can use those libraries without a GUI launching. This flag is sometimes necessary on remote systems that do not have a windowing system installed, since they'll exit with errors if a GUI tries to start up.

-Xoptions

JRuby provides a few extended options for advanced users, accessible by the -X flag. Passing the -X flag alone shows the available options.

Specifying -X-C turns off JRuby's compiler so that all code is interpreted. The opposite case is -X+C, which attempts to compile every piece of code as it loads and avoid the interpreter altogether. The default compile mode is just-in-time, which only compiles frequently called code.

The -X+O flag enables per-object tracking, which is used by Ruby's ObjectSpace#each_object method. The default, which you can explicitly specify with -X-O, is to disable object tracking in order to save the associated memory and CPU cost.

Data Processing

Now we're getting into some of the comparatively rare options. Don't spend too much time learning these by heart; just know you can flip to this section of the book if you encounter them in the wild.

-0*octal*

By now, you've seen several cases where you can throw together a Ruby script to parse a file given to you in some ad hoc text format. Up until now, we've been assuming that newline characters are what separates one record from the next. But there's no reason it can't be a different character.

You can specify the record separator by passing -0 with an optional octal byte value. For example, if you want to split a file on the letter *q*, you'd specify -0161, the octal value character code for *q*. Let's see what that looks like in action:

```
$ echo "fooqbarqbaz" | jruby -0161 -e '3.times { p gets }'
"fooq"
"barq"
"baz\n"
```

Notice that the final string still gets the standard \n line terminator, since there's no final *q* character to close out the string.

If you leave out the octal value, JRuby will use a record separator of \0, the null byte. If you specify -00 or provide a character code outside the 8-bit ASCII range, JRuby switches to "paragraph mode," with a record delimiter of two newline characters (\n\n).

-a, -n, and -p

These flags enable various line-processing options for processing data files or console input. The -n flag runs your specified script in a loop. At the top of the loop, JRuby implicitly calls gets (to wait for the user to

Charlie Says. . .
The Power of Line Processing

These flags can be especially useful for processing a data file quickly. They reduce the amount of boilerplate you need, like looping and splitting. Combined with flags like -0 and -F, you can create some pretty powerful one-liners.

enter something at the console) and assigns the resulting input to the $_ global variable.

The -a flag adds "autosplitting" to this loop: it calls Ruby's String#split on the input and stores the resulting array in the global variable $F. The -p option prints out the value of $_ at the end of each pass through the loop.

Here's what these flags look like in action:

```
⇒  $ jruby -n -e 'if $_ =~ /quit/; exit; else; puts "you said: #{$_}"; end'
⇐  hello
⇒  you said: hello
⇐  goodbye
⇒  you said: goodbye
⇐  quit
⇒

   $ jruby -a -n -e 'if $_ =~ /quit/; exit; else; puts $F; end'
⇐  hello goodbye
⇒  hello
   goodbye
⇐  quit
⇒

   $ jruby -p -n -e 'if $_ =~ /quit/; exit; else; $_ = "last line: #{$_}"; end'
⇐  hello
⇒  last line: hello
⇐  goodbye
⇒  last line: goodbye
⇐  quit
```

An experiment paints a thousand words. We highly encourage you to try these flags together or separately on a short test program.

-F *pattern*

The -F flag and the $; global are a matched set. They specify what character to use by default for splitting strings into arrays:

```
$ jruby -F bar -e 'p "foobarbaz".split'
["foo", "baz"]
```

Normally, JRuby will split strings on spaces if you call split without any parameters, but we've overridden the default here.

-i *extension*

Using the -i flag, you can process a large number of files at once "in place." Like the -n flag, it wraps a loop around your program. But instead of passing in input from the user, it passes in the contents of external files. The filenames are passed on the command line after the flag.

After each pass through the loop, JRuby overwrites the contents of the external file with your program's output. That's why this flag takes an extra parameter; it's a file extension so that JRuby can back up the input files. Here's what in-place processing looks like in action:

```
$ echo matz > /tmp/test
$ cat /tmp/test
matz
$ jruby -p -i.bak -e '$_.upcase!' /tmp/test
$ cat /tmp/test
MATZ
$ cat /tmp/test.bak
matz
```

Here, we've combined the -i flag with -p, so that for each file, the contents of the $_ variable will get written back out to the original file.

-l

You'll notice in the -0 example we saw earlier, the strings we processed still had their record terminators attached (the *q* and \n characters). If you want to clean that up without explicitly calling String#chop on each line, pass -l to JRuby. This flag calls chop on each line for you, which removes record separators (in the sense of the -0 flag) from the end of a string. Here's an earlier example, modified to use -l:

```
$ echo "fooqbarqbaz" | jruby -l -0161 -e '3.times { p gets }'
"foo"
"bar"
"baz"
```

It's yet another powerful tool for command-line data processing. Use it wisely![4]

C.2 Properties

JRuby, like many other JVM-based languages and libraries, also includes some properties that let you access internal or experimental settings. Although we don't have room to discuss every possible property, there are a few particular ones you may find useful. You can get the full list using jruby --properties.

Tweaking the Compiler

The first set of controls is for fine-tuning JRuby's just-in-time compiler.

jruby.compile.mode=JIT|FORCE|OFF

Normally, JRuby runs in JIT mode, meaning that it compiles frequently executed functions to JVM bytecode. You can force JRuby to compile all Ruby files at load time using FORCE, which is the same as running with -X+C. If you want to run everything interpreted and generate no bytecode (which you might want to do for restricted environments like applets or mobile devices), you can specify OFF (which is the same as -X-C).

jruby.jit.threshold=*invocation count*

As of JRuby 1.5, the default number of calls before a method will JIT is 50. If you want to make it happen sooner or delay compiling methods for more invocations, adjust this property appropriately.

jruby.jit.max=*method count*

This sets the maximum number of Ruby methods to JIT compile, which by default is 4096 per JRuby instance. Specifying 0 disables all JITing, and specifying -1 means no maximum count.

jruby.jit.logging=true|false

If you'd like to see a log of methods as they JIT, you can enable this property.

---

4. We should note that this feature is still a work in progress as of this writing.

jruby.jit.codeCache=*directory*

If you specify a codeCache directory, JRuby will also save JITed methods to disk. You can use this code cache in later runs to reduce the JIT-ing cost or to ship "pre-JITed" methods to one of those pesky restricted environments.

Configuring JRuby Features

The next few settings deal with code execution.

jruby.native.enabled=true|false

Normally, JRuby uses several native libraries to provide specific bits of functionality. For example, lower-level POSIX functions or C-based extensions require us to be able to load native code. On restricted environments or in more secure server settings, native libraries are often disallowed. Specifying true for this property will turn off those native libraries and try to use "pure Java" equivalents as much as possible.

jruby.compat.version=RUBY1_8|RUBY1_9

Like the --1.9 flag, this property can be used to explicitly specify the compatibility mode. The default is RUBY1_8.

jruby.objectspace.enabled=true|false

In C Ruby, the ObjectSpace module provides access to various aspects of memory management. For example, ObjectSpace.each_object makes it possible to walk through all objects in memory. Because of the way the JVM works, implementing this feature in JRuby is very expensive—especially for a rarely used debugging feature. If you're using a third-party library that depends on this feature for advanced Ruby techniques, you'll need to set this property to true.

jruby.launch.inproc=true|false

Ruby's system method is meant to launch an external process. But if that external process would be a call to ruby or jruby, JRuby will save you some time by reusing the same JVM (albeit with a different JRuby instance). If you really need to spin up a separate ruby process, set this property to true.

jruby.debug.fullTrace=true|false

This property is the equivalent of the --debug flag we discussed earlier. It enables execution tracing for set_trace_func, which many debugging libraries depend on.

Loading Files

A related issue to code execution is code loading; the final two options give you a window into that process.

jruby.debug.loadService.timing=true|false

Your app's startup performance takes a noticeable hit if you're loading complex files or doing a lot of up-front code generation. JRuby can help you identify the more obvious startup problems by logging how long each file takes to load (together with its dependencies). Set this property to true to enable load-time logging.

jruby.debug.loadService=true|false

If you have a pesky file being loaded from the wrong filesystem location and you can't figure out how JRuby is finding that file, you can turn on logging to show all locations searched along with failed and successful loads. You may be surprised what you see for large applications.

Calling External C Code

We've spent a lot of time in this book talking about calling Java from Ruby, and vice versa. And with good reason: it's one of the main reasons people come to JRuby. You may be wondering, though: are you stuck in the Java universe if you go with JRuby?

Not at all! JRuby is one of the many Ruby implementations that can call straight into C code—in fact, it's one of the best.

D.1 Foreign-Function Interface

There are several reasons you might want to call into native code from JRuby. For example:

- You may need to take advantage of some specific feature of your operating system.
- A piece of hardware you're using may come with no manual and no source code—just a DLL.
- Your Ruby code might be part of a larger program with parts written in different languages.
- You may be using a Ruby gem for image processing, XML parsing, or data access that leans on C code internally.

How do you connect to external code in these situations?

Extension API

In the old days, you'd write a small piece of glue code in C that would wrap the external code with a Ruby-like interface. This approach—using Ruby's extension API—is still supported in regular Ruby and is gradually making its way into JRuby as we write this book.

The advantages of the extension API are its speed and its status as the official way to plug C into Ruby. The disadvantage is that there's an extra layer of glue code. This layer takes time and effort to write. Moreover, it has to be compiled specifically for the end user's platform—often by the end user at installation time.

Ruby Standard Library

Ruby has evolved a couple of libraries that let you skip the middleman and talk straight to the external code you want. Two of these (Ruby/DL and Win32API) have become part of the Ruby standard library.

Because C functions must declare their argument and return types, Ruby code using one of these techniques has to be "decorated" with a little extra information about data types. The Ruby syntax for these decorations varies, but it's never felt flexible enough for C or comfortable enough for Ruby. Worse, there are subtle differences across Ruby versions.

Ruby/DL and Win32API are only partially supported in JRuby. We mention them mainly to set the stage for the preferred way of calling out to C: the FFI library.

FFI

FFI, short for Foreign-Function Interface, began as part of the Rubinius project (an advanced implementation of the Ruby language).[1,2]

We'll look at a couple of longer examples in a moment. But just to get a feel for FFI, here's how you'd call the pow() function in the C runtime library:

`ffi/pow.rb`
```ruby
require 'ffi'

module CMath
  extend FFI::Library
  ffi_lib 'libm'

  attach_function :pow, [:double, :double], :double
end

puts CMath.pow(2.0, 8.0) # >> 256.0
```

1. http://wiki.github.com/ffi/ffi
2. http://rubini.us

The syntax is such a natural fit for Ruby that the JRuby team decided to put FFI in the official JRuby build. That means if you code to this API, you can call into C from at least four different Ruby implementations.

A Windows Example

We're not going to cover all the ins and outs of FFI. But if we show off a couple of common scenarios, we can hit most of the high points.

Let's start with a really simple Windows example that just shows a couple of the basics of FFI: calling conventions and string parameters. The following code will print the title of the topmost window:

`ffi/windows.rb`

```ruby
require 'ffi'

module User32
  extend FFI::Library
  ffi_lib         'user32'
  ffi_convention :stdcall

  typedef :pointer, :hwnd

  attach_function :GetForegroundWindow, [], :hwnd
  attach_function :GetWindowTextA, [:hwnd, :pointer, :int], :int
end

FFI::MemoryPointer.new(:char, 1000) do |buffer|
  hwnd = User32.GetForegroundWindow
  User32.GetWindowTextA hwnd, buffer, buffer.size
  p buffer.get_string(0)
  # >> "jruby - Cmd"
end
```

As with the previous example, we gather related functions from one external library into a single module. Since this is a Windows library, we need to use the Windows stdcall calling convention.

Next, we specify the two functions we need based on their signatures. Notice that we can do simple type definitions so that the function declaration will use the "window handle" type familiar to Windows developers.

We've deliberately chosen an API call that takes a buffer so that we can talk about how to share strings with the C world. The call to Memory-Pointer#new allocates a buffer that stays in memory just for the lifetime of the attached block. Since this is just a generic pointer to raw storage, we have to tell FFI to interpret the result as a string, using the get_string call. If you save the program as windows.rb and run it, you should see something like this:

```
C:\> jruby windows.rb
"jruby - Cmd"
```

Ready for something a little more intricate? Let's move on to our second example.

A Mac Example (and More)

This program will get into a couple of FFI's more advanced features: callbacks and data structures. We're going to use the UNIX signal-handling system to set a timer and then wait for it to fire.

As before, we are going to call two C functions. Here are their C declarations:

ffi/defs.c
```
unsigned int alarm(unsigned int);
int sigaction(int, struct siginfo*, struct siginfo*);
```

FFI takes great pains to represent these functions legibly in Ruby:

ffi/posix.rb
```
module POSIX
  extend FFI::Library
  ffi_lib 'c'

  attach_function :alarm,     [:uint], :uint
  attach_function :sigaction, [:int, :pointer, :pointer], :int

  # remaining definitions will go here...
end
```

Those two :pointer parameters point to siginfo structures. This structure varies from platform to platform. We'll get to the Mac version of it in a minute. But first we need to talk about callbacks. UNIX signal callbacks can take one of two forms:

ffi/defs.c
```
typedef void (*handler_func)(int);
typedef void (*action_func)(int, struct siginfo*, void*);
```

Here's how to translate these two typedefs to Ruby. Note that this code needs to go inside the module declaration.

`ffi/posix.rb`
```
callback :handler_func, [:int], :void
callback :action_func,  [:int, :pointer, :pointer], :void
```

Now for the data structures that house those callbacks. The definition will look different if you're on Linux or another UNIX-like system. Caveat coder.

`ffi/defs.c`
```
union sigaction_u {
    handler_func sa_handler;
    action_func  sa_action;
};

struct sigaction {
    union sigaction_u sa_action_u;
    sigset_t          sa_mask;
    int               sa_flags;
};
```

FFI provides its own Struct and Union types to represent those C entities. Again, these definitions live in the POSIX module:

`ffi/posix.rb`
```
class SigActionU < FFI::Union
  layout :sa_handler, :handler_func,
         :sa_action,  :action_func
end

typedef :int,         :sigset_t

class SigAction < FFI::Struct
  layout :sa_action_u, SigActionU,
         :sa_flags,    :int,
         :sa_mask,     :int
end
```

We're almost ready to call all these elaborately built-up functions. FFI provides a Function class that we can pass into the C functions to serve as a callback. Here's how we set up the two structs we need: action for the input and out for the output.

`ffi/posix.rb`

```
handler = FFI::Function.new(:void, [:int]) { |i| puts 'RING!' }

action = POSIX::SigAction.new
action[:sa_action_u][:sa_handler] = handler
action[:sa_flags] = 0
action[:sa_mask] = 0

out = POSIX::SigAction.new
```

Finally, we can make our calls. sigaction() tells the OS which function to call when we receive a wakeup signal, and alarm() will fire that signal one second into the future:

`ffi/posix.rb`

```
SIGALRM = 14
POSIX.sigaction SIGALRM, action, out
POSIX.alarm 1

puts 'Going to bed'
sleep 2
puts 'Breakfast time'
```

When you run the program, you should see the messages one at time, with a brief delay in between.

```
$ jruby posix.rb
Going to bed
RING!
Breakfast time
```

If you're porting this code to another operating system, some of these data type definitions will need to change. The linux.rb file that comes with this book's source code shows one example of the kinds of modifications you might make.

Calling into an unsafe language from a safe one is, well, unsafe. But don't let that frighten you too much. Sometimes C gives you exactly the direct hardware access, high performance, or software interoperability you need.

JRuby for Sysadmins

We have talked a lot about developing applications and libraries with JRuby. What about other tasks, such as administering a system?

It turns out that JRuby is a great fit for running a single computer or an entire network. You get the benefits of Ruby's quick-scripting abilities and Java's monitoring libraries.

There's enough material on scripting your system with Ruby to fill an entire book. In fact, such a book already exists.[1] But we couldn't resist bringing up the subject here, too.

E.1 Automating Tasks

Ruby has a long history of helping sysadmins get their jobs done. It's no secret that Perl, the duct tape that holds networks together all over the world, was a big inspiration for Ruby. Several of Ruby's idioms came straight from Perl—the most famous of these is regular-expression matching.

You can use JRuby in the same kinds of situations where you'd use shell scripts, batch files, or Perl programs. For instance, let's say you're running a UNIX system where the corporate policy is that the company name has to be in everyone's email .signature file.[2]

---

1. *Everyday Scripting with Ruby* [Mar06], by Brian Marick
2. That doesn't sound like a place we'd like to work. But for this example, we'll assume the dental plan is outstanding.

Here's how you might generate a monthly report on signatures:

`jmx/check_sigs`

```
#!/usr/bin/env jruby
Dir['home/*'].each do |d|
  if `grep Initrode #{d}/.signature`.empty?
    puts "The .signature in #{d} isn't good for the company!"
  end
end
```

Just like any other UNIX shell script, you can use the first line of code—the *shebang* line—to associate this program with JRuby. You can then give yourself execute permission for this file and run it directly.

```
$ chmod u+x check_sigs
$ ./check_sigs
The .signature in home/ian isn't good for the company!
```

On Windows, there are a couple of extra setup steps, but nothing too tricky. Using Explorer, rename the file to check_sigs.rb and then associate .rb files with the jruby.exe program. Finally, add .rb to the end of your PATHEXT environment variable. Now you can run check_sigs directly from the command line:

```
C:\> set PATHEXT=%PATHEXT%;.rb
C:\> check_sigs
The .signature in home/ian isn't good for the company!
```

As you can see, Ruby can loop through directories and call out to other programs easily. These tasks are the bread and butter of day-to-day automation.

E.2 Monitoring Applications

Java has evolved a number of APIs that are useful to admins who have to keep application servers running and healthy. The best known of these is JMX, the Java Management Extensions library.[3] With JMX, you can gather statistics about a running program, either by compiling your monitoring code into it or by connecting to it remotely.

Because JRuby programs are running on the JVM, you can find out all sorts of performance information the same way you would with a regular Java program. Instead, let's measure something application-specific: hits to the home page of a web server.

---

3. http://java.sun.com/javase/technologies/core/mntr-mgmt/javamanagement

The JMX Interface

To provide our own custom statistics to a JMX client, we'll write our own *managed bean*, JMX's term for a data provider. We could call directly into the JMX APIs using the same Ruby/Java integration techniques we've been discussing throughout the book. But we'll save some time and use the jmx gem, which provides a few handy shortcuts:

```
$ jruby -S gem install jmx
```

Now, we just create a regular Ruby class that inherits from RubyDynamicMBean:

jmx/web_app.rb

```ruby
require 'rubygems'
require 'jmx'
require 'rmi'

class HitBean < RubyDynamicMBean
  def initialize(name, desc)
    super name, desc
    @hits = 0
  end

  def hit!
    @hits += 1
  end

  # rest of implementation goes here...
end
```

So far, this is just regular Ruby code. We're setting up our own API that the web server will use to increment the hit count. The next task is to add JMX hooks to retrieve the data. The following code goes inside the HitBean class definition, right after the hit! method:

jmx/web_app.rb

```ruby
r_attribute :hits, :int, 'Current hit count'

operation 'Clear the hit count'
returns :void
def clear
  @hits = 0
end
```

Much like Ruby's attr_reader directive makes an instance variable readable by other Ruby code, r_attribute makes values readable by JMX clients. In this case, we want JMX to be able to see the value of the @hits instance variable.

We're not limited to reading and writing variables. The operation directive makes a Ruby method callable from JMX. Here, we've provided a way to reset the counter to zero.

Once our bean has the JMX attributes and operations we want, it's time to connect it to a server:

`jmx/web_app.rb`
```
port = 9999
url = "service:jmx:rmi:///jndi/rmi://localhost:#{port}/jmxrmi"

registry  = RMIRegistry.new port
server    = JMX::MBeanServer.new
connector = JMX::MBeanServerConnector.new url, server
connector.start

bean      = HitBean.new 'jruby.HitBean', 'Web app hits'
domain    = server.default_domain
server.register_mbean bean, "#{domain}:type=HitBean"

at_exit do
  connector.stop
  registry.stop
end
```

Now we can move on to the application we'll be monitoring.

The Web App

After all that setup, the web server itself is pretty trivial. We'll use the Sinatra web framework, which is great at getting projects off the ground quickly.[4] First, install Sinatra:

```
$ jruby -S gem install sinatra
```

Add the following code to the end of the file you've been working in:

`jmx/web_app.rb`
```
require 'sinatra'

get '/' do
  bean.hit!
  "We're watching you"
end
```

---
4. http://www.sinatrarb.com/

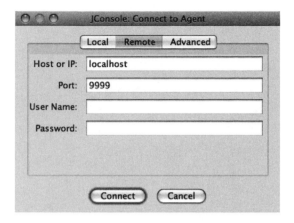

Figure E.1: LOGGING INTO JCONSOLE

This will increment the hit counter every time someone visits the page. The information will not be visible to users but will be available to administrators through JMX. Go ahead and run the app. Assuming you've saved the code in web_app.rb, you just run it like any other JRuby program:

```
$ jruby web_app.rb
```

Go to http://localhost:4567 in your web browser; you should see the text "We're watching you!" Hit Refresh a few times to bump up the internal hit count.

Remote Administration

Now that our web app is serving up statistics via JMX, we need a remote client to report the data. It would be easy enough to write one in JRuby, using the same jmx gem we've been discussing. But there's an even easier way: the jconsole command that comes with Java. When you launch it like this:

```
$ jconsole
```

...you should see a window like Figure E.1. On the Remote tab, fill in *localhost* and 9999 for the host and port, and then click Connect. The main window should fill in with details about the web app.

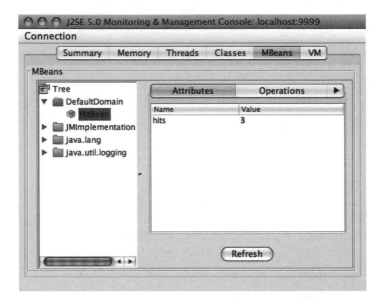

Figure E.2: Monitoring the app

Go to the MBeans tab. Underneath the DefaultDomain item, find the HitBean class you created for your app. You should see the hits attribute filled in with the number of times you viewed the web page, as in Figure E.2.

Take a few minutes to play around with the interface. Reload the web page a few times, and then click Refresh in JConsole to update the attribute. Switch over to the Operations tab and clear the hit count.

Of course, JConsole is far from the only JMX client that would work with this web app. In fact, the same jmx gem supports writing your own client in Ruby. Let's take a look at this technique.

Custom Clients

We could monitor our web app from a separate Ruby program:

jmx/web_watcher.rb

```
require 'rubygems'
require 'jmx'

client = JMX.connect :port => 9999
counter = client['DefaultDomain:type=HitBean']
```

```
loop do
  puts "The hit counter is at #{counter.hits.value}"
  puts "Type R to reset, or press Enter to continue"

  counter.clear if gets.strip.upcase == 'R'
end
```

As you can see, we're reading the hits attribute and calling the clear method just as if they belong to a regular Ruby object. Behind the scenes, the jmx gem is ferrying these calls to the remote process and delivering the answers to us.

This monitoring process does not know or care what language the main program is written in. You could easily command a stable of Java application servers full of Ruby and non-Ruby applications—all from the same remote client.

E.3 Wrapping Up

Over the last few pages, we've looked at a couple of different ways you can use JRuby to keep your system running smoothly. We wrote a Ruby script that runs like a batch file, only with the full power of a programming language behind it. And we grabbed some runtime statistics from a web application, without having to implement a separate administrative user interface.

Limelight Example Source

guis/limelight/bookie/stages.rb

```ruby
stage 'default' do
  default_scene 'bookie'
  title 'Bookie'
  location [200, 25]
  size [400, 400]
end

if ENV['BOOKIE_DEV']
  stage 'devtool' do
    default_scene 'devtool'
    title 'Dev Tool'
    location [50, 25]
    size [100, 100]
    background_color 'transparent'
    framed false
  end
end
```

guis/limelight/bookie/production.rb

```ruby
module Production
  attr_reader :chapter_contents

  def production_opening
    require 'redcloth'
    @chapter_contents = [{:title => '1', :text => ''}]
  end
end
```

guis/limelight/bookie/bookie/props.rb

```ruby
root do
  center do
    chapter_list :id => 'chapter_list'
    dual_pane :id => 'dual_pane' do
      tabs do
        tabs_shadow
        tabs_holder do
          tab_button :text           => 'Edit',
                     :id             => 'edit_tab',
                     :on_mouse_clicked => 'scene.dual_pane.edit!',
                     :styles         => 'left_tab'
          tab_button :text           => 'Preview',
                     :id             => 'preview_tab',
                     :on_mouse_clicked => 'scene.dual_pane.preview!',
                     :styles         => 'right_tab'
        end
      end
      preview_pane :id => 'preview_pane'
      edit_pane :players => 'text_area',
        :id => 'edit_pane'
    end
  end
  add_chapter :text => 'Add Chapter'
end
```

guis/limelight/bookie/bookie/styles.rb

```ruby
default_border_color     { border_color 'b9b9b9' }
default_background_color { background_color :white }

fill_parent {
  width '100%'
  height '100%'
}

bookie {
  extends :fill_parent
}

center {
  horizontal_alignment :center
  vertical_alignment :center
}

root {
  extends :default_background_color, :fill_parent
  text_color :white
  font_size 18
}
```

```
center {
  width '100%'
  height '90%'
}

chapter_list {
  width '10%'
  height '100%'
  bottom_margin 8
}

chapter {
  extends :default_border_color, :default_background_color, :center
  height 30
  width "100%"
  secondary_background_color 'f0f0f0'
  gradient :on
  bottom_border_width 1
  right_border_width 1
}

dual_pane {
  width '90%'
  height '100%'
}

edit_button {
  width '50%'
  height '10%'
}

preview_button {
  width '50%'
  height '10%'
}

add_chapter {
  extends :default_border_color, :default_background_color, :center
  width '22%'
  height '8%'
  rounded_corner_radius 4
  secondary_background_color 'f0f0f0'
  gradient :on
  gradient_angle 270
  border_width 1
  left_margin 4
  padding 4
}
```

```
tabs {
 width "100%"
 height '10%'
 horizontal_alignment :center
}

tab_button {
  extends :default_border_color, :default_background_color
  horizontal_alignment :center
  vertical_alignment :center
  secondary_background_color 'f0f0f0'
  gradient :on
  gradient_angle 270
  padding 5
  hover {
    secondary_background_color :sky_blue
  }
}

tabs_holder {
  extends :fill_parent
  float :on
  y '15%'
  x '37%'
}

tabs_shadow {
  extends :default_border_color
  extends :fill_parent
  top_margin '50%'
  left_margin 8
  right_margin 8
  top_border_width 1
  left_border_width 1
  right_border_width 1
  background_color 'f0f0f0'
}

left_tab {
  top_left_rounded_corner_radius 4
  bottom_left_rounded_corner_radius 4
  border_width 1
}

right_tab {
  top_right_rounded_corner_radius 4
  top_right_border_width 1
  bottom_right_rounded_corner_radius 4
  bottom_right_border_width 1
  left_border_width 0
```

```
    right_border_width 1
    top_border_width 1
    bottom_border_width 1
}

preview_pane {
    extends :default_border_color, :default_background_color
    width "100%"
    height "90%"
    left_border_width 1
    right_border_width 1
    bottom_border_width 1
    left_margin 8
    right_margin 8
    bottom_margin 8
    font_size 16
    font_face "times"
}

edit_pane {
    width "100%"
    height "90%"
    left_margin 8
    right_margin 8
    bottom_margin 8
}

###### Styles of styling text

p {
    top_margin 3
    bottom_margin 3
    border_width 1
    border_color :blue
}

br {
}

strong {
    font_style "bold"
}

em {
    font_style "italic"
}
```

guis/limelight/bookie/bookie/players/add_chapter.rb

```ruby
module AddChapter
  def mouse_clicked(e)
    contents    = production.chapter_contents
    title       = (contents.length + 1).to_s
    new_content = {:title => title, :text => ''}
    contents << new_content

    scene.chapter_list.repopulate
  end
end
```

guis/limelight/bookie/bookie/players/bookie.rb

```ruby
module Bookie
  prop_reader :chapter_list, :dual_pane
  prop_reader :preview_pane, :edit_pane
  prop_reader :preview_tab, :edit_tab

  def scene_opened(e)
    chapter_list.repopulate
    chapter_list.select(1, true)
    dual_pane.edit!
  end
end
```

guis/limelight/bookie/bookie/players/chapter.rb

```ruby
module Chapter
  attr_accessor :model

  def mouse_clicked(e)
    scene.dual_pane.current_chapter = @model
  end

  def select!
    style.background_color = :sky_blue
  end

  def deselect!
    style.background_color = :white
  end
end
```

guis/limelight/bookie/bookie/players/chapter_list.rb

```ruby
module ChapterList
  def repopulate
    remove_all
    production = scene.production
    build do
      production.chapter_contents.each do |chapter_model|
```

```ruby
          chapter :text => chapter_model[:title],
                  :model => chapter_model,
                  :id => "chapter_#{chapter_model[:title]}"
      end
    end
    update_selection
  end

  def update_selection
    selected = scene.dual_pane.current_chapter
    select(selected[:title]) if selected
  end

  def select(chapter, click_mouse=false)
    children.each { |prop| prop.deselect! }
    chapter = scene.find "chapter_#{chapter}"
    if chapter
      chapter.select!
      chapter.mouse_clicked(nil) if click_mouse
    end
  end
end
```

guis/limelight/bookie/bookie/players/dual_pane.rb

```ruby
module DualPane
  attr_reader :current_chapter

  def update_preview_pane
    preview_content = RedCloth.new(@current_chapter[:text]).to_html
    preview_content.gsub! /\<br\s+\/>/, "\n"
    scene.preview_pane.text = preview_content
  end

  def current_chapter=(chapter)
    save!
    @current_chapter = chapter
    scene.find("chapter_#{@current_chapter[:title]}").select!
    scene.edit_pane.text = @current_chapter[:text]
    update_preview_pane
    scene.chapter_list.update_selection
  end

  def edit!
    scene.preview_pane.style.height = "0"
    scene.edit_pane.style.height = "90%"
    scene.edit_pane.style.background_color = :sky_blue
    scene.preview_tab.style.background_color = :white
    scene.edit_tab.style.background_color = :sky_blue
  end
```

```ruby
  def preview!
    save!
    update_preview_pane
    scene.edit_pane.style.height = "0"
    scene.preview_pane.style.height = "90%"
    scene.preview_tab.style.background_color = :sky_blue
    scene.edit_tab.style.background_color = :white
  end

  def save!
    if @current_chapter
      @current_chapter[:text] = scene.edit_pane.text
      scene.preview_pane.text = @current_chapter[:text]
    end
  end
end
```

`guis/limelight/bookie/devtool/props.rb`

```ruby
refresh :players => "button", :text => "Refresh"
```

`guis/limelight/bookie/devtool/styles.rb`

```ruby
devtool {
  width "100%"
  height "100%"
  background_color :light_gray
  horizontal_alignment :center
  vertical_alignment :center
}
```

`guis/limelight/bookie/devtool/players/refresh.rb`

```ruby
module Refresh
  def mouse_clicked(e)
    production.theater.stages.map do |stage|
      scene = stage.current_scene
      production.producer.open_scene(scene.name, stage) if scene
    end
  end
end
```

Appendix G

Bibliography

[BLS94]   Jess Borgeson, Adam Long, and Daniel Singer. *The Com-
           pleat Works of Wllm Shkspr (Abridged)*. Applause Theatre &
           Cinema Books, New York, NY, 1994.

[CAD⁺09]   David Chelimsky, Dave Astels, Zach Dennis, Aslak Hellesøy,
           Bryan Helmkamp, and Dan North. *The RSpec Book*. The
           Pragmatic Programmers, LLC, Raleigh, NC, and Dallas, TX,
           2009.

[Dij76]   Edsger W. Dijkstra. *The problem of The Next Permutation*,
           chapter 13. Prentice-Hall, 1976.

[Fow03]   Martin Fowler. *Patterns of Enterprise Application Architec-
           ture*. Addison Wesley Longman, Reading, MA, 2003.

[HC07]   Cay S. Horstmann and Gary Cornell. *Core Java*. Prentice
           Hall, Englewood Cliffs, NJ, eighth edition, 2007.

[HT00]   Andrew Hunt and David Thomas. *The Pragmatic Program-
           mer: From Journeyman to Master*. Addison-Wesley, Reading,
           MA, 2000.

[Mar06]   Brian Marick. *Everyday Scripting with Ruby: For Teams,
           Testers, and You*. The Pragmatic Programmers, LLC,
           Raleigh, NC, and Dallas, TX, 2006.

[RTH08]   Sam Ruby, David Thomas, and David Heinemeier Hansson.
           Agile Web Development with Rails. The Pragmatic Program-
           mers, LLC, Raleigh, NC, and Dallas, TX, third edition, 2008.

[Tat06]   Bruce Tate. *From Java to Ruby: Things Every Manager Should Know.* The Pragmatic Programmers, LLC, Raleigh, NC, and Dallas, TX, 2006.

[TFH08]   David Thomas, Chad Fowler, and Andrew Hunt. *Programming Ruby: The Pragmatic Programmers' Guide.* The Pragmatic Programmers, LLC, Raleigh, NC, and Dallas, TX, third edition, 2008.

Index

The Pragmatic Bookshelf

Available in paperback and DRM-free eBooks, our titles are here to help you stay on top of your game. The following are in print as of December 2010; be sure to check our website at pragprog.com for newer titles.

Title	Year	ISBN	Pages
Advanced Rails Recipes: 84 New Ways to Build Stunning Rails Apps	2008	9780978739225	464
Agile Coaching	2009	9781934356432	248
Agile Retrospectives: Making Good Teams Great	2006	9780977616640	200
Agile Web Development with Rails	2009	9781934356166	792
Beginning Mac Programming: Develop with Objective-C and Cocoa	2010	9781934356517	300
Behind Closed Doors: Secrets of Great Management	2005	9780976694021	192
Best of Ruby Quiz	2006	9780976694076	304
Cocoa Programming: A Quick-Start Guide for Developers	2010	9781934356302	450
Core Animation for Mac OS X and the iPhone: Creating Compelling Dynamic User Interfaces	2008	9781934356104	200
Core Data: Apple's API for Persisting Data on Mac OS X	2009	9781934356326	256
Data Crunching: Solve Everyday Problems using Java, Python, and More	2005	9780974514079	208
Debug It! Find, Repair, and Prevent Bugs in Your Code	2009	9781934356289	232
Design Accessible Web Sites: 36 Keys to Creating Content for All Audiences and Platforms	2007	9781934356029	336
Desktop GIS: Mapping the Planet with Open Source Tools	2008	9781934356067	368
Domain-Driven Design Using Naked Objects	2009	9781934356449	375
Driving Technical Change: Why People on Your Team Don't Act on Good Ideas, and How to Convince Them They Should	2010	9781934356609	200
Enterprise Integration with Ruby	2006	9780976694069	360
Enterprise Recipes with Ruby and Rails	2008	9781934356234	416
Everyday Scripting with Ruby: for Teams, Testers, and You	2007	9780977616619	320
ExpressionEngine 2: A Quick-Start Guide	2010	9781934356524	250
From Java To Ruby: Things Every Manager Should Know	2006	9780976694090	160
FXRuby: Create Lean and Mean GUIs with Ruby	2008	9781934356074	240

Continued on next page

Title	Year	ISBN	Pages
GIS for Web Developers: Adding Where to Your Web Applications	2007	9780974514093	275
Google Maps API: Adding Where to Your Applications	2006	PDF-Only	83
Grails: A Quick-Start Guide	2009	9781934356463	200
Groovy Recipes: Greasing the Wheels of Java	2008	9780978739294	264
Hello, Android: Introducing Google's Mobile Development Platform	2010	9781934356562	320
Interface Oriented Design	2006	9780976694052	240
iPad Programming: A Quick-Start Guide for iPhone Developers	2010	9781934356579	248
iPhone SDK Development	2009	9781934356258	576
Land the Tech Job You Love	2009	9781934356265	280
Language Implementation Patterns: Create Your Own Domain-Specific and General Programming Languages	2009	9781934356456	350
Learn to Program	2009	9781934356364	240
Manage It! Your Guide to Modern Pragmatic Project Management	2007	9780978739249	360
Manage Your Project Portfolio: Increase Your Capacity and Finish More Projects	2009	9781934356296	200
Mastering Dojo: JavaScript and Ajax Tools for Great Web Experiences	2008	9781934356111	568
Metaprogramming Ruby: Program Like the Ruby Pros	2010	9781934356470	240
Modular Java: Creating Flexible Applications with OSGi and Spring	2009	9781934356401	260
No Fluff Just Stuff 2006 Anthology	2006	9780977616664	240
No Fluff Just Stuff 2007 Anthology	2007	9780978739287	320
Pomodoro Technique Illustrated: The Easy Way to Do More in Less Time	2009	9781934356500	144
Practical Programming: An Introduction to Computer Science Using Python	2009	9781934356272	350
Practices of an Agile Developer	2006	9780974514086	208
Pragmatic Guide to Git	2010	9781934356722	168
Pragmatic Guide to JavaScript	2010	9781934356678	150
Pragmatic Guide to Subversion	2010	9781934356616	150
Pragmatic Project Automation: How to Build, Deploy, and Monitor Java Applications	2004	9780974514031	176
Pragmatic Thinking and Learning: Refactor Your Wetware	2008	9781934356050	288
Pragmatic Unit Testing in C# with NUnit	2007	9780977616671	176
Pragmatic Unit Testing in Java with JUnit	2003	9780974514017	160

Continued on next page

Title	Year	ISBN	Pages
Pragmatic Version Control using CVS	2003	9780974514000	176
Pragmatic Version Control Using Git	2008	9781934356159	200
Pragmatic Version Control using Subversion	2006	9780977616657	248
Programming Clojure	2009	9781934356333	304
Programming Cocoa with Ruby: Create Compelling Mac Apps Using RubyCocoa	2009	9781934356197	300
Programming Erlang: Software for a Concurrent World	2007	9781934356005	536
Programming Groovy: Dynamic Productivity for the Java Developer	2008	9781934356098	320
Programming Ruby: The Pragmatic Programmers' Guide	2004	9780974514055	864
Programming Ruby 1.9: The Pragmatic Programmers' Guide	2009	9781934356081	944
Programming Scala: Tackle Multi-Core Complexity on the Java Virtual Machine	2009	9781934356319	250
Prototype and script.aculo.us: You Never Knew JavaScript Could Do This!	2007	9781934356012	448
Rails for .NET Developers	2008	9781934356203	300
Rails for Java Developers	2007	9780977616695	336
Rails for PHP Developers	2008	9781934356043	432
Rails Recipes	2006	9780977616602	350
Rapid GUI Development with QtRuby	2005	PDF-Only	83
Release It! Design and Deploy Production-Ready Software	2007	9780978739218	368
Scripted GUI Testing with Ruby	2008	9781934356180	192
Seven Languages in Seven Weeks: A Pragmatic Guide to Learning Programming Languages	2010	9781934356593	300
Ship It! A Practical Guide to Successful Software Projects	2005	9780974514048	224
SQL Antipatterns: Avoiding the Pitfalls of Database Programming	2010	9781934356555	352
Stripes ...and Java Web Development Is Fun Again	2008	9781934356210	375
Test-Drive ASP.NET MVC	2010	9781934356531	296
TextMate: Power Editing for the Mac	2007	9780978739232	208
The Agile Samurai: How Agile Masters Deliver Great Software	2010	9781934356586	280
The Definitive ANTLR Reference: Building Domain-Specific Languages	2007	9780978739256	384
The Passionate Programmer: Creating a Remarkable Career in Software Development	2009	9781934356340	200

Continued on next page

Title	Year	ISBN	Pages
The RSpec Book: Behaviour-Driven Development with RSpec, Cucumber, and Friends	2010	9781934356371	448
ThoughtWorks Anthology	2008	9781934356142	240
Ubuntu Kung Fu: Tips, Tricks, Hints, and Hacks	2008	9781934356227	400
Web Design for Developers: A Programmer's Guide to Design Tools and Techniques	2009	9781934356135	300

The Pragmatic Guide Series

Pragmatic Guide to JavaScript

JavaScript is now a powerful, dynamic language with a rich ecosystem of professional-grade development tools, infrastructures, frameworks, and toolkits. You can't afford to ignore it–this book will get you up to speed quickly and painlessly. Presented as two-page tasks, these JavaScript tips will get you started quickly and save you time.

Pragmatic Guide to JavaScript
Christophe Porteneuve
(150 pages) ISBN: 978-1934356-67-8. $25.00
http://pragprog.com/titles/pg_js

Pragmatic Guide to Git

New Git users will learn the basic tasks needed to work with Git every day, including working with remote repositories, dealing with branches and tags, exploring the history, and fixing problems when things go wrong. If youâĂŹre already familiar with Git, this book will be your go-to reference for Git commands and best practices.

Pragmatic Guide to Git
Travis Swicegood
(168 pages) ISBN: 978-1-93435-672-2. $25.00
http://pragprog.com/titles/pg_git

Agile Methods

Agile in a Flash

The best agile book isn't a book: Agile in a Flash is a unique deck of index cards that fit neatly in your pocket. You can tape them to the wall. Spread them out on your project table. Get stains on them over lunch. These cards are meant to be used, not just read.

Agile in a Flash: Speed-Learning Agile Software Development
Jeff Langr and Tim Ottinger
(110 pages) ISBN: 978-1-93435-671-5. $15.00
http://pragprog.com/titles/olag

The Agile Samurai

Faced with a software project of epic proportions? Tired of over-committing and under-delivering? Enter the dojo of the agile samurai, where agile expert Jonathan Rasmusson shows you how to kick-start, execute, and deliver your agile projects. You'll see how agile software delivery really works and how to help your team get agile fast, while having fun along the way.

The Agile Samurai: How Agile Masters Deliver Great Software
Jonathan Rasmusson
(275 pages) ISBN: 9781934356586. $34.95
http://pragprog.com/titles/jtrap

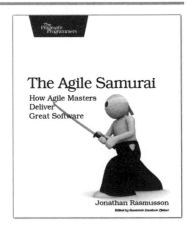

Ruby and Rails

Programming Ruby 1.9 (The Pickaxe for 1.9)

The Pickaxe book, named for the tool on the cover, is the definitive reference to this highly-regarded language.

• Up-to-date and expanded for Ruby version 1.9
• Complete documentation of all the built-in classes, modules, and methods • Complete descriptions of all standard libraries • Learn more about Ruby's web tools, unit testing, and programming philosophy

Programming Ruby 1.9: The Pragmatic Programmers' Guide

Dave Thomas with Chad Fowler and Andy Hunt
(992 pages) ISBN: 978-1-9343560-8-1. $49.95
http://pragprog.com/titles/ruby3

Agile Web Development with Rails

Rails just keeps on changing. Rails 3 and Ruby 1.9 bring hundreds of improvements, including new APIs and substantial performance enhancements. The fourth edition of this award-winning classic has been reorganized and refocused so it's more useful than ever before for developers new to Ruby and Rails. This book isn't just a rework, it's a complete refactoring.

Agile Web Development with Rails: Fourth Edition

Sam Ruby, Dave Thomas, and David Heinemeier Hansson, et al.
(500 pages) ISBN: 978-1-93435-654-8. $43.95
http://pragprog.com/titles/rails4

More Languages

Seven Languages in Seven Weeks

In this book you'll get a hands-on tour of Clojure, Haskell, Io, Prolog, Scala, Erlang, and Ruby. Whether or not your favorite language is on that list, you'll broaden your perspective of programming by examining these languages side-by-side. You'll learn something new from each, and best of all, you'll learn how to learn a language quickly.

Seven Languages in Seven Weeks: A Pragmatic Guide to Learning Programming Languages
Bruce A. Tate
(300 pages) ISBN: 978-1934356-59-3. $34.95
http://pragprog.com/titles/btlang

SQL Antipatterns

If you're programming applications that store data, then chances are you're using SQL, either directly or through a mapping layer. But most of the SQL that gets used is inefficient, hard to maintain, and sometimes just plain wrong. This book shows you all the common mistakes, and then leads you through the best fixes. What's more, it shows you what's *behind* these fixes, so you'll learn a lot about relational databases along the way.

SQL Antipatterns: Avoiding the Pitfalls of Database Programming
Bill Karwin
(300 pages) ISBN: 978-19343565-5-5. $34.95
http://pragprog.com/titles/bksqla

Fixing the Real World

Driving Technical Change

Your co-workers' resistance to new technologies can be baffling. Learn to read users' "patterns of resistance"—and then dismantle their objections. Every developer must master the art of evangelizing. With these techniques and strategies, you'll help your organization adopt your solutions—without selling your soul to organizational politics.

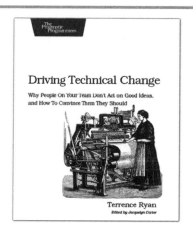

Driving Technical Change: Why People On Your Team Don't Act On Good Ideas, and How to Convince Them They Should
Terrence Ryan
(200 pages) ISBN: 978-1934356-60-9. $32.95
http://pragprog.com/titles/trevan

Debug It!

Debug It! will equip you with the tools, techniques, and approaches to help you tackle any bug with confidence. These secrets of professional debugging illuminate every stage of the bug life cycle, from constructing software that makes debugging easy; through bug detection, reproduction, and diagnosis; to rolling out your eventual fix. Learn better debugging whether you're writing Java or assembly language, targeting servers or embedded micro-controllers, or using agile or traditional approaches.

Debug It! Find, Repair, and Prevent Bugs in Your Code
Paul Butcher
(232 pages) ISBN: 978-1-9343562-8-9. $34.95
http://pragprog.com/titles/pbdp

The Pragmatic Bookshelf

The Pragmatic Bookshelf features books written by developers for developers. The titles continue the well-known Pragmatic Programmer style and continue to garner awards and rave reviews. As development gets more and more difficult, the Pragmatic Programmers will be there with more titles and products to help you stay on top of your game.

Visit Us Online

Home Page for Using JRuby
http://pragprog.com/titles/jruby
Source code from this book, errata, and other resources. Come give us feedback, too!

Register for Updates
http://pragprog.com/updates
Be notified when updates and new books become available.

Join the Community
http://pragprog.com/community
Read our weblogs, join our online discussions, participate in our mailing list, interact with our wiki, and benefit from the experience of other Pragmatic Programmers.

New and Noteworthy
http://pragprog.com/news
Check out the latest pragmatic developments, new titles and other offerings.

Save on the eBook

Save on the eBook versions of this title. Owning the paper version of this book entitles you to purchase the electronic versions at a terrific discount.

PDFs are great for carrying around on your laptop—they are hyperlinked, have color, and are fully searchable. Most titles are also available for the iPhone and iPod touch, Amazon Kindle, and other popular e-book readers.

Buy now at pragprog.com/coupon.

Contact Us

Online Orders:	www.pragprog.com/catalog
Customer Service:	support@pragprog.com
Non-English Versions:	translations@pragprog.com
Pragmatic Teaching:	academic@pragprog.com
Author Proposals:	proposals@pragprog.com
Contact us:	1-800-699-PROG (+1 919 847 3884)